MORE ADVANCE PRAISE FOR
DID BABE RUTH CALL HIS SHOT?

"*Did Babe Ruth Call His Shot?* is a lively, intriguing contribution to baseball literature. Delving into stories both familiar and unfamiliar, Aron's work is remarkably current, refreshingly well-balanced and always entertaining."

> —Jules Tygiel
> author of *Baseball's Great Experiment*

"Aron has written a compelling series of essays attempting to solve the most vexing 28 mysteries associated with the great game of baseball. Does he solve them once and for all? You'll have to read this fine, enjoyable book to find out."

> —Paul Dickson
> editor of *The Dickson Baseball Dictionary*

"Has Paul Aron read everything ever written about baseball? This appears to be the case, and he's therefore able to answer all the age-old questions . . . and new ones as well. I'm almost afraid Aron has taken the fun out of the game. There are no more mysteries. With this fiendishly clever book, everything is revealed."

> —Mike Bryan
> author of *Baseball Lives*

Did Babe Ruth Call His Shot?

And Other Unsolved Mysteries of Baseball

Paul Aron

WILEY

John Wiley & Sons, Inc.

Published by John Wiley & Sons, Inc., Hoboken, New Jersey
Published simultaneously in Canada

For general information about our other products and services, please contact our Customer Care Department within the United States at (800) 762-2974, outside the United States at (317) 572-3993 or fax (317) 572-4002.

Wiley also publishes its books in a variety of electronic formats. Some content that appears in print may not be available in electronic books. For more information about Wiley products, visit our web site at www.wiley.com.

Library of Congress Cataloging-in-Publication Data:

Aron, Paul, date.
    Did Babe Ruth call his shot? : and other unsolved mysteries
of baseball/Paul Aron.
        p.   cm.
    ISBN 0-471-48204-8 (cloth)
    1. Baseball—United States—History. 2. Baseball players—
United States—Biography. I. Title.

    GV863.A1A76 2005
    796.357'0973—dc22

                                        2004009417

Printed in the United States of America

10 9 8 7 6 5 4 3 2 1

Contents

Preface

You'd think it would be pretty easy to figure out whether Babe Ruth called his shot. After all, there were almost 50,000 witnesses at Wrigley Field. There were also sportswriters from across the country, and most of them filed stories within a day or two.

This was how Paul Gallico of the *New York Daily News* reported it: "Ruth pointed like a duelist to the spot where he expected to send his rapier home." Bill Corum of the Hearst newspapers was less flamboyant but equally clear. Ruth, Corum wrote, "pointed out where he was going to hit the next one, and hit it there."

Ruth's "called shot"—coming as it did at a crucial moment in the third game of the 1932 World Series between the Yankees and Cubs—immediately became part of his legend. Yet from the start, there were skeptics, among them Chicago catcher Gabby Hartnett and pitcher Charlie Root.

"Ruth did not point at the fence before he swung," Root insisted. "If he had made a gesture like that, well, anybody who knows me knows that Ruth would have ended up on his ass."

What really happened?

That's the question this book asks, not just about Ruth's called shot but also about Ed Delahanty's death and Moe Berg's spying and Satchel Paige's age and Fidel Castro's tryout. This is not the place to find out who were the best first basemen or what were the greatest teams or whether Pete Rose or Joe Jackson belong in the Hall of Fame. Those are important and fascinating issues, well worth discussing. But whatever your opinion on these issues, it's undeniably a matter of *opinion*.

Here, instead, are the facts. Ruth's called shot is by no means the only baseball fact open to dispute. Indeed, from the moment Abner Doubleday didn't invent the game, baseball history and legend have been inextricably intertwined. Maybe it's because when you gather 50,000 people at Wrigley or anywhere else, each is going to have a different view. Maybe it's because there has been so much written about baseball, so many good stories told and retold, that it takes a bit of detective work to uncover what really happened.

But the premise of this book is that it can be done. We can search for the original Casey at the Bat, maybe find Mudville on the map. We can investigate whether owners secretly introduced a rabbit ball to boost home run totals in the twenties and nineties, whether Branch Rickey was as good and Walter O'Malley was as evil as Brooklyn Dodger fans believed, and whether there was any truth to the smear campaign George Steinbrenner launched against Dave Winfield. We can examine the evidence against Gaylord Perry, who once said he didn't throw the spitter anymore. (To which Gene Mauch retorted: "He doesn't throw it any less, either.") We can look at the work of physicists experimenting to see whether a curveball is an optical illusion, of etymologists digging for the origins of "fungo," of economists studying the viability of small-market teams, of statisticians figuring out whether it pays to steal or makes more sense to play for a big inning.

And here's the best thing about all this: what really happened, at least when we're talking baseball, turns out to be just as fascinating and fun as any legend could hope to be.

Acknowledgments

For their advice and encouragement, thanks to Robert Adair, Jae Aron, Stephen Aron, Thomas Aron, Nick Bakalar, Allen Barra, Paula Blank, Mike Bryan, Rusty Carter, Paul Dickson, William Drennan, John Harvey, Bill O'Donovan, Steve Price, Ruth Sameth, John Simko, Mike Thompson, Bill Tolbert, David Wolff, Andrew Zimbalist, and especially John Thorn.

Thanks also to my agent, John Thornton, and my editor, Stephen Power.

Who Invented Baseball?

Albert G. Spalding was determined to establish that baseball was as American as apple pie and, well, baseball.

Spalding devoted his life to the game. As a pitcher, he led Boston to four pennants, and ended up 207–56. He went on to own the National League's Chicago White Stockings (who became the Cubs, not the White Sox) and the A. G. Spalding Company, which supplied baseballs to the American League and sporting goods to the rest of America. He was a publisher, too; the annual *Spalding's Official Base Ball Guide* was the game's most important record book. But his greatest and most lasting influence was as baseball's mythmaker.

There's the story he told, for example, about a delegation of Republicans who arrived in Springfield, Illinois, to inform Abraham Lincoln that the party had nominated him for president. Lincoln, Spalding explained, was "engaged in a game of Base Ball." So Lincoln informed the delegation they would have "to wait a few minutes until I make another base hit." As with most Spalding stories, this one was often repeated and never verified.

His most famous contribution to baseball mythology was, of course, Abner Doubleday. Doubleday, Spalding insisted, invented baseball. The time was 1839, the place small-town America. More specifically, Cooperstown, New York.

"Cricket is a splendid game," he wrote, "for Britons. Our British Cricketer, having finished his day's labor at noon, may don his negligee shirt, his white trousers, his gorgeous hosiery and his canvas shoes, and sally forth to the field of sport, with his sweetheart on one arm and his Cricket bat under the other, knowing that he may engage in his national pastime without soiling his linen or neglecting his lady."

"Not so the American Ball Player," he continued. "We have a game too lively for any but Americans to play."

Others, most notably the Spalding guides' English-born editor Henry Chadwick, disagreed. Chadwick argued baseball evolved from a British bat-and-ball game, though not cricket. Baseball's ancestor, Chadwick believed, was rounders. To be sure, there were differences: in rounders, bases were stones or posts, any number could play on each side, fielders had no set positions, and they retired runners by throwing the ball at them. But there was a "pecker" or "feeder" who threw the ball and there was a "striker" who tried to hit it. And the striker then circled the bases, albeit running clockwise. Besides, Chadwick didn't claim rounders and baseball were the same, just that the former was the latter's ancestor.

"From this little English acorn of Rounders," he wrote in 1868, in what seemed a pretty conciliatory way to put it, "has the giant American oak of Base Ball grown."

To Spalding, these were fighting words. In 1905, after years of squabbling with Chadwick, Spalding set up a special commission to establish baseball's origins once and for all. He appointed two senators and several businessmen. The chairman was one-time National League president A. G. Mills. The commission spent two years investigating without coming up with much. Then, in 1907, Spalding submitted letters from Abner Graves, then a mining engineer in Denver. Graves recalled how, in Cooperstown back in 1839, Abner Doubleday drew the first diagram of a diamond with all the fielders' positions marked.

"He went diligently among the boys in the town, and in several schools, explaining the plan, and inducing them to play Base Ball in lieu of other games," Graves wrote. "Doubleday's game was played in a good many places around town: sometimes in the old militia muster lot, or training ground, a couple of hundred yards southeasterly from the courthouse, where County Fairs were occasionally held."

For those who believed baseball was wholly American, Doubleday was an ideal choice. He was a military hero: he aimed the cannon for the Union's first shot of the Civil War at Fort Sumter, distinguished himself at Gettysburg, and retired as a major general. He later moved to San Francisco and built the nation's first cable car system. In case the commission didn't get it, Spalding spelled it out. "It certainly appeals to an American pride," he explained, "to have the great national game of Base Ball created and named by a Major General in the United States Army." And what better place for the game's origins than pastoral Cooperstown, the boyhood home of the great American novelist James Fenimore Cooper?

Doubleday himself could not testify, having been buried in Arlington National Cemetery since 1892. But Graves's word was enough for the commission. Its report concluded: "First—That Base Ball had its origin in the United States; Second—That the first scheme for playing it, according to the best evidence obtainable to date, was devised by Abner Doubleday."

Mills added his own interpretation of how it happened. "In the days when Abner Doubleday attended school in Cooperstown, it was a common thing for two dozen or more of school boys to join in a game of ball," he wrote. "Doubtless, as in my later experience, collisions between players in attempting to catch the batted ball were frequent, and injury due to this cause, or to the practice of putting out the runner by hitting him with the ball, often occurred."

Mills continued: "I can well understand how the orderly mind of the embryo West Pointer would devise a scheme for limiting the contestants on each side and allotting them to field positions, each with a certain amount of territory; also substituting the existing side and allotting them to field positions, each with a certain amount of territory; also substituting the existing method of putting out the base runner, for the old one of 'plugging' him with the ball."

In 1939, to commemorate the hundredth anniversary of the game's supposed invention, the National Baseball Hall of Fame and Museum opened in Cooperstown. The Doubleday story was now set in stone, or at least brick. Well before then, however, baseball historians were chipping away at its foundations. Some calculated that in 1839 Graves was five years old, making him an unlikely playmate for the twenty-year-old Doubleday. Others noted that Doubleday was at West Point, not Cooperstown, from 1838 to 1842. Moreover, Doubleday and Mills had been lifelong friends, yet the game's inventor apparently never mentioned his brainstorm to the National League president. Chadwick dismissed the whole Doubleday story as a "joke between Albert and myself."

The story was, indeed, pure fiction, as much a hoax as the Cardiff giant, the ten-foot-tall giant housed in Cooperstown's Farmer's Museum, just down the road from the Hall of Fame. Even the Hall, to its credit, conceded the story's appeal was mostly sentimental. Its exhibit on Doubleday includes the following: "In the hearts of those who love baseball, he is remembered as the lad in the pasture where the game was invented. Only cynics would need to know more."

Cooperstown, in fact, was an entirely inhospitable setting for baseball. As historian Alan Taylor recounted in his book *William Cooper's Town*, in 1816 the village trustees, intent on imposing the proper order on their streets, passed an ordinance banning ballplaying of any sorts in the town center. "Cooperstown," Taylor concluded, "can better claim to have tried to prevent the invention of baseball."

If not there, where? And who?

The Mills Commission itself provided an alternative to the Cooperstown-Doubleday myth. The place was Hoboken, New Jersey, the person was Alexander Joy Cartwright. Though the commission designated Doubleday as the game's inventor, it credited Cartwright with improving the rules and putting them down on paper. Wrote Spalding: "To Alexander J. Cartwright, beyond doubt, belongs the honor of having been the first to move in the direction of securing an organization of Base Ball

Players. It is of record that in the spring of 1845, Mr. Cartwright, being present and participating in a practice game of ball, proposed to others the formal association of themselves together as a Base Ball Club."

Cartwright was a member of a group of businessmen and clerks who called themselves the New York Knickerbockers. At first, the Knickerbockers played various bat-and-ball games on Manhattan's vacant lots. As the city built around them, the group crossed the Hudson River to a resort known as Elysian Fields. In 1845, Cartwright, a clerk at a Wall Street bank and then co-owner of a bookstore and stationery shop, organized the Knickerbockers into a club and codified the rules. Cartwright's game still varied considerably from modern baseball: the game ended not after nine innings but after one team scored twenty-one runs, and the batter was out if a fielder caught a ball on one bounce. Still, Cartwright's game, like Doubleday's, was recognizably baseball. The bases were laid out in a diamond, fielders were assigned positions, base runners were tagged out and not thrown at.

Hoboken has no Hall of Fame, only a small plaque claiming the game's origins. Nearby, in a small grass triangle known as Elysian Park, a sign reads, "No Ball Playing." Yet there is far more documentary evidence to back Hoboken's claim than Cooperstown's. The Knickerbocker Game Book, now in the New York Public Library's Spalding Collection, records variations of the rules in 1845 and 1846, as well as a primitive box score of the club's first match, against a team identified as the "New York Nine."

That game, according to the game book, took place June 19, 1846. The book doesn't say much about the opponents, who may have been cricket players or a pickup team with some outsiders and some Knickerbockers. In any case, the New York Nine had clearly mastered the game: they beat the Knickerbockers 23–1 in four innings. As Spalding put it, the Knickerbockers were admirable gentlemen, but "it does not appear that any of these were world-beaters in the realm of athletic sports." Indeed, he added, "there is reason to believe that these fine old fellows shone more resplendently in the banquet hall than on the diamond field."

By putting the rules down on paper, Cartwright (and his lesser-known colleagues William R. Wheaton, William Tucker, and Duncan Curry) assured that the Knickerbocker game would spread, first among other New York clubs, then to other parts of the country. In 1849, Cartwright joined the California gold rush, teaching the game on his way west. Later, Cartwright moved to Hawaii, and by 1852 the game was being played there. Even in Cooperstown, his significance was not denied: his portrait hangs in the Hall of Fame; Abner Doubleday's does not.

It was Cartwright's game that took hold. Yet that is not the same thing as saying that his was the original. Baseball historian John Thorn has made a strong case that Daniel "Doc" Adams played as great a role as Cartwright in creating baseball—and played it at least five years earlier. Thorn rediscovered an 1896 interview with Adams, in which the then-eighty-one-year-old recalled playing the game as early as 1839. Adams played on a club called the New York Base Ball club, many of whose members later formed the Knickerbockers.

Other bat-and-ball games were played in other places. In Philadelphia, for example, clubs played a version of "town ball," a game whose origins dated back to before the Revolution, when farmers would come to town to play. The Philadelphians had no foul territory and no limit on the number of players, and they laid out their bases on a square much smaller than today's infield. But they did have at least one feature of the modern game lacking in New York: in Philadelphia, pitchers threw overhand.

The Philadelphia game spread to Ohio and Kentucky as well as other parts of Pennsylvania, but the New York game eventually wiped it out. In May 1860, the Philadelphians started playing by Knickerbocker rules.

The Massachusetts version of town ball lasted longer, codifying its rules in 1858 and spreading throughout New England. In the Massachusetts game, pitchers threw overhand, and fielders had to catch the ball on the fly, but there were also many elements that would seem strange today: there were no foul lines, the bases were wooden stakes, the batter stood between first and "fourth base," runners were "plugged" or "soaked" by throws rather than tagged out, and the teams got only one out per inning. The game's biggest drawback, and the reason it lost out to the New York version, was that it took one hundred runs to win. An 1860 state championship game between the Unions of Medway and the Winthrops of Holliston took six days to reach that total. As one reporter noted, "The time occupied in playing the game under such rules was, we think, rather too much of a good thing."

By the end of the Civil War, most New England teams had adopted the Knickerbocker rules.

Increasingly, historians have come to agree with Henry Chadwick that all these early versions of baseball—whether New York's or Philadelphia's or Boston's—evolved over decades, even centuries. The history of these games is still largely unknown, partly because, unlike cricket, they were played by working-class people or children. These lives were rarely documented.

Still, some evidence remains. *A Little Pretty Pocket-Book*, published in 1744, contained a description of "base-ball" and a picture illustrating a game. One soldier at Valley Forge, for example, wrote in his journal that George Washington's troops passed the time by playing "base." In 1791, the town council of Pittsfield, Massachusetts, was sufficiently concerned about "the preservation of the windows in the new meeting house" to prohibit a slew of games within eighty yards of the building. The bylaw explicitly names baseball as one of the culprits. *A Boy's Own Book*, published in 1829, included a set of rules for rounders remarkably similar to those for baseball. In 1834, *The Book of Sports* printed the same rules for the game of "Base," adding that was the name "generally adopted."

All this is part of baseball's history, as are town ball, old cat, rounders, and other games played in England and colonial America. There was no single moment when Abner Doubleday or Alexander Cartwright or Doc Adams imagined an entirely new game.

Why, then, does the Doubleday story persist?

Partly it's because it appeals to America's nostalgia for its rural past. "Part of the agreeable nonsense about baseball being an echo of our pastoral past is the myth that Abner Doubleday invented the sport one fine day in 1839 in the farmer Phinney's pasture," wrote political columnist George Will. "The untidy truth is that the sport evolved from two similar, but interestingly different, games, based in two cities, New York and Boston."

Partly, too, there's a longing for that single moment of creation. Evolution, whether of humanity or baseball, is a more difficult story to grasp than one about Adam and Eve, or Abner Doubleday and Alexander Cartwright. "Creation myths," wrote paleontologist Stephen Jay Gould, "identify heroes and sacred places, while evolutionary stories provide no palpable, particular thing as a symbol for reverence, worship, or patriotism."

Yet evolutionary stories bring their own satisfactions. Asked Gould: "We may need heroes and shrines, but is there not grandeur in the sweep of continuity? Shall we revel in a story for all humanity that may include the sacred ball courts of the Aztecs, and perhaps, for all we know, a group of *Homo erectus* hitting rocks or skulls with a stick or femur? Or shall we halt beside the mythical Abner Doubleday, standing behind the tailor's shop in Cooperstown, and say 'behold the man'—thereby violating truth and, perhaps even worse, extinguishing both thought and wonder?"

To investigate further:

Gilbert, Thomas. *Elysian Fields*. New York: Franklin Watts, 1995. Though written for a young adult audience, this is a very thorough history of the game's early years.

Gould, Stephen Jay. *Triumph and Tragedy in Mudville*. New York: W. W. Norton, 2003. Gould's two great passions were biology and baseball.

Henderson, Robert. *Ball, Bat, and Bishop*. Champaign: University of Illinois Press, 2001. Originally published in 1947, this was one of the earliest and most thorough debunkings of the Doubleday myth. Henderson traces ball sports back to Egypt.

Seymour, Harold. *Baseball: The Early Years.* New York: Oxford University Press, 1960. The first of three volumes written by the man *Sports Illustrated* called "the Edward Gibbon of baseball history."

Spalding, Albert G. *America's National Game.* Lincoln: University of Nebraska Press, 1992. Originally published in 1911, this draws heavily on not only Spalding's recollections but also the writings and scrapbooks of Henry Chadwick. "No book has shaped our understanding of early baseball history more deeply," wrote historian Benjamin Rader.

Springwood, Charles. *Cooperstown to Dyersville.* Boulder, Colo.: Westview Press, 1996. A cultural anthropologist's study of American narratives of pastoralism and nostalgia. Dyersville, Iowa, is the site of the baseball field made famous by the movie *Field of Dreams.*

Thorn, John. "Doc Adams." Thorn's essay is part of the Society for American Baseball Research's biography project at *http://bioproj.sabr .org.* Thorn also was responsible for rediscovering Pittsfield's 1791 law.

Voigt, David Quentin. *American Baseball: From Gentleman's Sport to the Commissioner System.* Norman: University of Oklahoma Press, 1966. Like Seymour, Voigt wrote a multivolume history. He emphasizes the sociology and economics of the game.

2

Who Was the First Black in the Majors?

int: it wasn't Jackie Robinson.

Sixty-three years before Robinson joined the Dodgers, Moses Fleetwood "Fleet" Walker played 42 games for the Toledo Blue Stockings of the American Association, thirteen teams that were, if not quite on a par with the established National League, most definitely a major league. What's more, Walker was just one of several blacks who played in the majors or high minors during the 1880s. He may not even have been the first; evidence uncovered in 2004 points to William Edward White, who in 1879—five years before Walker's debut—played one game at first base for the National League's Providence Grays.

Walker—or White—is more than an answer to a trivia question. By investigating the lives of black baseball players of the 1880s, researchers have shed light on an era when race relations were much more in flux than before or after, when slavery was in the past but Jim Crow still in the future. "For a time," wrote historian C. Van Woodward, "old and new rubbed shoulders—and so did black and white. . . . It was a time of experiment, testing, and uncertainty—quite different from the time of repression and rigid uniformity that was to come toward the end of the century. Alternatives were still open and real choices had to be made."

                    *   *   *

Walker seemed to have the ideal background for integrating baseball. He was born in Mount Pleasant, Ohio, a station on the
Underground Railroad where free blacks regularly interacted with
Quaker abolitionists. The son of a doctor, he attended Oberlin
College, the first college in the United States to adopt an explicitly nondiscriminatory admissions policy. He starred on Oberlin's
baseball team for three years, then played two years at the University of Michigan. And Walker's skin was comparatively light,
making him more acceptable in some circles of white society.

    In 1883, Walker signed to play in Toledo, then in the North-
western League. He batted .251 and caught 60 games to help the
team win the pennant. He was one of the few players the team
held on to the next year, when it made the jump to the American Association. In 1884, now a major leaguer, Walker hit .263
(putting him in the top third of the league's hitters), playing
mostly at catcher and occasionally in the outfield. His younger
brother Welday Walker joined the team in midseason and hit
.222 in 5 games as a reserve outfielder.

    Fleet Walker was popular with the fans, at least according to
reports in the *Toledo Blade*, as well as newspapers in Baltimore
and Washington. But he also faced plenty of bigotry. During the
1883 season, when the National League champion White Stockings came to Toledo for an exhibition game, Chicago manager
and first baseman Cap Anson (who was also the first player to
get 3,000 hits) threatened to take his team home if Walker took
the field. Anson backed down when Toledo manager Charley
Morton sent Walker out to right field. In May 1884, according to
the *Blade*'s report of a game in Louisville, Walker was "hissed . . .
and insulted . . . because he was colored."

    Nor were Walker's teammates always supportive. "He was the
best catcher I ever worked with, but I disliked a Negro and when-
ever I had to pitch to him I used to pitch anything I wanted
without looking at his signals," recalled pitcher Tony Mullane,
who won 36 games for Toledo in 1884. "One day he signaled me

for a curve and I shot a fast ball at him. He said, 'I'll catch you without signals but I won't catch you if you are going to cross me when I give you signals.' And all the rest of that season he caught me and caught anything I pitched without knowing what was coming."

In September, before a game in Richmond, Morton received a letter threatening bloodshed if Walker played. Whether the threat would have been carried out can't be known, since by then Walker, who was suffering from broken ribs suffered in that pre–chest protector era, was spending most of his time on the bench. In October, Toledo released him, bringing an end to the brief pre-Robinson era of major league integration.

Walker continued to play in highly competitive minor leagues, as did a number of other blacks. In May 1887 there were seven blacks in the International League: Walker and pitcher George Washington Stovey in Newark, second baseman Bud Fowler and a pitcher named Renfroe (his last name is unknown) in Binghamton, second baseman Frank Grant (who led the league in hitting at .366) in Buffalo, second baseman Randolph Jackson in Oswego, and pitcher Robert Higgins in Syracuse.

"How far will this mania for engaging colored players go?" asked *Sporting Life*. "At the present rate of progress the International League may ere many moons change its title to 'Colored League.'"

It would not go much farther. In July, Anson brought the White Stockings to Newark, again for an exhibition game and again on the condition that no blacks would play. This time Anson prevailed; neither Walker nor Stovey took the field. The next day, the league voted not to sign any more Negro players. (The four teams with blacks on the roster voted against the measure; the other six voted for it.) At the beginning of 1888, the league backed away from a blanket ban, settling on an informal understanding that no team would sign more than one black. Still, it was increasingly clear that baseball's future was a segregated one.

Was Anson to blame? Sol White, a black star of the nineteenth century, believed Anson's threatened boycotts and general hostility played a key role in segregating baseball. Wrote White in his 1907 *History of Colored Baseball:* "His repugnant feeling, shown at every opportunity, toward colored ballplayers, was a source of comment throughout every league in the country, and his opposition, with his great popularity and power in baseball circles, hastened the exclusion of the black man from the white leagues."

Anson also may have prevented Walker from returning to the majors. According to White, in an exhibition game against New York, Walker threw out Giant captain John Montgomery Ward, prompting Ward to offer Walker a contract. That set off, White wrote, Anson's "strenuous and fruitful opposition."

Anson was undeniably racist and influential. But he also was all too representative of the majority of players and owners. Most historians have agreed with Robert Peterson, author of *Only the Ball Was White*. "That [Anson] had the power and popularity to force Negroes out of organized baseball almost singlehandedly," Peterson argued, "is to credit him with more influence than he had, or for that matter, than he needed."

Amid increasing hostility, Walker hung on with Syracuse in 1888 and 1889. In 1888, when Anson again refused to play against him in an exhibition game, it was no longer considered newsworthy, except in the Negro press. By the end of 1889, Walker was the only black in the International League, the last one until Robinson went to Montreal.

Exiled from baseball, Walker's life spiraled downward. In April 1891 he got into a fight with a group of white men near a saloon and fatally stabbed a bricklayer named Patrick Murray. A jury found him not guilty of murder. Walker took a job as a mail clerk, and in 1898 was charged with mail robbery. This time he was found guilty and sentenced to a year in jail.

Walker later edited a newspaper with his brother Welday and owned or operated an opera house and movie theater in Cadiz, Ohio, but his experiences in and out of baseball clearly undercut whatever optimism he might once have felt about race relations. In 1908 Walker published a booklet called *Our Home Colony; A Treatise on the Past, Present and Future of the Negro Race in America*. The booklet advocated that blacks move to Africa. "The only practical and permanent solution of the present and future race troubles in the United States is entire separation by emigration of the Negro from America," wrote the onetime pioneer of integration. "The Negro race can find superior advantages, and better opportunities . . . among people of their own race."

The Society for American Baseball Research (SABR) has committees of researchers investigating nineteenth-century baseball and Negro baseball. Neither committee had any reason to investigate William Edward White. The former could not have been impressed by White's career totals: one game, four at-bats, one hit, twelve plays at first base without an error. The latter also had no reason to look at White, since the 1880 census listed him as a white man. Instead, it was left to SABR's biographical committee, whose researchers were compiling birth, death, and other records on every major leaguer, to discover that White may have been black.

SABR researcher Peter Morris knew White was playing for Brown University in Providence when he filled in for the Grays on June 21, 1879. Brown records indicated that White was born in 1860 in Milner, Georgia, and that his father was A. J. White. The 1880 census listed an Andrew J. White in Milner. He had no wife or children, but his household included a mulatto woman named Hannah White. The 1870 census showed that White had seventy slaves, including Hannah White and her nine-year-old son William.

Next Morris tracked down a photo of the 1879 Brown team. William White's skin appeared to be darker than that of his teammates. Finally, in January 2004, Morris traveled to the Zebulon, Georgia, courthouse. There he found A. J. White's will, which left his estate to "William Edward White, Anna Nora White, and Sarah Adelaide White, the children of my servant Hannah." The will also mentioned that William and a sister were "now at School in the North."

All this added up to William Edward White being the son of a white slaveholder and a mulatto slave. Perhaps deciding that Georgia was no place for his quarter-black son, A. J. White sent William White north to Providence, where he could pass as white. But when William White took the field for the Grays, he was most likely not only the first black, but also the only former slave to play in the majors.

This raised another question: was White's major league career cut short because someone found out he was black? There's no proof that was the case, and White may very well have been called up only as an emergency replacement for the Grays' regular first baseman, Joe Start, who newspapers reported had a broken finger. But it's worth noting that White, according to the *Chicago Tribune*'s report of the game, "played the position with remarkable activity and skill for an amateur." And the *Providence Journal* reported that White "was as expert and effective, as ever, catching some widely-thrown balls with great ease."

The *Journal* added that White "will be a valuable substitute for the unfortunate Start." But the next day right fielder Jim O'Rourke moved to first, abruptly ending White's major league career.

To investigate further:

Fatsis, Stephen. "Mystery of Baseball: Was William White Game's First Black?" *Wall Street Journal*, January 30, 2004. The *Journal* broke the story of how Morris, along with other SABR researchers and Civil War historian Bruce Allardice, tracked down White's roots.

Malinowski, W. Zachary. "Who Was the First Black Man to Play in the Major Leagues?" *Providence Journal*, February 15, 2004. A follow-up to Fatsis's story, offering more details on White's still-sketchy life before and after June 21, 1879.

Peterson, Robert. *Only the Ball Was White*. New York: Oxford University Press, 1992. A groundbreaking history of black players and teams, originally published in 1970.

Thorn, John, ed. *The Armchair Book of Baseball II*. New York: Charles Scribner's Sons, 1987. This excellent anthology includes Jerry Malloy's excellent essay "Out at Home," which tells how baseball drew the color line in 1887. Malloy's essay originally appeared in the Fall 1982 edition of the SABR journal *The National Pastime*.

Zang, David. *Fleet Walker's Divided Heart*. Lincoln: University of Nebraska Press, 1995. A valuable though occasionally overwritten biography.

3

Who Was Casey at the Bat?

D eWolf Hopper was already a famous comic actor when, in August 1888, he stepped on the stage of Wallack's Theater, at Broadway and Thirtieth Street, and first announced that the outlook wasn't brilliant for the Mudville nine that day. The poem was an instant hit, and Hopper made it part of his standard repertoire. He later estimated he must have recited the poem more than ten thousand times.

"Casey" became, if not America's best poem, at least its best loved. "Love has its sonnets galore," wrote A. G. Spalding in 1911. "War its epics in heroic verse; Tragedy its somber story in measured lines, and Base Ball has 'Casey at the Bat.'"

Naturally, people wanted to know who Casey was. And naturally, the place to look was Mudville.

Alas, the town wasn't on any map.

Grantland Rice, a sportswriter whose fame in the early part of the twentieth century rivaled Casey's, explained why. In an introduction to his poem "Mudville's Fate," Rice wrote that "the celebrated Son of Swat put the township on the blink by whiffing in the championship game, thus wiping out all interest in a hitherto thriving baseball center." As the poem put it:

> For after Casey fanned that day the citizens all left,
> And one by one they sought new lands, heartbroken
>   and bereft. . . .

Martin Gardner, better known for his work on math puzzles than baseball ones, posited that local leaders changed the name in an effort to bring joy back to Mudville. It didn't work. "The town continued to deteriorate rapidly," he wrote, tongue in cheek. "By 1907 it had disappeared entirely and Casey, with his wife and eight children, had moved to nearby Bugville." Gardner warned that Mudville should not be confused with Mudlick, Kentucky, Mud Butte, South Dakota, Mudford, West Virginia, Muddy Creek Forks, Pennsylvania, Mud Camp, Kentucky, or Mud, Illinois.

The lack of a Mudville, however, did not discourage would-be Caseys from stepping forward. Indeed, it opened up the possibility of alternative settings. Detroit, for example, where, according to O. Robinson Casey of Syracuse, he had inspired the poem by striking out with the bases loaded in a 1885 game against Minneapolis. But there was no record of an O. Robinson Casey playing for Detroit that year. Besides, according to the poem, the bases weren't loaded when Casey came to bat (Blake was on second, Flynn on third).

The only Casey on the Detroit roster that year was Dan Casey, a pitcher who went on to a respectable career in Philadelphia, and then became a streetcar conductor in Binghamton, New York. Dan Casey recalled that the neighborhood where the Phillies later played was often very muddy. He also noted that he was preceded in the lineup by two weak-hitting infielders, Charlie Bastian and Joe Mulvey. These, he concluded, must have been the poem's Blake and Flynn. Dan Casey also remembered striking out on August 21, 1887. Two runners were on base.

The problem with this story was that no game was played that day. Moreover, it was hard to see Dan as a particularly mighty Casey. Though he won 96 games over seven years as a pitcher, his lifetime batting average was .162. His home run total was 1.

There were plenty of other claimants, not necessarily with a first or last name of Casey. Ultimately, there was only one way to identify the real Casey: ask the poet.

The problem was that no one—not even Hopper—knew who wrote the poem.

*   *   *

In his memoirs, Hopper recalled how he first came to read the poem. He knew that on that evening in August, members of the New York Giants and Chicago White Stockings would be attending his show, a comic opera called *Prince Methusalem*. He was trying to think of an appropriate encore for that audience, when a friend, the novelist Archibald Clavering Gunter, suggested a poem he'd clipped from the *San Francisco Examiner* during a recent West Coast trip. Hopper quickly memorized it.

"On his debut Casey lifted the audience, composed largely of baseball players and fans, out of their seats," he wrote. "When I dropped my voice to B flat, below low C, at 'the multitude was awed,' I remember seeing [Giant catcher] Buck Ewing's gallant mustachios give a single nervous twitch. And as the house, after a moment of startled silence, grasped the anticlimactic denouement, it shouted its glee."

Hopper was of course curious who wrote the poem. The only clue on the *Examiner* clipping was the byline "Phin."

As with Casey, the poem's fame brought forth many a pretender. Among the first was Will Valentine, a newspaper editor and poet who contributed parodies to the *Sioux City Tribune*. Valentine once roomed with a businessman named F. T. Wilstach. Later, Wilstach remembered that he was there one day in 1882 when Valentine wrote "Casey." Wilstach said Valentine then published the poem in the *Tribune* years before it somehow worked its way to San Francisco and the *Examiner*. But Wilstach failed to produce a copy of the paper with the poem.

Then there was George D'Vys, who said he'd played for a Somerville, Massachusetts, sandlot team called the Mudville Nine. D'Vys said he was inspired by a strikeout of his hero, King Kelly of the White Stockings. D'Vys claimed he sent the poem to the *Sporting Times* in 1888—anonymously, he explained, because his father disapproved of poetry. Unlike Wilstach, D'Vys was able to produce a July 29, 1888, copy of the publication with the poem.

Yet the story didn't ring true. D'Vys said he'd sent the poem to O. P. Caylor, who didn't become editor of the *Sporting Times* until 1890, two years after the newspaper published the poem. Moreover, the published version included only eight very mutilated stanzas, indicating that perhaps someone at the *Sporting Times*, as at many other papers across the country, had heard Hopper or read the *Examiner* and then written down some poorly remembered version. Most damningly, for D'Vys though not the newspaper, the *Sporting Times* poem explicitly stated that it was adapted from one that had appeared in the *Examiner.*

Besieged by forgeries, Hopper despaired of learning the poet's true identity. Then, about five years after he'd started reciting the poem, he was scheduled to do so in Worcester, Massachusetts. In his memoirs, Hopper recalled how a Mr. Hammond asked the actor to join him after the performance at the Worcester Club. Hammond promised to introduce him there to Casey's author.

That he did.

"Casey's long-lost parent proved to be Ernest L. Thayer, known to all Worcester as Phinney Thayer, the son of a wealthy textile-mill owner," wrote Hopper. "In his modesty Thayer waited so long before advancing his rightful claim to the poem that it has been challenged by innumerable others. I have met or corresponded with most of these pretenders in my time, and none has yet offered me the slightest proof or corroborative evidence to authorship, while Mr. Thayer has shown me three other manuscripts worthy of Casey's creator, and overwhelming supporting evidence."

Thayer had been editor of Harvard's *Lampoon* when the magazine's business manager was William Randolph Hearst, soon to be publisher of the *San Francisco Examiner.* Thayer followed Hearst west, contributing a series of ballads to the newspaper as Phin. Hearst paid him five dollars for each, including "Casey," which appeared in the *Examiner* on June 3, 1888.

Thayer, who was independently wealthy, wasn't interested in making money off the poem. He didn't even like the poem much. "During my brief connection with the *Examiner*," he later said, "I put out large quantities of nonsense, both prose and verse. . . . In general quality Casey (at least in my judgment), is neither better nor worse than much of the other stuff. Its persistent vogue is simply unaccountable, and it would be hard to say, all things considered, if it has given me more pleasure than annoyance. The constant wrangling about the authorship, from which I have tried to keep aloof, has certainly filled me with disgust."

Hopper was much amused to discover that Thayer, though unquestionably the poet, could not recite the poem. At his club in Worcester, Thayer's fellow members insisted he perform.

"I have heard many another give Casey," Hopper wrote. "Fond mammas have brought their young sons to me to hear their childish voices lisp the poem, but Thayer's was the worst of all. In a sweet, dulcet Harvard whisper he implored Casey to murder the umpire, and gave this cry of mass animal rage all the emphasis of a caterpillar wearing rubbers crawling on a velvet carpet."

Who, then, was Thayer's Casey?

The poet adamantly denied he had a particular ballplayer in mind. Responding to a *Syracuse Post-Standard* inquiry about the claim of O. Robinson Casey, Thayer wrote that the original Casey was a boy who had bullied him years earlier.

"The poem has no basis in fact," Thayer told the *Post-Standard*. "The only Casey actually involved, I am sure about him, was not a ballplayer. . . . While in high school, I composed and printed myself a very tiny sheet, less than two inches by three. In one issue, I ventured to gag, as we say, this Casey boy. He didn't like it and he told me so, and, as he discoursed, his big, clenched red hands were white at the knuckles."

"I suspect the incident, many years after, suggested the title for the poem," Thayer said. "It was a taunt thrown to the winds. God grant he never catches me."

Thayer's words did not put an end to the parade of would-be Caseys, or, for that matter, Mudvilles. In 1952, the chamber of commerce in Stockton, California—a mere train ride from San Francisco—decided that Thayer had written the poem after seeing a game at the local ballpark. They staged a reenactment, with boxer Max Baer playing Casey. The chamber noted that four of the five players named in the poem—Cooney, Barrows, Flynn, and Blake—played in the California State League during the 1880s, albeit not for Stockton. The chamber conveniently failed to mention that no one in the league was named Casey.

In 2000, Stockton's minor league team, then a Milwaukee Brewers affiliate, renamed itself the Mudville Nine. Clearly Thayer, who died in 1940, would not have the last word on his creation.

And in one respect he ought not to have it. For despite Thayer's modest assessment of the poem, Casey's popularity is by no means, as its author thought, "unaccountable."

"It is not great poetry," Gardner conceded. "Parts of it are certainly doggerel. Yet it is almost impossible to read it several times without memorizing whole chunks, and there are lines so perfectly expressed, given the poem's intent, that one cannot imagine a word changed for the better."

"Fans loved every syllable of it," agreed baseball historian Lee Allen, "possibly because it echoed the frustrations that they knew so well. . . . Certainly if Casey had won the game for his team with a hit, the verse would soon have been forgotten."

Wrote Hopper: "There are one or more Caseys in every league, bush or big, and there is no day in the playing season that this same supreme tragedy, as stark as Aristophanes for the moment, does not befall on some field."

To investigate further:

Allen, Lee. *The Hot Stove League*. Kingston, N.Y.: Total Sports Publishing, 2000. Originally published in 1955, and still one of the best collections of baseball anecdotes. Allen includes the full text of Thayer's reply to the *Syracuse Post-Standard*.

Gardner, Martin, ed. *The Annotated Casey at the Bat*. Chicago: University of Chicago Press, 1967. Not just Thayer's original, but also the best of its sequels and parodies, including Grantland Rice's "Casey's Revenge" ("But Mudville hearts are happy now, for Casey hit the ball"), J. A. Lindon's "A Village Cricket Casey" ("It had been a sticky wicket at Cowpat-under-Slosh . . ."), Les Desmond's "O'Toole's Touchdown" ("But there is no joy in Hokus, O'Toole crossed the wrong goal line!"), and Ray Bradbury's "Ahab at the Helm" ("It looked extremely rocky for the Melville nine that day . . .").

Hopper, DeWolf. *Once a Clown, Always a Clown.* Garden City, N.Y.: Garden City Publishing Co., 1927. "When my name is called upon the resurrection morn I shall, very probably, unless some friend is there to pull the sleeve of my ascension robe, arise, clear my throat and begin: "'The outlook wasn't brilliant . . .'"

4

Was Ed Delahanty Murdered?

E d Delahanty was by no means the only baseball player to die violently and strangely.

There was Lyman Bostock, the Angel outfielder who was shot in 1978 by an insanely (and mistakenly) jealous husband. There was Len Koenecke, the Dodger outfielder who in 1935 died on a plane—not in a crash, but in a fight with the pilot. And, of course, there was Ray Chapman, the Indian shortstop who in 1920 was killed by a Carl Mays fastball. Mays never fully shook off suspicions that he was aiming for Chapman's head.

In Delahanty's time especially, violence was very much a part of the game. Players fought with umpires, fans, and each other. John McGraw, an Oriole shortstop and later Giant manager, routinely used his spikes to stomp on umpires' feet.

"In the early days of baseball, it was not terribly uncommon for players to meet . . . violent deaths," baseball historian Richard Topp said. "These players often came from the lowest strata of society and were ill-equipped to deal with the fame and money and lifestyle."

Amid all this, Delahanty's death stood out. For one thing, he was a future Hall of Famer, a slugger who rarely struck out, who won a batting title in each league and had a lifetime average of .346. In a deadball era, he hit 101 home runs. So far did his balls travel that others' home runs were known as "Delahanty bunts."

Once, when Cy Young tried to intentionally walk him, Delahanty reached across the plate and hit a home run. Another time, he broke a third baseman's ankle with a low line drive. When Babe Ruth came on the scene, the player he was most often compared to was Ed Delahanty.

So, on July 9, 1903, when Delahanty's body was found floating below Niagara Falls, it was understandably the source of a great deal of excitement and speculation. More than a hundred years later, it still is.

Once police identified the body under the falls, they retraced the steps that led him there. They found two key witnesses. One was John Cole, the conductor aboard a train en route from Detroit to New York, that Delahanty boarded on the afternoon of July 2. (Cole didn't recognize him at the time; only after Delahanty's death did the conductor realize his passenger was the famous ballplayer.) The passenger quickly caused trouble. He refused to stop smoking, or to move to the smoking car. He tried to push down a wood partition. Later that night, for no apparent reason, he started grabbing sleeping passengers by the ankles and pulling them from their berths.

Finally, Cole had had enough. The train stopped on the Canadian side of the Niagara River, and Delahanty was told to get off.

Delahanty apparently headed across the International Bridge, where he encountered Sam Kingston, a night guard. Kingston told police that he saw a man, apparently drunk, on the bridge. Kingston ordered him off the bridge, there was a brief struggle, and the man fled. Then Kingston heard a splash in the water. Later, Kingston told a reporter that the man was "the worse for liquor."

Did a drunken Delahanty cause trouble on the train and bridge, and then trip into the water?

Possibly. Delahanty had been known to go on drinking binges. In fact, when he failed to show up for a game in Detroit a few days before his death, his Washington Senator teammates shrugged it off. Their star had disappeared before, usually to drink or gamble or both. Newspapers, in those days reluctant to taint the image of a superstar, reported that he was "under the weather."

There was also talk of suicide, especially from nervous rail-road officials. Kingston pushed this version, telling reporters that "he must have climbed over the girders, then onto the pier and jumped off."

But many, especially Delahanty's family, suspected foul play. Frank Delahanty, then twenty years old and an outfielder in the New York State League, examined his brother's body and wondered why a tie was still around Ed's neck, but the diamond pin that had held it in place was gone. Two rings Ed wore also were gone, along with other jewelry family members said the victim had with him. Frank suspected that Ed had been robbed, then pushed from the bridge. When Kingston later changed his story to emphasize Ed's drunkenness and deny any sort of physical confrontation with him, Frank became even more suspicious.

A Niagara Falls newspaper, the *Cataract Journal,* also was skeptical of the official story. "Railroad officials say that he jumped from the bridge but there is another surmise that he was held up by the bridge tender, then an altercation and struggle ensued between the two men and that Delahanty either fell off or was shoved off the bridge."

Ed's widow, Norine, sued the railroad for kicking her husband off the train, and was awarded $3,000. Still, no criminal charges were brought against Cole or Kingston or anyone else. Police concluded that whatever jewelry the victim might have had on him had been washed away by the Niagara River. Officially, the case was closed.

Indeed, there was a strong case for suicide. It had not been a good year for Delahanty. True, he was hitting .333 when he disappeared. But his fielding was abominable, so much so that the *Washington Post* labeled it "suspicious." Washington manager Tom Loftus tried moving Delahanty from right to left field, but he was even less comfortable and competent there. Moreover, the Senators were slumping, so much so that when Loftus was suspended for a fight in St. Louis, reporters joked he was being rewarded with five days away from the Senators.

In Detroit, Ed wrote a letter to Norine and enclosed an accident insurance policy, made out to their daughter. If he was thinking about suicide, his drinking must have made things worse.

He also must have been embarrassed by a July 1 headline in the *Detroit Times*, "Big Fellow Decides to Cut Out the Booze." It was bad enough to be depressed and drunk without the whole world reading about it.

Wrote a *Buffalo Courier-Express* poet:

He had the blues,
So he quaffed some booze
And turned up dead
In just necktie and shoes.

Blues and booze may very well have led to Delahanty's death, but there was more to Delahanty's depression. If a fielding slump and a losing record were enough to spark a suicide, the Senators would have been defunct long before club owners moved the original team to Minnesota in 1960 and a later version to Texas in 1971. Delahanty also had financial woes, many of which could be traced to the turn-of-the-century war between the National League and the upstart American League.

In 1899, Delahanty hit .410 for the Philadelphia Phillies, topping the National League. He made only $2,400. So it was not surprising that when the Senators offered him $4,000 a year for 1902 and 1903, Delahanty jumped to the American League. Alas, Delahanty liked to gamble as well as drink, and he lost much of his salary at the track.

Then his luck seemed to turn. The National League wanted him back, in the person of John McGraw, who was eager to have Delahanty in the Giant outfield. After the 1902 season, in which Delahanty led the American League with a .376 average, McGraw offered him $6,000 a year for three years. Delahanty jumped again. He also accepted a $4,000 advance from the Giants.

At this point the owners had had enough of this interleague free agency. The two leagues agreed to stop raiding each other's players, and they ordered players back to their 1902 teams. They also ordered Delahanty to return the $4,000 advance to the Giants. Delahanty, alas, had already lost that money at the track. That meant he owed the Giants most of what he stood to earn playing, again, for the Senators. This was certainly a depressing prospect.

The interleague war may have contributed even more directly to Delahanty's death. Near the end of June, while the Senators were playing in Cleveland, Delahanty may have picked up a copy of the *Cleveland Press* and seen the headline "Base Ball War Is on Again." McGraw had ordered two of his preseason signees to leave their American League teams and come to New York. Delahanty might very well have assumed he was next and may have decided to see McGraw. After all, as many of his teammates later pointed out, the train he boarded in Detroit was bound for New York. The chance to play for the Giants must have elated Delahanty, but—coupled with his drinking—it may have increased his agitation. Certainly that was the state in which Cole and Kingston described him.

"We couldn't prove anything," Frank Delahanty said, "but I understand what started the whole thing was that he was going to leave the team and go to New York to play for the Giants. He was going to jump back to the National League. If he had made it, the baseball war between the two leagues would have started all over again."

Wrote *Sporting Life:* "The American League players as a mass sincerely mourn Delahanty's unfortunate death, and attribute it to the management of the New York National League Club."

Senators owner Fred Postal agreed: "John T. Brush, president of the New York National League baseball team, is responsible for the death of Edward Delahanty."

McGraw responded that the American League was to blame for invalidating Delahanty's deal with the Giants and sending him back to the Senators.

The American League got the last word that fall. In the first World Series between the leagues, the Boston Pilgrims defeated the Pittsburgh Pirates, 5 games to 3.

To investigate further:

Alexander, Charles. *John McGraw.* New York: Viking, 1988. A scholarly study of baseball's "rowdy" era, and one of its rowdiest players and managers.

Fitzpatrick, Frank. "A Baseball Mystery Is 85 Years Old." *Philadelphia Inquirer,* July 3, 1988. Eighty-five years earlier, another *Inquirer* columnist had written: "Poor old Del has been called out by the inexorable umpire."

Sowell, Mike. *July 2, 1903.* New York: Macmillan, 1992. Through Delahanty's life and death, Sowell chronicles the war (and peace) between the leagues. This chapter is much indebted to him.

Summers, Robert. "His Ticket Said New York City, but Fate Said Niagara Falls." *Buffalo Courier-Express,* September 8, 1974. Continuing the *Courier-Express*'s poetic tradition, the newspaper wrote: "Baseball lost its brightest star when they kicked him off the Pullman car."

5

Did Merkle Touch Second?

The 1908 National League pennant race came down to the final game between the Chicago Cubs and the New York Giants. The Cubs had shortstop Joe Tinker, second baseman Johnny Evers, and first baseman-manager Frank Chance, whose double-play-making skills were immortalized by Giant fan Franklin Adams:

> These are the saddest of possible words
> Tinker to Evers to Chance
> A trio of bear Cubs and fleeter than birds
> Tinker to Evers to Chance

The Giants had arguably the era's greatest manager, John McGraw, and arguably its greatest pitcher, Christy Mathewson. Alas, the Giants also had Fred Merkle.

For much of the season, Merkle appeared to be an asset. Before spring training, McGraw lauded him as the fastest base runner he ever saw. Only nineteen, Merkle was used primarily as a utility infielder, but he made the most of his opportunities. In June, his pinch-hit home run won a game, and he was briefly a hero. Then came the infamous game of September 23.

Merkle started at first in place of regular Fred Tenney, who had a bad back. The Cubs and Giants went to the bottom of the ninth tied 1–1. With two outs, Merkle singled, sending third baseman Moose McCormick to third. Merkle's teammate Fred Snodgrass described what happened next.

"The next man up was Al Bridwell, our shortstop," Snodgrass told oral historian Lawrence Ritter. "Al hit a line single into center field. McCormick, of course, scored easily from third—he could have walked in—with what appeared to be the winning run."

"Merkle started for second base, naturally," continued Snodgrass. "But the minute he saw the ball was a safe hit, rolling toward the fence out in right center, with McCormick across the plate and the game presumably over and won, he turned and lit out for the clubhouse. . . . And that was Merkle's downfall."

What Merkle forgot, but the Cubs didn't, was that a force-out at second would invalidate the winning run. As Merkle headed toward the clubhouse and prematurely celebrating Giant fans headed onto the field, Tinker somehow got hold of the ball. In true poetic tradition, he threw it to Evers, who, the *New York Herald* wrote, "stood proudly on second base holding the ball aloft, while [umpire Hank] O'Day, who had run down to second to see the play, was immediately surrounded by Chicago players." O'Day called Merkle out.

With fans on the field and darkness approaching, there was no way to continue the game. O'Day called it a tie. Two weeks later, when the season ended with the two teams tied for first, the Giants and Cubs replayed the game that the Giants thought they'd already won. The Cubs won, 4–2, with Mordecai "Three Finger" Brown (whose curveball was much aided by a boyhood farm accident) outpitching Mathewson. The Cubs went on to win the World Series.

As for Merkle, he was saddled with the nickname Bonehead, unnecessarily, since Merkle itself came to be a synonym for stupidity. Rarely a day went by—or at least a day when he reached first—without some fan loudly reminding him to touch second. The National League Board of Directors, in upholding O'Day's decision, left no doubt who was to blame. "There can be no question that the game should have been won by New York had it not been for the reckless, careless, inexcusable blunder of one player, Merkle."

"I wished that a large, roomy, and comfortable hole would open up and swallow me" was how Merkle put it.

Did Merkle deserve such a fate? From the start, there have been some witnesses who claimed Merkle *did* touch second, and some who said Tinker never got the ball to Evers. Others have questioned whether O'Day's ruling was fair, even if Merkle never made it to second.

Broadcaster Keith Olbermann proposed September 23 as a national day of amnesty, in Fred Merkle's memory. "Not forgiveness; forgiveness requires guilt," explained Olbermann. "But amnesty means merely an acknowledgment that something that could deserve blame, might in fact be far more complicated."

Not surprisingly, more Chicago reporters tended to remember Evers at second, while more of New York's saw Merkle there.

Wrote the *Chicago Tribune*, the day after the game: "The facts gleaned from active participants and survivors are these: [Cub center fielder Solly] Hofman fielded Bridwell's knock and threw to Evers for a force play on the absent Merkle. But [Giant pitcher and third base coach Joe 'Iron Man'] McGinnity cut in and grabbed the ball before it ever reached the Trojan." (Evers came from Troy, New York.)

"Three Cubs landed on the Iron Man from as many directions at the same time and jolted the ball from his cruel grasp," the *Tribune* continued. "It rolled among the spectators who had swarmed upon the diamond like an army of starving potato bugs.

"Some say Merkle eventually touched second base," the *Tribune* concluded, "but not until he had been forced out by Hofman to McGinnity to six potato bugs to [pitcher] 'Kid' Kroh to some more Cubs, and the shrieking, triumphant Mr. Evers."

Evers credited teammates Harry Steinfeldt and Floyd Kroh with recovering the ball after McGinnity tossed it into the crowd. "I can see the fellow who caught it yet . . . a tall, stringy middle-aged gent with a brown bowler hat on," he recalled. "Steinfeldt and . . . Kroh . . . raced after him. 'Gimme the ball for just a minute,' Steinfeldt begged him. 'I'll bring it right back.' The guy wouldn't let go and suddenly Kroh solved the problem. He hit the customer right on top of that stiff hat, drove it down over his eyes and as the gent folded up, the ball fell free and Kroh got it. I was yelling and waving my hands out by second base and Tinker relayed it over to me and I stepped on the bag."

Here's how the *New York Evening Journal* reported the same events: "Merkle did make a run for the clubhouse to escape the onrushing fans . . . but he turned after going only a few feet and broke for second. Hofman did return the ball, but it went far over Evers' head, hit Tinker in the back and went on to [Cub catcher Johnny] Kling. Merkle was then on second."

Players and managers also tended to split on partisan lines. Chance saw Merkle forced; McGraw saw him touch second en route to the clubhouse. Merkle said he touched second; Evers said Merkle never did. Mathewson told the *New York Evening Mail* that he and Merkle were headed toward the clubhouse when he heard Chance call to Hofman to throw the ball to second. At that point, according to Mathewson, he grabbed Merkle by the arm and told him to go to second.

"Merkle touched the bag," Mathewson insisted. "I saw him do it."

Mathewson's status as, in Ritter's words, "the very embodiment of the all-American boy," perhaps lends his testimony a bit more weight. Yet, on balance, the evidence seemed to favor the Cubs. For one thing, no one questioned that Merkle was heading to the clubhouse before he did (or didn't) turn back toward second. At the very least, then, he could be called out for running out of the baseline.

Then there's McGinnity. The Giant's claim was that McGinnity threw the ball into the stands, that no Cub could have retrieved it, and that the ball that Evers triumphantly held at second could not therefore have been the game ball. That may be true. But if it is, what McGinnity did was clearly interference. That, too, was reason enough to call Merkle out.

Finally, there's the fact that the umpire called Merkle out. Giant fans maintained he couldn't have seen the play, but O'Day's official report on the game indicated both that Merkle didn't touch second and that McGinnity interfered with the play. National League president Harry Pulliam, in rejecting the Giants' appeal, insisted that the umpire's decision on a question of fact is final.

"The question of whether there was a force play or not cannot be substantiated by evidence of spectators," Pulliam wrote. "It rests solely with the umpire. . . . This whole controversy hinges on a simple question—Was Merkle forced out at second base? Umpire-in-chief O'Day says he was. O'Day is no novice, and there is no reason to doubt his accuracy in his decision."

The league's Board of Directors agreed. "To set aside an umpire's decision by evidence from persons in attendance, would, in our mind, be establishing a dangerous precedent," its report concluded. "We can, therefore, come to no other conclusion than that the New York club lost a well-earned victory as the result of a stupid play of one of its members."

Was Merkle really that stupid?

McGraw never thought so. Teammate Chief Meyers told Ritter: "McGraw never consulted anybody except Merkle on a question of strategy or something of that sort. He never asked Matty, he never asked me. He'd say, 'Fred, what do you think of this?' The bonehead! What a misnomer! One of the smartest men in baseball, Fred Merkle."

McGraw always believed the Giants were robbed, not because Merkle touched second (though McGraw thought he did) but because he didn't have to. If there was a realistic possibility of a force-out, of course runners had to beat the throw. But if the winning run had already crossed the plate and the defense had no chance of a force, it was common practice for runners to veer off the field before touching the bag. What Merkle did was no different from what many others had done before, without any consequences. And with the fans already mobbing players on the field, this was surely not the time suddenly to stand on ceremony.

"I think that under the circumstances any ballplayer on any ball club would have done the same thing Merkle did," said Bridwell, the man who would have had the game-winning RBI if Merkle hadn't been called out. "They did it all the time in those days."

"Any other player on the team would have undoubtedly done the same thing under the same circumstances, as the custom had been in vogue all around the circuit during the season," agreed Mathewson. "It was simply Fred Merkle's misfortune to have been on first base at the critical moment."

Bill Klem, who umpired the final game of the 1908 season and went on to become one of the profession's elder statesmen, went farther. "The intent in this rule applied to infield grounders and such," Klem told *Collier's* magazine in 1951. "It does not apply to cleanly hit drives to the outfield that make a force-out impossible unless the runner on first drops dead."

Klem said that O'Day "was accepting a technicality and ignoring perhaps a half a century of custom, usage, tradition, and the intent of the rule."

Indeed, fewer than three weeks before Merkle's gaffe, the same situation had arisen with the same umpire, and the ruling had been just the opposite. On September 4, with the Pirates batting in the bottom of the tenth, rookie Doc Gill failed to touch second after the game-winning hit. Evers grabbed the ball, tagged the base, and asked O'Day to call Gill out. O'Day ruled that the run counted, and the Pirates won.

Why the difference? O'Day never explained. Probably he, like everyone else that day except Evers, had been heading off the field, and he may have felt he couldn't call a play he hadn't seen. In any case, the Cubs protested, and Pulliam characteristically backed O'Day, arguing that questions pertaining to a force play rested "solely with the umpire."

Neither O'Day nor Pulliam gave any indication that the rule in question needed clarification, or that they might rule differently in the future. Still, had Merkle known what Evers had done in Pittsburgh, he might have gone directly to second, just to be on the safe side. That's led some to blame Merkle's manager. Wrote baseball historian David Nemec: "Since the Gill incident was widely reported, it should have been incumbent upon McGraw to remind his players of what Evers had tried to do against the Pirates, particularly when a repeat attempt was imminent with two out in the ninth and Giants runners on the corners."

McGraw was certainly a stickler for the rules when it benefited the Giants, and he was never averse to telling his players what to do. "It is indeed puzzling," wrote baseball historian David Anderson, "that a manager who would dictate what his players ate for breakfast, as McGraw did, should have overlooked the situation. . . . And considering O'Day's presence on the diamond that fateful day, the oversight was particularly egregious."

But neither McGraw nor Merkle could have known that a rule that was not enforced on September 4 would be enforced on September 23. And that's led many to sympathize with both.

"The saga has always seemed to me a microcosm not just of baseball or of celebrity, but of life," said Olbermann. "The rules sometimes change while you're playing the game. Those you trust to tell you the changes often don't bother to. That for which history still mocks you would have gone unnoticed if you had done it a year or a month or a day before."

In 1987, when umpire Joe Brinkman nullified a home run by Kansas City third baseman George Brett because of pine tar too high on his bat, the Royals used much the same logic in protesting that it was unfair suddenly to enforce a previously ignored rule, especially at a crucial moment in the pennant race. Unlike Pulliam, American League president Lee MacPhail agreed and overturned the umpire's decision.

So maybe history should give Merkle a break, too.

Snodgrass, who may have been more prone to forgiving blunders after he dropped a crucial fly ball in the 1912 World Series, which the Giants then went on to lose to the Red Sox, thought it was unfair to say that Merkle cost the team the pennant in 1908.

"McGraw never did, and neither did the rest of us," he said. "How could you blame Merkle, when we lost the play-off game, and besides that we lost five other games *after* the Merkle incident? If we had won any one of those five games we would have won the pennant in the regular season, and we wouldn't even have had to play a play-off game."

Despite the constant heckling, Merkle went on to play for another fourteen years in the majors, and then to manage in the minors, a sign of, if nothing else, considerable resilience. Pulliam, on the other hand, may never have recovered from the turmoil that trailed his decision. On July 19, 1909, he shot himself in the head.

Representatives from every major league team attended the funeral—except for the Giants.

To investigate further:

Alexander, Charles. *John McGraw*. New York: Viking, 1988. Sure, he stood by Merkle. But he may have lost the moral high ground by, as Alexander suspects, trying to bribe Klem to throw the final game of the season.

Anderson, David. *More Than Merkle*. Lincoln: University of Nebraska Press, 2000. A history of the 1908 season, when the American League race also came down to the final day.

Fleming, G. H. *The Unforgettable Season*. New York: Holt, Rinehart, & Winston, 1981. The 1908 season as seen through masterfully edited contemporary newspaper accounts.

Golenbock, Peter. *Wrigleyville*. New York: St. Martin's Press, 1997. Golenbock's oral history of the Cubs includes extensive excerpts from Evers's 1910 book *Touching Second*. Evers's Cobb-like intensity, incidentally, inspired others besides Adams to poetry. Wrote Ogden Nash in his "Line-up for Yesterday: An ABC of Baseball Immortals": "E is for Evers,/His jaw in advance;/Never afraid/To Tinker with Chance."

Mathewson, Christy. *Pitching in a Pinch*. New York: Stein & Day, 1977. Stories and strategies from the man who made baseball respectable. Originally published in 1912.

Nemec, David. *The Rules of Baseball*. New York: Lyons & Burford, 1994. An anecdotal look at how the rules came to be.

Ritter, Lawrence. *The Glory of Their Times*. New York: Macmillan, 1966. Classic oral history.

6

Did Cobb Win the 1910 Batting Race?

Going into the final day of the 1910 season, Ty Cobb seemed sure to win the "Chalmers 30," a luxury car that Hugh Chalmers, owner of the company that bore his name, had promised the winner of the American League batting title. This would be Cobb's fourth straight title. Cobb, bothered by some eye problems, chose to sit out the Tigers' game in Chicago.

Napoleon Lajoie, who had led the league in hitting in 1901, 1903, and 1904, was also having another superb season. Lajoie was twelve years older than Cobb, and this looked like his last shot at another title. He was the sentimental favorite. But Cobb was hitting .383, Lajoie .376. To top Cobb, Lajoie, whose Indians were playing in St. Louis, had to go 8 for 8.

Which is exactly what he did.

How he did it was an immediate scandal. "St. Louis Team 'Lays Down' to Let Lajoie Win," headlined the *Detroit Free Press*, which attributed Lajoie's hits to "the hate-Ty-Cobb-campaign." The *St. Louis Post* agreed: "All St. Louis is up in arms over the deplorable spectacle," the paper reported. "The obvious frame-up to beat Cobb out of the title surely will place a period upon the career of whatever officials of the home team ordered this gross affair."

Lajoie's first hit, a drive to left, appeared legitimate. The remaining seven were all bunts. Lajoie had no trouble beating them out, since the Browns' third baseman, Red Corriden, was playing on the outfield grass. After the game, Corriden explained that he was afraid of Lajoie's line drives. "I want to remain in baseball for some time," he said. "I might have got some of Lajoie's bunts, and at the same time a broken nose or lost a couple of teeth." Brown manager Jack O'Connor said Lajoie, by bunting every time up, "outguessed us."

These were pretty lame explanations, and American League president Ban Johnson promised a full investigation.

It would not have taken much investigating to learn that Lajoie was one of the best-liked players of the era. "After Ed [Dela-hanty] died . . . the big hero of all the kids in Cleveland became . . . the Cleveland second baseman," infielder Tommy Leach told oral historian Lawrence Ritter. "He was a pleasure to play against. . . . Even when the son of a gun was blocking you off the base, he was smiling and kidding with you. You just *had* to like the guy."

It would have taken even less investigating to learn what other players thought about Cobb. No one was as zealously and as universally disliked. Cobb did not play for fun, and it was no fun to play with him. "Baseball is a red-blooded sport for red-blooded men," he wrote in his autobiography. "It's no pink tea, and mollycoddles had better stay out. It's a contest and everything that implies, a struggle for supremacy, a survival of the fittest."

Cobb denied intentionally sharpening his spikes, but his slides bloodied many an infielder. After Cobb spiked Frank "Home Run" Baker in a 1909 game, Philadelphia manager Connie Mack called him "a no-good ruffian" and "a malefactor no league can afford." Ernest Hemingway, who went hunting with him, said Cobb "had a screw loose."

Even his fellow Tigers couldn't stand him. No one would room with him on road trips, no one sat next to him in the dugout. After Lajoie's 8-for-8 performance moved him past Cobb, eight Tigers whipped off a congratulatory telegram.

"You can't turn that kind of competitive drive on and off," said teammate Charlie Gehringer. "He was the same off the field as he was on; he was always fighting with somebody. He was a holy terror."

Sam Crawford, who played beside Cobb in the Tiger outfield, thought the Georgia Peach was still fighting the Civil War. "As far as he was concerned, we were all damn Yankees before he even met us."

Al Stump, who ghosted Cobb's autobiography and later wrote a biography of him, asked why he fought so hard. "I did it for my father," Cobb answered. "They killed him when he was still young. . . . He never got to see me play. Not one game, not an inning. But I knew he was watching me . . . and I never let him down. *Never.*"

What Cobb didn't mention was that the "they" who killed his father was his mother. The killing, which took place the very week Cobb was called up to the majors, is still shrouded in mystery. At her murder trial, Amanda Cobb testified that on the evening of August 8, 1905, W. H. Cobb told her he was going out of town and left the house. Amanda Cobb went upstairs, locked the windows, and went to bed. At about 10:30 P.M. she woke up to see someone trying to open one of the bedroom windows. Assuming it was a burglar, she took a shotgun and fired. Then she shot again.

Her story left a lot of questions. Why did she lock the windows, when it had been in the nineties during the day and was still hot and humid? Why, according to witnesses who heard the shots, was there a considerable interval between them? Why was W. H. Cobb, who presumably had a key to his house, outside the bedroom window? And why was his body found with a revolver in his pocket?

Some suspected Amanda Cobb hated her husband, who had married her when she was only twelve years old. Possibly, but the practice was not then unheard of in small-town Georgia, and there was no evidence that that was the case. The gossip around town was that Amanda Cobb had a lover, and that her husband had told her he was going out of town so he could sneak back home, catch them in the act, and shoot one or both of them. But there was no proof of this either, and Amanda Cobb was alone when she shot her husband. Prosecutors never mentioned a lover, and the jury found Amanda Cobb not guilty.

Still, the killing and the scandal surely strengthened Cobb's resolve to prove himself. "I know for a fact that he never got over it," Cobb's childhood friend Joe Cunningham told Stump. "It was always on his mind that his father never would see him in action, crowds cheering him. . . . After the shooting, I figure that much of what he did on the diamond was for W. H. Seemed he was out to pay tribute to him in death."

"The thing is, W. H. opposed his playing ball," Cunningham added. "But he cared enough to let Ty go and prove he was a man. Ty owed him for that and he never stopped paying back."

For Johnson, of course, the issue wasn't why Cobb hated everyone, or why everyone hated Cobb. The league president just wanted to know who hated him enough to fix the batting race. It seemed unlikely that Corriden, a rookie, had acted on his own, and the third baseman soon admitted that O'Connor, the manager, had given the order to play deep. St. Louis coach Harry Howell also was implicated; an anonymous note informed Johnson that Howell had offered the official scorer a suit of clothes to score any of Lajoie's questionable at-bats as a hit.

Johnson banned Howell for the attempted bribe, but he absolved Corriden of any blame. He was spared having to hand down a formal decision on O'Connor, since Brown owner Robert Lee Hedges fired the manager at the end of the season. (The team had finished last, anyway.) O'Connor never managed or coached in the majors again.

As for the batting title, Johnson announced his decision on October 16, a week after the game. Since the scorer had ignored Howell's attempted bribe, and since there was no formal ruling against O'Connor or Corriden, there were no grounds for disqualifying Lajoie's hits. The umpires and scorers had considered the game legitimate, and Johnson stuck by their decisions. Both Cobb and Lajoie had been criticized for what they did the final

day of the season—Cobb for not playing (some people suspected, wrongly, that his eye problems were exacerbated by his
desire to keep up his average), and Lajoie for "the St. Louis incident," Johnson said. Somehow this made it all balance out.

"It is a matter of comment that Lajoie frequently resorted to
the bunt in the latter stages of the pennant race," Johnson added
somewhat disingenuously.

So Lajoie's final average stood at .384.

Did Lajoie get the car? Not yet. For Johnson also had ordered
a review of Cobb's stats and, he now announced, Cobb's final
average was not .383 but .385, giving him the title. Fortunately,
Hugh Chalmers was a generous man, or at least one who'd mastered public relations. Both Cobb and Lajoie would get a Chalmers 30.

Everyone was happy, even Cobb. The following spring a
Detroit writer asked him how he felt about the congratulatory
telegram his teammates sent Lajoie. "Oh, when I pass some of
them on the street," he answered, "I just honk the horn of my
new car at them."

So matters stood until 1981, when researchers at the *Sporting
News* took a new look at the 1910 box scores. They discovered
Johnson's statistician had incorrectly credited Cobb twice for a
2-for-3 game on September 24, and also left out hitless at-bats
on May 26 and August 10.

Recalculated, Cobb's final average was .382. Seventy-one
years later, Lajoie was now the batting champion.

The new research also raised questions about Johnson's
investigation. Did the league president err in Cobb's favor to
avoid giving a tainted title to Lajoie? The *Sporting News* didn't
know, and perhaps it's unfair to assume that in those days there
weren't plenty of other errors in the statistics, some of which
might very well have been in Lajoie's favor. But there's no doubt
that based on what's now known—and if you count Napoleon
Lajoie's admittedly dubious final day—Ty Cobb did not deserve
a Chalmers 30.

To investigate further:

Alexander, Charles. *Ty Cobb*. New York: Oxford University Press, 1984. Scholarly but readable.

Cobb, Ty, with Al Stump. *My Life in Baseball*. Garden City, N.Y.: Doubleday, 1961. Surprisingly revealing; Cobb comes across as extraordinary—and extraordinarily disagreeable.

MacFarlane, Paul. "After 70 Years, Researchers Prove Lajoie Really Did Win." *Sporting News*, April 18, 1981. Statisticians Leonard Gettelson and Pete Palmer, in a separate study, also uncovered the 1910 errors.

Ritter, Lawrence. *The Glory of Their Times*. New York: Macmillan, 1966. Oral history at its best.

Stump, Al. *Cobb*. Chapel Hill, N.C.: Algonquin Books, 1994. He was "the most spectacular, enigmatic, and troubled of American sports figures." He was also, Stump believed, psychotic.

7

Did Shoeless Joe Throw the Series?

The career of "Shoeless Joe" Jackson—whose talent, according to his fellow players, rivaled that of Babe Ruth—came to an abrupt end when he was banned from the game after the 1919 Black Sox scandal. That was the year gamblers bribed the heavily favored Chicago White Sox to throw the World Series.

A year later, Jackson testified before a Cook County grand jury, and the *New York Evening World* published its famous account of the player encountering a group of boys outside the courthouse.

"A man, guarded like a felon by other men, emerged from the door," reported Hugh Fullerton. "He did not swagger. He slunk along between his guardians, and the kids, with wide eyes and tightened throats, watched, and one, bolder than the others, pressed forward and said, 'It ain't so, Joe, is it?' "

Jackson, according to Fullerton, gulped back a sob before answering, "Yes, kid, I'm afraid it is."

Jackson always denied this story. More to the point, he denied he ever played anything but his best, pointing to his .375 Series batting average, his 5 runs scored, and his 6 runs batted in. Since then, Jackson has become a mythic figure, sometimes a symbol of guilt and sometimes of innocence. He is the basis for the Faustian Joe Hardy in the musical *Damn Yankees* and the more-sinned-against-than-sinning Roy Hobbs in the novel and movie

The Natural. As an illiterate cotton mill worker whose natural ability took him from a small South Carolina town to Chicago, Jackson is a symbol of innocence; corrupted by the big city, he is a symbol of our fall from grace. In the movie *Field of Dreams*, he emerges from an Iowa cornfield, the perfect symbol of a lost America. Even his nickname seemed to fit perfectly his image as bumpkin and phenom, a man without the sense or money to wear shoes but with so much talent that he didn't need them.

Amid Jackson's apotheosis, baseball historians have continued to debate the question whether it actually is or ain't so.

Rumors that the Series was fixed surfaced even before it began. In fact, by the first game, so much money had been bet on the underdog Cincinnati Reds that White Sox fans could get even odds on their team. After the Reds won the Series, White Sox owner Charles Comiskey offered a $20,000 reward for evidence of a fix.

Almost a year later, the reward tempted Billy Maharg, one of the gamblers involved in bribing players, to tell his story, and a Cook County grand jury convened to investigate. The first player to crack was Eddie Cicotte, a pitcher who told the grand jury he'd taken $10,000 to lose two Series games.

On September 28, 1920, Jackson appeared before the grand jury, and his own testimony is among the most damning evidence against him. Jackson told the grand jury that White Sox first baseman Chick Gandil was the first to approach him about the fix. Assistant state's attorney Hartley Repogle questioned Jackson:

Q. How much did he promise you?
A. $20,000 if I would take part.

Q. And you said you would?
A. Yes, sir.

Q. When did he promise you the $20,000?
A. It was to be paid after each game.

Q. How much?

A. Split up in some way. I don't know just how much it
   amounts to, but . . . it would amount to $20,000. Finally
   [White Sox pitcher Lefty] Williams brought me this
   $5,000, and threw it down.

Later the same day, Jackson seemingly contradicted himself.
He told the grand jury that he'd always played his best.

Q. Did you make any intentional errors yourself?

A. No, sir, not during the whole Series.

Q. Did you bat to win?

A. Yes.

Q. And run the bases to win?

A. Yes, sir.

Q. And fielded the balls at the outfield to win?

A. I did.

Still, Jackson's earlier admission, along with similar statements
from Cicotte and Williams, seemed enough at least to bring the
Black Sox to trial. State's attorney Robert Crowe, who took over
the case from Repogle, certainly expected to go to court. But
when Crowe examined the grand jury's files, he discovered that
the critical portions of the players' testimony were missing from
the record. This was not just mysterious but also damn suspicious. Gone, too, were the waivers of immunity the players had
signed before testifying. And Cicotte, Williams, and Jackson now
denied that they'd ever confessed to anything.

Crowe proceeded nonetheless, and the fraud and conspiracy
trial of eight White Sox, including Jackson, opened in June 1921.
Instead of the players, Crowe called to the stand Maharg and
another gambler, Bill Burns, who in return for immunity described
their roles in the fix. But the prosecution's case was undercut by
the judge's instructions to the jury. There was no law on the
books that specifically outlawed throwing baseball games. So
Judge Hugo Friend explained that to find the defendants guilty,

the jurors had to be convinced the players had intentionally harmed Comiskey's business and defrauded the public. This was a difficult standard of proof for prosecutors to meet, especially since during the 1920 season, Jackson and his teammates had finished a close second, baseball fans continued to stream into Comiskey Park, and Comiskey was making more money than ever. Besides, even if the Black Sox had thrown the Series, prosecutors hadn't presented evidence that the players were motivated by anything other than greed. It took the jury only three hours to find all eight not guilty.

The celebration, however, was short-lived. Baseball's new commissioner, Kenesaw Mountain Landis, didn't think much of the jury's verdict or of leniency in general. (As a judge, Landis once sentenced a seventy-five-year-old to fifteen years in jail. When the man said he couldn't serve that long, Landis told him to "do the best you can.")

The same evening the jurors pronounced their verdict, Landis gave his. "Regardless of the outcome of juries," he said, "no player that throws a ball game, no player that entertains proposals or promises to throw a game, no player that sits in a conference with a bunch of crooked players where the ways and means of throwing games are discussed, and does not promptly tell his club about it, will ever again play professional baseball."

Neither Jackson nor any of the seven other Black Sox would ever again play major league baseball.

Jackson sued Comiskey for the salary he lost after the owner dropped him and the other Black Sox from the roster. The case went to court in January 1924. This time it wasn't enough for Jackson to show he hadn't damaged Comiskey's business; he had to convince a jury he wasn't in on the fix.

The story Jackson now told differed from the one presented to either the 1920 grand jury or the 1921 jury. Jackson claimed he knew nothing about the fix during the Series; the other players, without his permission, used his name to impress the gamblers. Indeed, Jackson went on, he did not know there was a fix until Lefty Williams gave him the $5,000 after the last game of the Series. Gamblers Maharg and Burns appeared in court again, this time to confirm that Jackson wasn't present at any of their meetings with the players. Williams also testified that he hadn't spoken to Jackson about the fix until he handed over the money.

Moreover, Jackson explained, once he learned of the fix he tried to tell Comiskey about it. With the $5,000 in his pocket, Jackson went to Comiskey's office, but the owner wouldn't see him. Jackson backed up this testimony by producing a letter he'd dictated to Comiskey suggesting that the Series was crooked. Comiskey never responded. The villain of this story was clearly Comiskey, who tried to cover up the fix to protect the value of his team. Only after Maharg blew the lid off the scandal did the owner change course and turn on the players.

Comiskey's lawyer, George Hudnall, struck back with the most startling revelation of the trial. He pulled out of his briefcase the grand jury testimony in which Jackson admitted discussing with Gandil the fix and his $20,000 share. Here was the document that had disappeared after the grand jury hearing. Jackson responded by explaining that, yes, he had sort of confessed, but only because Comiskey's lawyer had advised him no jury would believe the truth. Jackson had taken the lawyer's word that he wouldn't be prosecuted if he confessed.

If the grand jury testimony embarrassed Jackson, it was also awkward for Comiskey. How, after all, did his lawyer come to be in possession of the missing document? Questioned by Jackson's lawyers, Comiskey said he didn't know. But reporters then and historians later couldn't help but note how conveniently the grand jury testimony disappeared when Comiskey was still hoping to hold on to his star players, and how conveniently it reappeared when he was trying to avoid paying back wages to one of those players. Most historians assumed that Comiskey, probably with the help of some of the gamblers, either paid off some clerk or simply stole the documents.

The 1924 jury, like the 1921 one, found for Jackson. They awarded him $16,711.04. Again, however, there was little time to celebrate. Once the jury was out of earshot, Judge John Gregory declared that Jackson was a liar. His 1921 and 1924 stories couldn't both be true, so he must have lied one of those times. Either way, Gregory wasn't going to let a perjurer walk away with a victory in his court. He immediately set aside the verdict.

After the trial, Comiskey offered an out-of-court settlement, thus precluding any more awkward questions about how he happened to have the grand jury testimony. Jackson took an undisclosed (and presumably small) amount of money and went home to South Carolina.

Comiskey's reputation, deservedly, never recovered. Many baseball historians focused on how he not only covered up the fix, but also to some extent caused it. In an era before big-money baseball salaries, Comiskey paid players significantly less than other owners paid theirs. Jackson, clearly one of the best players of all time, never made more than $6,000 a year. Cicotte, according to Eliot Asinof's *Eight Men Out*, was driven to throw the Series at least partly because of Comiskey's penuriousness. In 1917, Comiskey promised the pitcher a $10,000 bonus if he won 30 games; when Cicotte reached 29, the owner ordered him benched. (Other historians dispute Asinof's story on the grounds that Comiskey would never have promised to pay anyone $10,000.) Even before 1919, some people called his team the Black Sox, because Comiskey, unlike other owners, wouldn't pay to clean their uniforms.

Historians also have done much to put the scandal in its historical context. When Landis banned the eight players, his clear implication was that he had solved the problem, that baseball's record until 1919 was pure and that it now would be again. But these were hardly the first players to get mixed up with gamblers. In addition to the eight Black Sox, fourteen others were banned from the game for similar reasons between 1917 and 1927. The record for the most thrown games probably goes to Hal Chase, a first baseman in New York, Chicago, and Cincinnati. Three of Chase's managers accused him of dishonesty before he was finally banned for bribing an umpire. With a tip of the hat to Asinof's classic, statistician-historian Bill James referred to the players who were banned as the "twenty-two men out." That figure doesn't count the many others who were allegedly involved in gambling, but against whom there wasn't enough evidence to take any action.

But back to Jackson. That some blame has fallen on Comiskey and others does not ultimately answer the question of how much belongs to Jackson. To some of his recent defenders, most notably historian Donald Gropman, Jackson is blameless. The story Jackson told at the 1924 civil trial was the truth; the 1921 grand jury testimony was solely the result of an illiterate mill-hand being duped by Comiskey's sophisticated lawyer. Two juries found Jackson not guilty, and so did Gropman. And, as Gropman and others have stressed, there's that .375 batting average. Jackson's 12 Series hits weren't matched until 1960.

A majority of recent historians, however, have found Jackson guilty, though to varying extents. He *did* take the $5,000 from Williams, even if we accept Jackson's word that he didn't know in advance it was coming and that he tried to tell Comiskey about it. Jackson was illiterate but not stupid. When he returned to South Carolina, he opened a successful dry-cleaning business, employed more than twenty people, and bought a home and two cars. He knew what the money was for, and he kept it.

Whether he actually earned the money by playing less than his best remains a mystery. It's possible, as some historians have suggested, that he intended to throw the games but had so much natural talent and so much love for the game that once he took the field, he couldn't stop himself from hitting. It's also possible, as others have noted, that he was capable of playing even better than he did. His hits were plentiful, but most of them didn't come with the game on the line. He was not charged with any errors, but three triples fell near him.

In the press box, with rumors rampant during the Series, Hugh Fullerton circled on his scorecard those plays he considered suspicious. Some involved Jackson. But, like so much else about Shoeless Joe, what Fullerton wrote has added as much to the myth as to the reality. Even Fullerton's famous story about the boy who said "it ain't so" has often been denied, including by Jackson.

"No such word . . . was ever said," Jackson later claimed. "The fellow who wrote that just wanted something to say. When I came out of the courthouse that day, nobody said anything to me. The only one who spoke was a guy who yelled at his friend 'I told you the big son of a bitch wore shoes.'"

To investigate further:

Asinof, Eliot. *Eight Men Out*. New York: Holt, Rinehart, & Winston, 1963. This was a classic of baseball history long before John Sayles made it into a fine movie.

Fleitz, David. *Shoeless*. Jefferson, N.C.: McFarland, 2001. A comprehensive biography that concludes Jackson was guilty.

Frommer, Harvey. *Shoeless Joe and Ragtime Baseball*. Dallas: Taylor, 1992. A less thorough defense than Gropman's, though the appendix— which contains the entire text of Jackson's 1921 grand jury testimony—is useful.

Gropman, Donald. *Say It Ain't So, Joe!* New York: Citadel Press, 1995. Originally published in 1979, this remains the best defense of Jackson.

James, Bill. *The New Bill James Historical Baseball Abstract*. New York: Free Press, 2001. James is usually thought of as a statistician, but his history goes way beyond the numbers.

8

What Caused Ruth's "Bellyache"?

Babe Ruth was, folkorist Tristram Coffin wrote, "a mass market Achilles." Biographer Marshall Smelser called him "our Hercules, our Samson, Beowulf, Siegfried." And as with all such heroes, his appetites were as legendary as his deeds.

Breakfast, awed onlookers reported, consisted of eighteen eggs, three big slices of ham, and a dozen slices of buttered toast. During five or six hours spent with outfielder Harry Heilmann and infielders Fred Haney and Joe Dugan, Ruth once consumed four porterhouse steaks, four orders of salad with Roquefort dressing, four orders of fried potatoes, four slices of apple pie à la mode, eight hot dogs, and four bottles of Coke.

Recalled Ty Cobb: "I've seen him at midnight, propped up in bed, order six club sandwiches, a platter of pigs' knuckles, and a pitcher of beer. He'd down them all while smoking a big black cigar. Next day, if he hit a homer, he'd trot around the bases complaining about gas pains and a bellyache."

It all seemed to catch up with him in 1925. In January he weighed 256 pounds, well above normal and with a beer belly that, though now part of his image, was distinctly lacking in his younger days. In late March, when the Yankees boarded the train that would take them north from spring training (with stops along the way to play exhibition games against the Dodgers), he had a fever and stomach cramps. On April 7, as the train wound its way along a bumpy track, several players were nauseous, Ruth especially so. When the train stopped in Asheville, North Carolina, Ruth got off and fainted. Doctors said he was suffering from influenza and indigestion. The team headed to Greenville, but Ruth was sent directly to New York, where he fainted again, this time remaining unconscious.

"Ruth never did anything in a small way," wrote sportswriter Paul Gallico. "He was carted from the train on a stretcher and taken to the hospital, where he very nearly died. Few if any American citizens have ever had such a death watch or caused so much public concern while lying on a sick-bed." In London, the *Evening News* printed his obituary.

At St. Vincent's Hospital, Dr. Edward King reassured reporters that Ruth had the flu, prescribed rest, and predicted he'd be ready for opening day the next week. "The big fellow doesn't take care of himself," he said. "He leads an active life and eats heartily."

A week later, though, Ruth was no better. King announced that Ruth had an intestinal abscess, and on April 17 Dr. George Stewart operated on him. Ruth didn't return to the lineup until June, and in July he was hitting .250 with only a few home runs. He appeared washed up, as did the Yankees, who finished next to last.

In the words of *New York Tribune* writer W. O. McGeehan, this was "the bellyache heard round the world." Immediately, the story spread that it was brought on by hot dogs Ruth ate on the train, somewhere between twelve and eighteen by varying accounts. But this, another writer quipped, was a little hard to swallow: you don't end up in the hospital for seven weeks because of indigestion.

"I was a mighty sick man," Ruth wrote in his autobiography, but that wasn't much of an explanation.

"You know," said Ruth, talking about his autobiography, "you can't put everything in a story, so I left out a few things. Maybe there should have been two books, one for kids and one for adults."

Reporters could not help but suspect that what had been left out was venereal disease. Ruth's appetite for sex was almost as notorious as his for food, and—though publicly presented as a zest for late nights on the town—it was very much a part of his Herculean image. If Hercules could sleep with all fifty of the king's daughters in a single night, why not Babe? His roommate Ping Bodie once famously remarked that he roomed with the Babe's suitcase.

Reporter Rud Rennie parodied manager Miller Huggins's never-ending search for his outfielder:

I wonder where my Babe Ruth is tonight?
He grabbed his hat and coat and ducked from sight?
He may be at some cozy roadside inn,
Drinking tea—or maybe gin.
He may be at a dance, or may be in a fight.
I know he's with a dame,
I wonder what's her name?
I wonder where my Babe Ruth is tonight?

Ruth's wife, Helen, found none of this funny. In late April she was herself hospitalized at St. Vincent's with what doctors described as "a nervous condition brought on by worry about the illness of the Yankee slugger." That may very well have been the case, but it also was clear that the marriage was in trouble, and the two soon separated, though they remained on friendly terms.

Off the record, Ed Barrow, the Yankees' general manager, told reporters what really ailed the Babe was syphilis. Others suspected gonorrhea, and both were certainly possible. But this didn't quite add up, any more than indigestion. Abdominal surgery would be a strange treatment for venereal disease, and Ruth definitely had a surgical scar.

That brings us back to Dr. King's diagnosis: an intestinal abscess. It was such an imprecise term that one can't blame skeptics for suspecting something more sinister. Some even hinted Ruth was poisoned. But it's much more likely that the abscess was some sort of groin injury, or an inflammation or obstruction of the intestine. Either could have required surgery and then convalescence.

Why, then, didn't doctors come right out and say so? Ruth's second wife, Claire Hodgson, suggested he hurt his groin sliding into first base and that it was too embarrassing to describe the details. "It was simpler to let the public think that the great star was just a hog," she said.

Perhaps it was not his injury but some aspect of Ruth's convalescence that seemed embarrassing. A colostomy, for example, might have seemed to the baseball and medical establishments of 1925 indelicate to discuss in public.

For all the talk about the Babe's eating and sexual habits, they probably had nothing to do with what hospitalized him that spring. And yet, ironically, his hospitalization did lead him to change his ways.

Not completely, to be sure. That August, Huggins suspended him for "misconduct off the field," including "drinking and a lot of other things besides." But there were fewer late nights, and once he married Claire Hodgson, there were fewer—or at least much more discreet—affairs. In a fall 1925 article in *Collier's*, Ruth admitted he'd been "a Babe and a Boob" and said he was done with "the pests and the good-time guys." He was never again as out of shape as he'd been that spring, and he was certainly not washed up. From 1926 to 1931, Ruth hit .354, averaging 50 home runs and 155 runs batted in a year.

"From the ashes of 1925," wrote biographer Robert Creamer, "Babe Ruth rose like a rocket."

To investigate further:

Coffin, Tristram. *The Old Ball Game*. New York: Herder & Herder, 1971. Baseball as folklore.

Creamer, Robert. *Babe*. New York: Simon & Schuster, 1974. Not only the best biography of Ruth but also one of the best biographies of any sports figure.

Gallico, Paul. *Farewell to Sport*. New York: Alfred A. Knopf, 1944. "God gave his alias as Babe Ruth," explained Gallico, who gave up sportswriting to write fiction, including *The Poseidon Adventure*.

Meany, Tom. *Babe Ruth*. New York: A. S. Barnes, 1947. An old-fashioned, anecdotal (and fun) sports biography.

Ritter, Lawrence, and Mark Rucker. *The Babe*. New York: Ticknor & Fields, 1988. An elegant pictorial biography.

Ruth, Babe, as told to Bob Considine. *The Babe Ruth Story*. New York: E. P. Dutton, 1948. A conventional sports autobiography for an unconventional player.

Ruth, Mrs. Babe, with Bill Slocum. *The Babe and I*. Englewood Cliffs, N.J.: Prentice-Hall, 1959. A loyal but surprisingly candid and often touching portrait by Ruth's second wife.

Smelser, Marshall. *The Life That Ruth Built*. New York: Quadrangle, 1975. A meandering and overly long biography that was the last and the least of the spate of midseventies biographies. Smelser deserves credit, however, for debunking the myth that the Baby Ruth candy bar was named after one of President Grover Cleveland's daughters. That has always been the claim of the Curtiss Candy Company, but Smelser noted that the candy first appeared in 1921, just as Ruth came to fame and seventeen years after Ruth Cleveland died.

Sobol, Ken. *Babe Ruth and the American Dream*. New York: Random House, 1974. Some cynicism is called for in any biographer of Ruth, but Sobol just doesn't seem to like him very much.

Wagenheim, Kal. *Babe Ruth*. Westport, Conn.: Praeger, 1974. A fine biography that had the misfortune of being published the same time as Creamer's definitive work.

9

What Caused the Home Run Surge?

To traditionalists—and baseball always has had its share of them—the rising home run totals of the 1920s were ruining "scientific baseball" and "inside baseball," if not the game itself. Gone were the sophisticated strategies of bunting and stealing, squeeze plays and playing for a single run; all that mattered now was brute strength. One magazine warned of "The Growing Problem of the Home Run." Another's headline: "Baseball Shudders at the Home Run Menace."

"The way they play today," complained Ty Cobb, "it's as if two golfers decided to forget all about the course—with its doglegs, sand traps, roughs, and putting greens—and instead just went out to see who could hit the ball the farthest at a driving range."

The home run totals of Babe Ruth alone had reached epidemic proportions. In 1918, Ruth tied for the league's lead with 11. The next year he set a major league record with 29. In 1920, he hit 54. Others followed, hitting for average as well as power. In 1922, Rogers Hornsby hit .401 along with a National League record 42 homers. Batting averages were up 50 points from the previous decade.

What caused the power surge? Most fans assumed the owners had introduced a "rabbit ball." "They fixed up a ball," wrote sportswriter Ring Lardner, "that if you don't miss it entirely it will clear the fence." Explained another baseball writer in the mid-1920s: "The whole matter of liveliness is due to tighter winding. . . . If the balls are wound tight, they will travel, high, wide and handsome; if wound loosely, they won't go far." Many suspected a conspiracy. The homer totals, wrote baseball historian Frank Graham in 1943, were "fattened on a lively ball introduced surreptitiously into the American League." Fifty years after it was allegedly introduced, the rabbit ball was still standard wisdom. According to the sixth edition of *The Baseball Encyclopedia*: "To take advantage of the popularity of a young star named Babe Ruth, the ball was made much livelier."

Yet at no point did the powers-that-be admit that they'd tampered with the ball. American League president Ban Johnson suggested that maybe, unbeknownst to the owners, the manufacturers had at the end of World War I been able to buy better-quality materials, such as Australian wool. No one took this seriously. Cynics joked about a "kangaroo ball," and as early as 1920 one New York sportswriter, describing a Ping Bodie home run, reported that "Ping jarred the ball right where the Australian wool was thickest." The manufacturers persistently denied any changes. Proclaimed the A. J. Reach Company, which had been supplying balls to the National League since 1876: "We never experiment with our patrons."

What was needed, it was clear, was a careful look at the balls themselves.

In the middle of the 1920 season, a group that identified itself as "friends of Babe Ruth" took the task upon itself. Members gathered a number of balls Ruth had hit into the stands and took them to the U.S. Bureau of Standards. The bureau had the right equipment for the job, having been responsible for choosing baseballs for servicemen during World War I. Engineers used bouncing wells, propulsion tubes, and impact wells to compare the 1920 balls with some from 1917. They found no change in the balls.

A year later, National League president John Heydler, a former statistician, conducted his own investigation. He reached the same conclusion as the bureau, and it was met with the same skepticism.

A few reporters decided to go to the source: the Reach Company's Philadelphia factory. In 1926, a *Popular Mechanics* reporter found nothing suspicious. "About the only basis we have for believing that the ball is more lively now than formerly," he wrote, "is the increasing number of home runs and the longer hits being made." Three years later, a *Chicago Tribune* reporter toured the same plant with Tom Shibe, whose father founded the company. The ball could be made more lively," Shibe explained, "but you can see for yourself what an expensive outlay would be involved in changing machinery and materials."

The reporter tried out the bouncing well himself, and found each ball bounced the requisite three feet, eight inches. "You didn't see them putting Mexican jumping beans inside the ball at any time, did you?" Shibe asked. He continued: "You've seen them making baseballs just as they have been doing since 1910."

Baseball historians hoped the 1910 change might provide some clues as to what happened later. That was the year Reach added cork to the rubber core of its ball. The intent, the company announced, was to create a longer-lasting ball. It turned out to be a livelier ball as well. In 1911, the first year it was used, Cobb led the American League at .420, with Shoeless Joe Jackson not far behind at .408. The league batting average jumped 30 points. The league ERA rose from 2.53 in 1910 to 3.34.

Back then, it seemed clear, changes in the ball made a difference. The 1920 *Reach Guide* even attributed that year's offensive records, in part, to the 1910 corking. The problem with this theory was that the offensive surge of 1911 lasted only two years. In 1912, Cobb hit .410, but that was the last time anyone hit over .400 until 1920. By 1913, batting and pitching records were back to where they'd been in 1910. So it was reasonable to ask: why, if a livelier ball was introduced in 1911, did the dead-ball era last a decade longer?

Another openly admitted alteration also raised more questions than answers. In 1925, Reach and Spalding, which produced the

American League ball, added a "cushioned cork center." The next year batting averages dropped 12 points in the National League, 11 in the American. Homers fell by 31 percent in the National League and by 20 percent in the American. But, again, without any additional changes to the ball, the trend reversed itself. Hitters quickly stormed back, and by 1929 they set new records for total homers in both leagues.

One reason why many fans and reporters suspected a conspiracy was that Reach and Spalding tended to be secretive about their business dealings. For example, in the 1920s, few knew that Spalding had bought Reach. A great deal of time was wasted discussing the differences between National League and American League balls, when in fact they were produced by the same company to identical specifications. Still, when it came to changes in the ball—in 1911 and in 1925—the company was quite open about what it was doing and why. Nor has anyone ever presented any evidence that additional changes were ordered in some smoke-filled room of 1919.

"The inference is that at dead of night the under-secretary of the club owner sneaks to a private telephone, summons the manufacturer, and bids him pour a little strychnine of digitalis into the old apple to make its heart action quicker," sportswriter Paul Gallico sarcastically explained in 1927. "The factory gets out the ball bearings, the block rubber, and the go-juice, and the home run epidemic follows."

So yes, the ball was changed a couple of times, and yes, the changes seemed to have at least a temporary effect. But there was no conspiracy. For the game to change as radically as it did during the 1920s, there must have been other factors at work.

The minisurge of 1911–1913 provided more clues. These were the years when a pitcher named Russ Ford perfected the emery ball. It took only a small scratch, Ford realized, to make the ball dive. By 1914, the technique had spread throughout the majors. Spitballs, too, were increasingly prevalent. As more pitchers mastered these trick pitches, both of which were legal, they regained their control over batters and counteracted the effects of the cork-centered ball. Fielders helped their pitchers out by adding their own blend of tobacco and spit to the ball as they threw it around.

"We hardly ever saw a new baseball, a clean one," recalled Fred Snodgrass, an outfielder for the Giants and Braves through 1916. "If the ball went into the stands and the ushers couldn't get it back from the spectators, only then would the umpire throw out a new one."

After the 1919 season, the owners outlawed tampering with the ball and limited each team to two spitball pitchers. Then, in 1920, a Carl Mays pitch killed Cleveland shortstop Ray Chapman. Mays threw a fastball, not a spitter, but the ball was rough and dirty. The former may have contributed to the pitch getting away from Mays, the latter to Chapman's inability to see it in time. The owners responded with a more general ban on trick pitches and a directive to umpires to put clean balls in play. The rules changes immediately benefited hitters.

The new rules included a grandfather clause that let seventeen pitchers, for whom the spitter had always been their primary pitch, continue to throw it. The subsequent careers of these seventeen highlighted what a relief it must have been for hitters to face no other spitballers. In 1921, William "Spittin' Bill" Doak led the National League in winning percentage and ERA, while Burleigh Grimes tied for the lead in wins. In the American League, Red Faber led the league with an ERA of 2.48 (compared to the league average of 4.28).

There was a chorus of complaints from pitchers who could no longer throw a dirty ball. According to the 1922 *Reach Guide*, "they were unable to curve the new balls, because they were not able to get a proper grip on them." No longer weighed down by foreign substances, balls were also slightly lighter and therefore livelier.

It was, of course, Babe Ruth who showed most clearly what could be done with a clean ball. As early as 1921, the conservative *Baseball Magazine*, no fan of the new offense, realized that the Babe was as much a cause as an effect.

"The livelier ball may have influenced the situation to some extent," wrote F. C. Lane. "But the livelier ball is a thing so elusive that offers the scantiest evidence. . . . We are irresistibly impelled, therefore, to see in Babe Ruth the true cause for the amazing advance in home runs."

As the writer-statistician pair John Thorn and Pete Palmer noted, Ruth's breakout 1919 season came in spite of a shortened schedule (140 games), Fenway Park's deep right-center field (20 of his 29 homers came on the road), and the fact that some of the slugger's energy was still expended on the mound (he pitched 133 innings). The rest of the Red Sox hit only 4 homers, and league totals stayed around where they'd been for the decade.

"If Ruth benefited from a rabbit ball being sneaked into play in 1919," wrote baseball historian William Curran, "he was the only one in Organized Baseball to cash in."

In 1919, managers and batters were still thinking of bunts and steals, not homers. For years, they'd been taught that anyone who tried to hit the long ball was likely to pop out. Ruth changed all that, especially after he was traded to New York and the homer-friendly Polo Grounds. Wrote Curran: "Regulars spent the winter of 1920–21 pondering Babe Ruth's 54 home runs, and, more important, his new $52,000 salary."

It was not so many years later that Ralph Kiner, when advised he could raise his average by choking up, replied, "Cadillacs are down at the end of the bat."

Despite the criticism of traditionalists, most fans then and now loved home runs. American League attendance jumped 5 million in 1920, setting a new record. The Yankees drew 1,289,422, also a new record.

"People in every big city in the land," wrote baseball historian Robert Smith, "suddenly discovered that baseball could be as exciting, in its summery way, as all-night drinking and dancing, airplanes, fast automobiles, and reckless gambling on the Stock Exchange. The Babe became almost a symbol of the age."

By 1930, all hitters seemed Ruthian. The National League average was .303. Hack Wilson had 190 RBIs. Babe Herman hit .393 with 241 hits, 48 doubles, 11 triples, 35 homers, and 130 RBIs—and failed to lead the league in any category. The Philadelphia Phillies had two outfielders hitting over .380—and finished last. The *Sporting News* called for the owners to curb "the home run burlesque."

This time the owners did intervene. Before the opening of the next season, National League president John Heydler openly introduced a new ball with raised stitches and a heavier cover. The impact was immediate.

"The ball just plain felt bigger in your hand," said Carl Hubbell. "It was easier to grip."

The National League average dropped to .277 in 1931, and homers dropped 45 percent. By 1941, averages were back to where they'd been in 1919.

Home runs, of course, did not disappear. Even in 1968, when Bob Gibson's ERA sunk to 1.12 and Carl Yastrzemski was the only American Leaguer to hit over .300 (at .301), Frank Howard still managed 44 homers. Still, there was no doubt that offense was on the wane. In 1976, homers had dropped to 1.15 per game. Then, in the 1980s, the numbers started to rise again, and in 1987 they soared to 2.12 a game, a new record. And then, of course, in seemingly less time than you could say Roger Maris, there were Mark McGwire's 70 and 65, Sammy Sosa's 66 and 64 and 63, and finally Barry Bonds's 73.

"Sure, 'records are made to be broken,' " complained natural and baseball historian Stephen Jay Gould. "But truly great records should endure for a little while, at least long enough to potentiate the stuff of legend across a single generation: 'Son, I remember when . . . Oh, yeah, Dad, you were there? Really, honest?!' "

There were many explanations. New stadiums with smaller dimensions tended to favor hitters. Colorado's Coors Field alone was so friendly to hitters that statistician Bill James found it colored the stats of the entire league.

Not surprisingly, many fingers again pointed at the ball.

"The rabbit ball is back-back-back-back-back," wrote the *Seattle Times*. "A hanger? Sure. That deserves to go 450 feet," moaned Indian pitcher Dave Burba in 2000. "But not a good pitch. It's starting to become a joke the way these guys are hitting them." Even some hitters agreed. "I liked it when home runs were special," said Chicago first baseman Mark Grace. "It's becoming almost easy."

Yet the manufacturer—this time it was the Rawlings Sporting Goods Company—again maintained that the ball was the same. Rawlings asserted it tested a statistically accurate random sampling of each shipment of balls, firing them from an air cannon at a wall of white ash. Independent tests confirmed that the "coefficient of restitution" (the ratio of striking to rebound velocity) was "totally within the range of major-league standards."

If it wasn't the ball, maybe it was the *bat*. Longer, thinner bats meant quicker swings and bigger sweet spots. And the new aluminum bats were nothing but one big sweet spot. True, aluminum bats were outlawed in the majors, but players who grew up using them also grew up with a new confidence in their hitting.

"Young hitters were always taught either to lay off the outside pitch or to go with it and guide it to the opposite field," wrote James. "If you try to 'drive' that ball, they were told, you're going to wind up with a ground ball to second base (if you're right-handed) or shortstop (if you're a lefty)."

Playing with the forgiving aluminum bats allowed in college, batters figured they might as well swing away at outside pitches. "What the hitters learned from using the aluminum bats," James continued, "was not that they couldn't hit the outside pitch hard, but that they could." This was a change in attitude almost as revolutionary as that of the 1920s, when hitters first discovered the long ball. Starting in the late 1980s, batters crowded the plate, went for outside pitches, and homered to the opposite field. James noted that opposite-field homers have more than tripled since 1987.

Pitchers, meanwhile, were learning the opposite lesson. Recognizing that aluminum bats let batters make solid contact with an inside pitch, they stopped trying to jam them and started giving hitters the outside pitches they now relished. That trend was boosted by umpires' lower tolerance for brushback pitches.

"The vogue of 'the high hard one' and the glamour of 'getting in his kitchen' . . . has waned," wrote sportswriter Tom Boswell. "Gradually, the knees and the outside corner became the target of most 'quality' pitches. Anything up or in that got hit was dismissed as a mistake, while any homer off a low or outside pitch was excused as 'a pitcher's pitch' that somehow ended up traveling 400 feet."

Now batters owned the outside and the inside of the plate. And, like Kiner, they knew it paid to swing for the fences—even if it meant more strikeouts.

Grumbled Al Lopez, a catcher in the thirties and a manager in the fifties and sixties: "We had big guys. Hack Wilson was a strong guy. Hornsby was a great hitter. Bill Terry was a great hitter. . . . They made contact with the ball. Today, I think, everybody's swinging from their heels. . . . They don't feel bad about striking out. They just walk back to the bench like they're supposed to do it."

Increasingly, though, the focus was not on doctoring the ball or bat but the players themselves. Weight training aimed at specific muscles was one method. "Assiduous, specialized work," wrote Gould, "rigorously followed by those few surpassingly gifted athletes who combine the three essential attributes of bodily prowess, personal dedication, and high intelligence, can probably raise Greenberg's 58 to McGwire's 70."

Steroids were another method. During his record-breaking 1998 season, McGwire admitted using androstenedione, which was weaker than other steroids and then legal. By 2003, 5 to 7 percent of major leaguers tested positive for steroid use—this despite knowing in advance that they'd be tested. Equally telling was that this first year of testing also was the first year since 1994 that no one hit 50 homers.

The scandal worsened in 2004 when Greg Anderson, Bonds's personal trainer, was indicted as part of a federal probe of a California company accused of distributing the illegal steroid tetrahydrogestrione. Bonds claimed that he thought Anderson was giving him a nutritional supplement and a rubbing balm, but even if he didn't know they were steroids, it's likely that's what they were. "I know that you can't put something in your body to make you hit a fastball, changeup, or curveball," said Hank

Aaron, "but, at that age, you have to ask: Did he accomplish all of this by rejuvenating his strength . . . with those substances?"

"When Bonds goes from 49 to 73, you just wonder," said Hall of Fame pitcher Jim Palmer.

To investigate further:

Curran, William. *Big Sticks*. New York: HarperCollins, 1990. An elegant history of baseball in the twenties that effectively debunks the myth of the lively ball.

Gould, Stephen Jay. *Triumph and Tragedy in Mudville*. New York: W. W. Norton, 2003. Gould's scientific approach didn't interfere with his passion for the game: "I don't care if the thin air of Colorado encourages home runs. I don't care if expansion has diluted pitching. I don't care if the ball is livelier and the strike zone smaller. And I especially don't care if McGwire helps himself train by taking an over-the-counter substance regarded as legal by major league baseball. . . . Mark McGwire . . . can only inspire wonderment in us all."

James, Bill. *The New Bill James Historical Baseball Abstract*. New York: Free Press, 2001. Decade-by-decade analysis from the man who revolutionized the way we look at baseball. Make sure to get this significantly updated and improved edition, not the 1985 original.

Mead, William. *Two Spectacular Seasons*. New York: Macmillan, 1990. Baseball in 1930, "the year the hitters ran wild," and 1968, "the year the pitchers took revenge."

Ritter, Lawrence. *The Glory of Their Times*. New York: Macmillan, 1966. The classic oral history of baseball's early days.

10

Did Babe Ruth
Call His Shot?

B y 1932 Babe Ruth was already past his prime. At thirty-eight, he was no longer the best hitter in baseball. Still to come, however, was the single most dramatic—and most disputed—moment of his career: his "called shot."

The setting was Chicago, the third game of the World Series between the Cubs and the Yankees. The Yankees had won the first two in New York, and the Cub players and fans were restless and surly, tossing insults and lemons onto the field. In the fifth inning, with the score tied, Ruth came to bat; from the Chicago stands came cries that Ruth was old, he was fat, he was washed up. The Chicago pitcher, Charlie Root, threw two strikes and the jeering intensified.

Here's how Ruth, in his autobiography, recalled what happened next:

> While [Root] was making up his mind to pitch to me, I stepped back again and pointed my finger at those bleachers, which only caused the mob to howl that much more at me.
>   . . . Root threw a fast ball. . . . I swung from the ground with everything I had and as I hit the ball every muscle in my system, every sense I had, told me that I had never hit a better one, that as long as I lived nothing would ever feel as good as this.

I didn't have to look. But I did. That ball just went on and on and on and hit far up in the center-field bleachers in exactly the spot I had pointed to.

A crucial home run in the World Series is itself a guarantee of at least temporary fame; this "called shot"—a home run before which the batter predicted not just the exact pitch he'd hit but the exact place it would land—was a story destined for immortality.

But did it actually happen?

You'd think this mystery would be a cinch to solve. After all, almost fifty thousand people were at Wrigley Field when Ruth came to bat. Sportswriters from across the country witnessed the game, and the next few days' newspapers were filled with reports of the home run. In the *New York World-Telegram*, Joe Williams wrote that "with the Cubs riding him unmercifully from the bench, Ruth pointed to center field and punched a screaming liner to a spot where no ball ever had been hit before."

A couple of days later, Paul Gallico wrote in the *New York Daily News* that "Ruth pointed like a duelist to the spot where he expected to send his rapier home." A day after that, Bill Corum wrote for the Hearst newspapers that Ruth "pointed out where he was going to hit the next one, and hit it there."

Given Ruth's history as a great hitter and showman, the story seemed credible. This wasn't even the first time Ruth had called his shot. Back in 1926, another story went, he'd visited a dying boy in the hospital and promised to hit a home run for him; the next day he hit a home run and the boy miraculously recovered. The facts in that case were not quite so dramatic: in reality, Johnny Sylvester had been hospitalized after falling from a horse and was by no means dying, and Ruth didn't visit him in person until after he hit the home run. But he had sent him an autographed ball along with a promise to try to hit one for him, and then he did hit a home run the next day. Not so fantastic, when you think about it: for a hitter with 714 lifetime home runs and a tremendous love of the spotlight, it was to be expected that some of the home runs were going to come after some of the promises.

Still, the 1932 World Series called shot was in a class by itself. In this instance Ruth had called the specific pitch and the specific spot to which he'd hit it. The odds against success were astronomical; even Ruth, in an interview with sportswriter John Carmichael, once admitted there was an element of luck involved.

"Ruth could do those things, take those chances and get away with them, because he was The Babe and because his imagination told him that it was a fine, heroic, and Ruthian thing to do," wrote Gallico. "And he had the ability to deliver."

Inevitably, there were skeptics.

Foremost among them were the two Chicago Cub players nearest the action. Gabby Hartnett, the catcher, was the only player near enough to hear what Ruth said; according to Hartnett, Ruth's words were "It only takes one to hit," referring to the one strike he had left. But Hartnett said Ruth pointed his finger at the Chicago players riding him from the dugout, *not* at the center-field bleachers.

Charlie Root, the pitcher, vehemently denied Ruth pointed to center field. Root even turned down the opportunity to play himself in a movie version of Ruth's life that included the called shot. "Ruth did not point at the fence before he swung," insisted Root. "If he had made a gesture like that, well, anybody who knows me knows that Ruth would have ended up on his ass."

So, it seemed, the eyewitness testimony canceled itself out. For every witness who saw Ruth call his shot, there was one to swear he didn't. More objective evidence, in the form or a 16-millimeter home movie taken by spectator Matt Kandle Sr., was tantalizing but inconclusive. Ruth is definitely seen pointing—but whether at the pitcher, or the Cub bench, or the center-field bleachers is impossible to say.

Among serious baseball historians, however, the consensus that emerged was that Ruth did *not* point to center field. These historians pointed out that, of all the sportswriters present at the game, only one—Joe Williams, whose *World-Telegram* article is quoted above—mentioned the called shot in an article written that day. One other, John Drebinger of the *New York Times*, said Ruth "notified the crowd that the nature of his retaliation would be a wallop right out of the confines of the park," but this story didn't specify that Ruth pointed to center field. According to Ruth's premier biographer, Robert Creamer, the story that Ruth pointed to center field originated with Williams and then was picked up by Gallico and Corum and other writers who either respected Williams or who just couldn't resist such a good story.

Over time, Williams himself backed away from his initial story. It was Williams, in a February 1950 column, who quoted Gabby Hartnett's story and—though Williams still said he had "a distinct memory that [Ruth] did motion in the general direction of the stands in right center"—he admitted he now had doubts as to what the gesture meant. Fifteen years after that column, a 1965 Williams column recalled a conversation in which the sportswriter casually asked Ruth whether the called shot was the greatest thrill of his career. No, Ruth replied (according to Williams), his greatest thrill had been striking out Cobb, Crawford, and Veach with the bases full. Williams surmised that Ruth had deliberately ducked the question; Ruth couldn't bring himself to debunk his own legend, but he also didn't want to lie to Williams.

Not that Ruth had anything to be ashamed of. If, as Hartnett reported and as seems most likely, Ruth merely predicted he was going to hit a home run but didn't point to where it would land, or perhaps merely held up one and then two fingers to remind Root he still had two and then one pitch to go, this would still be a fitting capstone to his career. George Washington deserves to be a legendary figure, even if he never chopped down a cherry tree; so does Babe Ruth, even if he never pointed to center field.

To investigate further:

Creamer, Robert. *Babe.* New York: Simon & Schuster, 1974. The rush of Ruth biographies in the mid-1970s, which also included Smelser's, Sobol's, and Wagenheim's, can probably be attributed to the fact that Hank Aaron was then challenging Ruth's lifetime home-run record.

Gallico, Paul. *Farewell to Sport*. New York: Alfred A. Knopf, 1944. "I suppose in fifty or sixty years the legend will be that Ruth could call his shots any time," wrote Gallico. "But once is sufficient for me, and I saw him do that."

Meany, Tom. *Babe Ruth*. New York: A. S. Barnes, 1947. Meany, who once worked for Joe Williams, was an eyewitness to the called shot and a true believer.

Ritter, Lawrence, and Mark Rucker. *The Babe*. New York: Ticknor & Fields, 1988. Includes stills from Matt Kandle's home movie.

Ruth, Babe, as told to Bob Considine. *The Babe Ruth Story*. New York: E. P. Dutton, 1948. "What annoyed me was their spitting," Ruth said of the Chicago fans who inspired his shot, "their spitting and their bad aim. Poor Claire received most of it."

Williams, Peter, ed. *The Joe Williams Baseball Reader*. Chapel Hill, N.C.: Algonquin, 1989. A collection of Williams's columns through which you can trace the birth, growth, and abandonment of the called-shot story.

11

Was Moe Berg a Spy?

Sportswriters loved to tell stories about Moe Berg, the eccentrically bookish catcher for the Dodgers, White Sox, Indians, Senators, and Red Sox.

"As soon as Professor Moe Berg of the Boston Red Sox Department of Languages and Obscure Sciences can be located," wrote John Kieran of the *New York Times*, "this observer plans to consult him about an obscure item that popped up in the recent baseball news."

What was irresistible was the contrast between Berg's intellectual prowess (he graduated from Princeton and then got a law degree from Columbia; he was fluent, by some accounts, in a dozen languages) and his baseball mediocrity (he hit .243 lifetime with 6 home runs, and he spent most of his career warming up pitchers in the bullpen).

"It will be remembered," continued Kieran, "that Professor Berg, the Red Sox catcher who officiates only in the second games of doubleheaders and not even then if it is a hot day, is a licensed barrister. . . . Professor Berg was, allegedly, a big league ballplayer in the summertime. Anyway, he had a uniform and was allowed to travel with the team."

Berg reveled in his image as the game's resident intellectual. Once, when he was called in from the bullpen for a rare appearance behind the plate, he stopped by the dugout and asked,

"Gentlemen, does everyone still get three strikes out there?" Another time, just after Berg joined the Senators, writer Shirley Povich pointed him out to Washington outfielder Dave Harris.

"I just want to tell you he speaks seven languages," Povich said.

"Yeah, I know," Harris answered, "and he can't hit in any of them."

His reputation spread in 1939, when he made a series of guest appearances on the radio game show *Information, Please!* and successfully fielded questions on such arcane topics as a bordereau (a document such as that used in the Dreyfus affair) and poi (a Hawaiian root).

Yet for all Berg's fame, it was difficult to know him. He rarely socialized with players, and with writers his tales were more apt to impress than to reveal anything personal. Red Sox teammate Ted Williams dubbed him "the mystery man." Casey Stengel agreed: "Nobody ever knew his life's history. I call him the mystery catcher. Strangest fellah who ever put on a uniform."

By 1939, Berg's final year as a player, it was clear that his mind was, more than ever, on nonbaseball matters. "Europe is in flames," he told *New York Times* writer Arthur Daley. "All over that continent men and women and children are dying. Soon we too will be involved. And what am I doing? I'm sitting in the bullpen, telling jokes to the relief pitchers."

Berg would often leave the team to visit Washington, D.C., and players began to wonder why. "Some of the fellows thought Moe was an undercover man for the government," recalled Lefty Grove. "He had mysterious meetings and we didn't know what he was doing."

"We ballplayers felt Moe had some kind of relationship with the government, but we didn't know what it was," agreed Red Sox pitcher Elden Auker. "And Moe was basically a very mysterious man away from the ballpark, so that added to the intrigue."

Grove and Auker were by no means the only ones to suspect that the catcher was a spy.

Berg's cloak-and-dagger-like activities dated back to 1934, when the catcher—along with such players as Babe Ruth, Lou Gehrig,

Lefty Gomez, Charlie Gehringer, and Jimmie Foxx—toured Japan. Berg brought with him a movie camera, which he carried with him seemingly everywhere.

On November 29, when his teammates took on a Japanese all-star team at the Omiya Grounds north of Tokyo, Berg was not there. This in itself was not significant; Berg spent as little time on the field in Japan as he did in Brooklyn or Chicago or Boston. In this case, though, he was not in the bullpen.

Instead, dressed in a black kimono, Berg entered St. Luke's Hospital in Tokyo, where he told a nurse he wanted to visit the U.S. ambassador's daughter. He then climbed to the top of the hospital bell tower, pulled out his movie camera, and filmed the surrounding city, including its industrial and military complexes.

Seven years later, the films ended up in the hands of U.S. military intelligence, and in a 1942 letter to his sister, Berg bragged about the government's reaction. "The movies were received triumphantly," he wrote. "They wondered how I got them—now they can make pinpoint recognition of warehouses, gas tanks, docks, factories, etc."

For his 1974 biography of Berg, journalist Louis Kaufman interviewed Samuel Berg, who said he didn't know whether his brother had been working for the government when he was in Japan. Still, Samuel Berg seemed to assume his brother had been a spy in Japan.

"Moe was from an era and background that held strong loyalties to the country," Samuel Berg told Kaufman. "This trait was reflected in Moe, I feel, when the government made requests of him. I'm sure that he was flattered that the government asked him to serve."

Kaufman concluded that the films played a critical role in planning Lieutenant Colonel Jimmy Doolittle's attack on Tokyo.

That seems unlikely. For Doolittle to rely on eight-year-old footage to plan his 1942 raid would have been foolhardy. The triumphant reception Berg described was probably nothing more than an effort to be polite to an ardent but amateur patriot. Berg's 1994 biographer, Nicholas Dawidoff, found "no archival or trustworthy published evidence . . . to suggest that Berg's films were put to any use during World War II."

Still, Samuel Berg was quite right in assuming that his brother would be flattered by a government request to serve. That request came in 1942, when Nelson Rockefeller, then the coordinator of the Office of Inter-American Affairs, asked Berg to help improve relations to the south by teaching sports in Central and South America. Berg eagerly accepted and spent the first part of 1943 traveling throughout the region.

As in Japan, Berg decided on his own to act as something more than a cultural ambassador. "In all my visits and talks with [Brazilian military officials]," he wrote Rockefeller in 1943, "I made clear that although I was making an official trip my status with them was unofficial and off the record."

Wrote Dawidoff: "By poking around in this way, Berg had turned his soft propaganda assignment into a secret operation and delicately imposed himself on a new profession. He was acting, more or less, as a spy."

Later in 1943, Berg got the chance to formalize that role when he signed on with the Office of Strategic Services. The OSS was the forerunner of the CIA.

In one sense, Berg was an absurd choice as a spy. The fame that attracted the attention of OSS director "Wild Bill" Donovan seemed to disqualify Berg from any undercover work. Even in Japan Berg was well known from his 1934 tour. Yet his penchant for secrecy was undeniable, and in baseball-free Europe he could easily blend into the background. That's where he went to work.

The extent and importance of Berg's spying has been a subject of much dispute. Kaufman, ever eager to elevate his hero's status, described how Berg entered occupied Florence in a German officer's uniform, inspected a factory where Germans were studying ways to compress fissionable material, then reported back to Washington. Historian Thomas Powers, in his 1993 book on Germany's secret efforts to build an atomic bomb, debunked Kaufman's version. It turned out that Berg did indeed enter the Florence factory, but only after Allied troops had taken the city.

Powers also described an incident that showed what an amateur Berg remained. In May 1944, Berg was seated next to army major George Shine on a flight from Washington, D.C., to London. According to Shine, as Berg moved about his seat or got up to go to the bathroom, a pistol kept falling out of his pocket. Shine finally offered to hold it for him.

Yet Powers also determined that Berg *did* play a crucial role in various operations designed to discover how close German scientists were to creating an atomic bomb. The German project was a cause of great concern to the Allies, especially since Hitler regularly referred to a *Wunderwaffe* in the works, and they feared that the brilliant physicist Werner Heisenberg was working on the bomb. When Berg arrived in Rome in June 1944, he held a series of meetings with Italian scientists. Speaking to them in Italian, Berg learned that at least as far as they knew, the Germans were years away from a bomb.

More dramatically, in December 1944, Berg was sent to Zurich—in neutral Switzerland—to attend a Heisenberg lecture there. His mission, if he heard anything indicating a German A-bomb was imminent, was to shoot Heisenberg on the spot. Berg's knowledge of German and physics was limited, but he listened intently.

Berg's notes on the lecture made clear he was not sure what to do. "As I listen, I am uncertain,—see: Heisenberg's uncertainty principle—what to do to H.," he wrote.

At a dinner after the lecture, Berg overheard a conversation in which another scientist said to Heisenberg that the Germans would lose the war. "Yes," Heisenberg conceded, "but it would have been so good if we had won." To Berg, the implication was clear: if Heisenberg thought the Germans had lost, there was no German A-bomb in the works. The gun stayed in his pocket.

Berg was later recommended for the Medal of Merit, the highest honor given civilians during wartime. Lieutenant Colonel Howard Dix's letter of recommendation quoted Major General Leslie Groves, who headed the U.S. atomic-bomb project, as saying that "the guidance obtained through work in Switzerland . . . permitted him [Groves] to gauge the pressure placed upon his scientists and he was thereby able to gauge the ability of the United States to produce two usable bombs before the war was over without 'killing off' his own scientists."

Berg's report from Switzerland may have reached the White House. Kaufman's version, for which no source is cited and which Powers considered apocryphal, had Groves telling Roosevelt of Heisenberg's remark that Germany had lost.

"Fine, just fine. Let us pray Heisenberg is right," Roosevelt responded. "And, General, my regards to the catcher."

With the end of World War II (and of the OSS), Berg was out of work. The CIA didn't want him—Berg's type of solo operation didn't fit the agency's more disciplined approach to intelligence. So Berg wandered from ballpark to ballpark, occasionally visiting the press box and chatting with writers. When they would ask what he was up to, he would exhibit his usual secrecy, often putting a finger to his lips and implying he wasn't at liberty to say.

Dawidoff captured the desolation of Berg's postwar life. "For an accomplished man who was doing nothing and wished people to believe otherwise, spying was an ideal cover. Nobody could dispute it," Dawidoff wrote. "For a private man who was loath to reveal anything about himself, spying was also an excellent means of warding off questions. Yet when Berg left the false impression that he worked for the CIA, it was not just a matter of petty dissembling calculated to save face and veil personality. It was also symptomatic of a man suffering a protracted bout of wishful thinking."

In the OSS, Berg's achievements were real and substantial, but they were by nature secret, and even after the war, difficult to describe. What he had discovered, after all, was that the Germans did *not* have the bomb; what he had done, therefore, was *not* kill Heisenberg. This must have seemed, at least to Berg, a dubious claim to fame. So he haunted the ballparks where he had once achieved, amid his unimpressive career stats, a genuinely impressive renown.

For Berg, baseball—as much as espionage—had always been a cover, a chance to imply he was something more than a baseball player, even when he was not. One of Berg's few published works, an essay called "Pitchers and Catchers" which appeared in the September 1941 *Atlantic Monthly*, perhaps inadvertently revealed how well the game suited his furtive nature.

Berg wrote about Lefty Grove. In 1935, with a game on the line and Washington's Heinie Manush at the plate, the count went to 3 and 2. Manush knew to look for either a fastball or curve. They were the only pitches Grove threw.

"Heinie broke his back striking out on the next pitch, the first fork ball Grove ever threw," Berg wrote. "For over a year on the side lines, in the bullpen, between pitching starts, Lefty had practiced and perfected this pitch before he threw it, and he waited for a crucial spot to use it."

Explained Berg: "With every move the pitcher is trying to fool the hitter, using his skill and wiles, his tricks and cunning, all his art."

To investigate further:

Berg, Moe. "Pitchers and Catchers." *Atlantic Monthly* 168, no. 3 (September 1941). When *New York Times* columnist Ira Berkow asked Berg if he'd ever written for publication, Berg referred only to a treatise on Sanskrit. Then Berkow came upon a collection of *Atlantic Monthly* articles, including this one. When he next saw Berg, he confronted him with the book and the lie. "You caught me," Berg said.

Dawidoff, Nicholas. *The Catcher Was a Spy*. New York: Pantheon, 1994. A subtle and unsettling portrait.

Kaufman, Louis, Barbara Fitzgerald, and Tom Sewell. *Moe Berg*. Boston: Little, Brown, 1974. Not always reliable, but lots of good stories.

Powers, Thomas. *Heisenberg's War*. New York: Alfred A. Knopf, 1993. Powers' controversial thesis is that Heisenberg was anti-Nazi and intentionally undermined the German effort to build a bomb.

12 What Caused the Feud between Williams and the Press?

H ere is the replacement for Babe Ruth," announced Dan Daniel in the *New York World-Telegram* when Joe DiMaggio arrived for his first spring training with the Yankees, in 1936. That set the tone for the coverage that would follow. Briefly, during DiMaggio's 1938 holdout, reporters portrayed him as greedy. Except for that, he was almost always a symbol of quiet dignity and pride, a Hemingway hero, literally. This was not surprising. Baseball reporters still thought of themselves as owing more to the teams, who paid all their expenses on the road, than to their newspapers, let alone their readers. The quickest way to lose your job was to write some dirt about a player, particularly a player tagged as the next Ruth. Besides, for select writers, there was the thrill of a night on the town with DiMaggio. A reporter might even learn what showgirl DiMaggio picked up that night, though he surely wouldn't mention it in print.

In Boston, none of this applied. Far from worshiping their greatest player, the Boston press attacked Ted Williams, relentlessly and brutally. In 1947, the *Boston Globe*'s Mel Webb didn't even rank Williams among the top ten on his Most Valuable Player ballot. That meant the award went to DiMaggio, though Williams won the Triple Crown and bested DiMaggio in every offensive category. In 1957, the writers again voted Williams second, this time to Mickey Mantle, though Mantle had fewer homers and hit 23 points lower.

Williams himself summed up his experience with the press. "I can still remember the things they wrote, and they *still* make me mad," he wrote in his 1969 autobiography, *My Turn at Bat*. "How I was always trying to get somebody's job—the manager's, the general manager's, the guy's in the radio booth—and I never coveted another man's job in my life. Or how I didn't hit in the clutch, and yet drove in more runs per time at bat than anybody who ever played this game except Babe Ruth, and got on base more times per at-bat than anybody *including* Babe Ruth. I was a draft dodger. I wasn't a 'team' man. I was 'jealous.' I 'alienated' the players from the press. I didn't hit to left field. I took too many bases on balls. I did this, I did that. And so on. And so unfair."

The irony of this was that in contrast to the aloof and often surly DiMaggio, Williams made for a great interview. "He was intelligent, enthusiastic, knowledgeable, and, by unpredictable turns, witty, charming, gracious, opinionated, belligerent, and almost eloquent," recalled Tim Horgan of the *Boston Herald*. "He even speaks in home runs," agreed *Los Angeles Times* columnist Jim Murray.

What, then, accounted for the lasting enmity between Williams and those he derisively dubbed the "knights of the keyboard"? Who started it?

Williams blamed Harold Kaese of the *Boston Transcript*. In May 1940, Ted's sophomore season, Kaese learned that Boston manager Joe Cronin planned to bench Williams for loafing in the field. After complaining about Williams's "extreme selfishness, egoism, and lack of courage," Kaese asked: "Can you imagine a kid, a nice kid with a nimble brain not visiting his father and mother all of last winter?"

Williams was, in fact, deeply ashamed of his parents. Like DiMaggio, Williams's parents were poor. But DiMaggio's family was large and loving, while Williams was raised by a mother who devoted herself to the Salvation Army, often at the expense of her children. To Williams, this part of his life was off-limits to the press. Kaese realized he was crossing a line, and he cut the offending line. But an editor saw the deleted stick of type and put it back in. The battle was joined.

"Before this, I was willing to believe a writer was my friend until he proved otherwise," Williams wrote in his autobiography. "Now my guard's up all the time, always watching for critical stuff."

Other criticisms of Williams's personal life followed. At one point, frustrated by a sophomore slump, Williams said he'd rather be a fireman than a baseball player. It was a silly remark, and the press jumped all over it. Then Williams and Red Sox owner Tom Yawkey were seen shooting pigeons at Fenway Park. Grounds-keepers routinely did so, but this time someone called the Humane Society. Now Williams was feeling truly persecuted. He said he'd rather play in New York.

In 1942, when Williams received an exemption from the draft because he was supporting his mother, the headline writers were indignant. Williams eventually enlisted in the navy. In 1948, Williams's wife gave birth to his daughter in Boston while Williams was fishing in the Everglades. The newspapers were again aghast, but this time Williams didn't back down. He briefly visited mother and child, then returned to Florida. "To hell with the public," he told reporters. "They can't run my life." One shudders to think what Williams would have thought about the coverage, after he died in 2002, of the battle between his oldest child, who wanted him cremated, and his younger two, who wanted him frozen. (The younger two prevailed, and his remains were placed in a cyronics facility in Arizona.)

There also was plenty of negative press about what Williams did on the field. The main knock, from the start, was that he was selfish. Sure, he chalked up impressive numbers, but in the eyes of many reporters that just proved he was more interested in his own success than that of the team. After Indian manager Lou Boudreau shifted his defense to the right in 1946, Williams continued to try to pull the ball. Writers blamed him for trying to bulk up his power numbers instead of bunting down the unprotected third-base line, or at least trying to hit to left.

"Defeat with him starring is preferable to victory when he must stand in the shadow of another," maintained Dave Egan of the *Boston Record*. Egan, who called Williams the "inventor of the automatic choke," rarely failed to note when one of his home runs came with the Red Sox way ahead or behind. Egan repeatedly pointed out Williams's big-game failures, including his playoff and World Series average of .232. This was highly selective. There were plenty of big games where Williams came through—in the final three games of 1948, for example, when the Sox tied the Indians for the pennant and Williams went 6 for 8, or in the final 11 games of 1949, when the Sox caught the Yankees and Williams won four games with home runs. Still, Williams was stuck with a reputation of not coming through in the clutch.

In a 1951 *Sport* magazine article, Joe Williams concluded that the only hope the Red Sox had of winning was to trade Williams. "All Williams is interested in is his hitting," he wrote. "This is another way of saying that all Williams is interested in is Williams."

For much of this, Williams had himself to blame. From the moment he arrived in Boston as a rookie and announced, "All I want out of life is that when I walk down the street folks will say 'There goes the greatest hitter who ever lived,'" he dared anyone to say otherwise. If they did, he would surely note it.

"His sense of hearing is so acute he hears every blunt remark," Bob Considine wrote for UPI. "And his eyes are so sharp he can read between the lines of every Boston baseball writer's story." (When Williams enlisted, a navy doctor administered a physical, including a hearing test. "Hell," Williams later said, "if he only knew I could hear a heckler at Fenway in the fortieth row, he'd know my ears were okay.")

He was often moody and always impatient—with himself as well as with others. He didn't care about the needs of the press, and unlike other athletes who felt the same way, he didn't pretend to care. When things went wrong, he was, biographer Michael Seidel wrote, "like the great Greek warrior Achilles, who spent a fair time sulking in his tent."

"His career was marked by an overriding paradox," Seidel believed. "Williams's theory of hitting depended on split-second assessments of ordained hitting zones and an almost eerie self-discipline regarding the nature and frequency of his swings. But away from the plate he seemed to swing savagely and wildly at whatever sucker pitches were tossed up to him."

So any negative story had legs. Reporters could count on Williams to respond, even if his response was sometimes to refuse to talk to reporters. In his autobiography, Williams conceded he was partly at fault. "I was never able to be dispassionate, to ignore the things people said or wrote or implied," he said. "I am certainly in the upper bracket of sensitivity, maybe the top 3 percent. In a crowd of cheers I could always pick out the solitary boo."

But Williams also recognized that Boston's baseball reporters were especially bloodthirsty.

"Certainly any professional sport has to have press coverage, has to have color written about the teams, has to have its adversity written up, but you can do all that without being unfair, without picking on somebody, without making a damn mountain out of a molehill, without putting somebody on the spot," he wrote. "In Boston they weren't content to do it that way. The Boston writers would come around pumping, pumping, always after something controversial, always listening at the keyhole, always putting somebody on the spot."

Williams was right about that. "Boston's newspapering in the late forties and into the late fifties was probably the worst of any major city in America," wrote reporter and historian David Halberstam. "It specialized in sensationalism, parochialism, prejudice, and ignorance."

Worst of all, Halberstam believed, was the *Record*'s Dave Egan. "What he did, especially to Williams, was not pleasant for anyone who cares about the American press," Halberstam wrote. "His coverage amounted to a vendetta."

True enough. Egan was a bitter drunk who knew just how to bring out the worst in Williams. But he also was a provocative writer in an era when most avoided any sort of provocation. The heart of the problem was not any given writer, but the sheer numbers of them. Williams stepped into the middle of a circulation war. Boston had seven major newspapers: besides the *Record* there were the *Post, Herald, Globe, American, Traveler,* and *Christian Science Monitor,* not to mention smaller and foreign papers. That meant more than forty baseball writers, all desperate for something new and different to say about Boston's left fielder.

"They ought to put numbers on their backs," Williams once said. "There's so many of them it's the only way you could figure out who they were."

Unlike the Yankees, who were quick to punish anyone who criticized DiMaggio, Red Sox management did little to protect Williams. They neither offered him advice nor pressured the writers to back off. Williams resented this. "I didn't know how to handle [the press]," he wrote. "Joe Cronin did. . . . He could suave those writers to death. If it were me, if I'd been the general manager, I'd have nipped it right now."

Of course, Williams admitted, it helped that the Yankees were winning. "You get good press when you're winning, and we were losing and there were forty-nine million newspapers in Boston, from the *Globe* to the Brookline Something-or-Other, all ready to jump us for it."

Williams was almost as uncompromising in his attitude toward Boston's fans as he was toward its writers. Most famously and stubbornly, he refused to tip his cap after a home run. Even after his final home run (in his final at-bat), despite the pleas of his manager and teammates, Williams would not relent.

"Gods do not answer letters," explained novelist and essayist John Updike, who was at the game.

Updike's essay, though a literary masterpiece, didn't get this quite right. Williams wanted the fans and writers to think he was above it all, that he cared nothing for their cheers or boos. But he cared. If he hadn't, it would have been a lot easier to give them what they wanted. Catcher Birdie Tebbetts suggested as much to Williams. As Williams recounted it, Tebbetts suggested he "put one over on 'em" by tipping his hat and smiling while yelling "Go to hell, you S.O.B.s."

"That kind of appealed to me a little bit, and I said I might just do it," Williams said. "But there was a rainout the next day, and by the time I hit my next home run, the mood had passed."

What Williams most resented was what he called "frontrunning." He couldn't forget that the same people cheering his home run had booed him when he made an error and would do so again. His relationship with the fans reached its nadir in 1956. Angered because fans had booed and cheered him in the same inning, he showed his contempt by spitting at the crowd three times. The newspapers had a field day, with headlines such as "Great Expectorations" and "The Night the Spit Hit the Fan."

But Williams forgave the fans (unlike the writers). The next night, he homered to right, and as Fenway held its breath, he stretched out his arm and clamped it over his mouth, as if to restrain himself. The fans loved it . . . and him. This was a turning point in his relationship with the fans, who were always more forgiving than the writers.

In his final playing years, wrote Halberstam, "he had mellowed and the world had largely come round to him." Williams earned a reputation for helping younger players, and he had lasting friendships with many former teammates. He even maintained amicable relationships with some of the younger Boston writers. But mellow, no, that could never describe him. It was his single-minded drive, his refusal to give in, that defined him and made him a great hitter. "Joe DiMaggio might have hit in 56 consecutive games," Halberstam wrote, "but he never won 33,277 arguments in a row, like Ted Williams, the undisputed champion of contentiousness."

Williams did not compromise. Even when he relaxed, he wasn't truly relaxed. He was as intense (and almost as accomplished) a fisherman as he was a hitter. The player he ought to be compared with is not DiMaggio, but Ty Cobb. Williams was in many ways more likable, but he shared Cobb's intensity, his search for perfection at the plate. Some writers speculated that Williams courted criticism because he knew it would make him angry. Then he could channel that anger, whether at fans or writers, into an even greater drive to succeed. "His career was a case study in exacerbation," wrote Seidel. "Williams nurtured his rage," wrote Roger Kahn.

After every injury, after every slump, after every insult, he came back. "I hit better mad," was how Williams himself put it to a *Globe* reporter in 1950. "The boos stir me up," he told the *Sporting News* in 1957.

Given the pain the press inflicted on him, it's unlikely Williams consciously sought out bad press. Certainly he did not want newspapers to remind him of his unhappy childhood; his desire to put his past behind him was part of what drove him. But it's also clear that he was not just the victim of a vicious circulation battle or of fickle fans. His battles with the press and the public, too, drove him.

"Baseball gives every American boy a chance to excel, not just to be as good as someone else, but to be better," Williams said when he was inducted into the Hall of Fame in 1966. "This is the nature of man and the name of the game."

To investigate further:

Baldassaro, Lawrence. *The Ted Williams Reader.* New York: Fireside, 1991. Williams has attracted more good writing than any other player. This anthology includes two classic works on Williams's last game: John Updike's "Hub Fans Bid Kid Adieu" and Ed Linn's "The Kid's Last Game."

Cramer, Richard Ben. *The Seasons of the Kid.* New York: Prentice Hall Press, 1991. An expanded version of an *Esquire* profile that, as editor Daniel Okrent put it, "merges Updike's awe-struck regard with Linn's piercing iconoclasm." Lavishly illustrated.

DiMaggio, Dom, with Bill Gilbert. *Real Grass, Real Heroes.* New York: Kensington, 1990. The 1941 season, as recalled by Joe's brother and Ted's friend.

Halberstam, David. *Summer of '49.* New York: William Morrow, 1989. Yankees vs. Red Sox, DiMaggio vs. Williams.

————— . *The Teammates*. New York: Hyperion, 2003. Former Sox teammates Dominic DiMaggio and Johnny Pesky travel to Florida to visit a dying Williams; lightweight but moving.

Johnson, Dick, and Glenn Stout. *Ted Williams*. New York: Walker, 1991. An illustrated portrait with essays by Stephen Jay Gould, Donald Hall, George Higgins, and others.

Linn, Ed. *Hitter*. San Diego: Harcourt Brace, 1993. Whoever else he was—the Kid, the Splendid Splinter, Teddy Ballgame—he was always a hitter.

Montville, Leigh. *Ted Williams*. New York: Doubleday, 2004. Admirably nuanced.

Seidel, Michael. *Ted Williams*. Chicago: Contemporary Books, 1991. A comprehensive biography.

Williams, Ted, with John Underwood. *My Turn at Bat*. New York: Fireside, 1988. Originally published in 1969, and you can still feel the anger. Even the titles of their autobiographies are tellingly different: DiMaggio's was *Lucky to Be a Yankee*.

13

Why Did Rickey
Sign Robinson?

I n 1903 the Ohio Wesleyan baseball team, coached by Branch
Rickey, visited South Bend, Indiana. The hotel there refused to
assign a room to a black player named Charley Thomas.
Finally, Rickey suggested a cot be put in his room, as if Thomas
were his servant. That night Rickey returned to his room to find
Thomas on the cot, in tears.

"His whole body shook with emotion," Rickey told Dodger
publicist Arthur Mann in 1945. "I sat and watched him, not
knowing what to do until he began tearing at one hand with the
other—just as if he were trying to scratch the skin off his hands
with his fingernails."

Rickey asked Thomas what he was doing.

"It's my hands," he sobbed. "They're black. If only they were
white, I'd be as good as anybody then, wouldn't I, Mr. Rickey? If
only they were white."

Rickey then promised Thomas "the day will come when they
won't have to be white." Forty-two years later, Rickey kept his
promise by signing Jackie Robinson to a contract with the Brooklyn Dodgers.

The Charley Thomas story—as told first to Mann and retold
many times by Rickey himself—is as much a part of baseball lore
as anything Robinson achieved on the field. Reporters quickly
sought out Thomas, then a successful dentist in Albuquerque,
and Thomas confirmed the 1903 incident.

Robinson's biographer Arnold Rampersad compared Rickey's story to that of Abraham Lincoln going down the Mississippi, seeing slavery, and vowing to end it. Rickey himself seemed to encourage the comparison by hanging a portrait of Lincoln in his office. It was a story, historian Jules Tygiel wrote, almost biblical, or at least sermonlike—so much so that it seemed to invite skepticism.

If Charley Thomas left such a mark on Branch Rickey, many asked, why—when he became president of the St. Louis Cardinals in 1917—did he do and say nothing about the segregation at Sportsman's Park, both on the field and in the stands? Why did he wait until Brooklyn, forty-two years after Thomas's humiliation—to do something about it?

Rickey went to great lengths to conceal his plans to sign Jackie Robinson. In May 1945, five months before the deal, he held a press conference to announce that he was establishing a new Negro League—the United States League. Rickey's scouts would henceforth be on the lookout for Negro players to fill the roster of his own entry in the league, the Brooklyn Brown Dodgers.

The assembled reporters were not sure what to make of the new league. Some feared it would perpetuate baseball's color line. Others suspected it was Rickey's attempt to drive the established Negro Leagues out of business. In reality, of course, the new league never came to be, and the Brown Dodgers turned out to be merely a cover for Rickey's scouts as they checked out black players for the Dodgers.

Robinson himself was told nothing of Rickey's plans until August 1945, when Dodger scout Clyde Sukeforth ushered him into Rickey's office. As Robinson recalled the meeting in his 1972 autobiography, it was only then that Rickey revealed he was considering him for the Dodgers. Rickey told Robinson he had investigated him thoroughly, checking out his character as well as his playing ability.

Then Rickey subjected Robinson to his final test. Taking on in turn the roles of hostile teammates, opponents, fans, hotel clerks, and others, Rickey goaded Robinson with racial epithets and acted out the types of situation that reduced Charley Thomas to tears. Robinson asked whether he was looking for someone who was afraid to fight back. Rickey answered he wanted a player "with guts enough *not* to fight back."

"Could I turn the other cheek?" Robinson wondered. "I didn't know how I would do it. Yet I knew that I must." He agreed to play for the Montreal Royals, the top Dodger farm club.

Robinson's decision to accept Rickey's terms set Robinson on the path that would make him a civil rights hero and also ulti- mately put him at odds with many in the movement. By the late sixties, militant civil rights leaders such as Malcolm X were openly hostile toward the stoic turn-the-other-cheek suffering that Robinson epitomized. This was in large part unfair to Robinson, who had no real choice in the matter if he wanted to play in the majors. Nor was Robinson, prior to his deal with Rickey, afraid to confront whites. In 1944, for example, while he was serving at Camp Hood in Texas, a bus driver demanded that Lieutenant Robinson move to the back of the bus. Like Rosa Parks, Robinson refused, which led to his court-martial. (He was acquitted.) Robinson was equally aggressive after 1949, when Rickey told him he was free to be himself. He argued with um- pires and managers at least as much as anyone else, and he bluntly criticized baseball's continuing discrimination.

Still, there was no denying Robinson's instincts were essen- tially conservative. In July 1949 he spoke in front of the House Un-American Activities Committee and denounced the pro- Russian statements of Paul Robeson, a black activist and singer. In 1960 Robinson supported Richard Nixon for president, and four years later Nelson Rockefeller. In both cases, he did so out of a conviction that blacks should seek influence in both parties; still, his support for Republicans cost him much prestige among liberals, and many went so far as to call him an Uncle Tom.

Rickey, too, had conservative instincts, however radical inte- gration seemed at the time. In a 1947 address to black leaders, Rickey proclaimed, "the biggest threat to [Robinson's] success— the one enemy likely to ruin that success—is the Negro people themselves." He urged blacks not to congregate in large groups at ballparks or to hold any special gatherings or celebrations that white fans might find threatening. There were to be no Jackie Robinson Days. Above all, baseball integration must not be touted as a victory for communism. "If any individual, group, or segment of Negro society uses the advancement of Jackie Robinson in baseball as a symbol of social 'ism' or schism, a triumph of race over race," Rickey warned, "I will curse the day I ever signed him to a contract, and I will personally see that baseball is never so abused and misrepresented again."

At times, Rickey so distanced himself from anything that sounded revolutionary that it was hard to imagine that his motive for signing Robinson had anything to do with social justice. This led many historians to conclude—Charley Thomas notwithstanding—that what really motivated Rickey was greed.

Among those most cynical about Rickey's motives were many former Negro Leaguers. This was the same Rickey, they noted, who had made the Cardinals a perennial contender by creating the farm system, which at one point consisted of as many as fifty teams. This let him harvest top players without having to outbid richer teams. Sportswriter Roger Kahn called this the game's "production line" and compared Rickey's influence on the business of baseball to Henry Ford's on the business of cars.

Negroes, the theory went, were just his latest source of raw—and cheap—talent. With the exception of Satchel Paige, Negro stars were passed over for young prospects. Indeed, the greatest irony of integration was that it spelled the demise of the Negro Leagues and the end of the line for its often well-paid stars, men such as Josh Gibson and Buck Leonard and Cool Papa Bell. In St. Louis, Rickey could do nothing to take advantage of black players; the city, the southernmost in the major leagues at the time, was "stony soil," he later said. In Brooklyn, Rickey seized his opportunity.

And Rickey was after not just Negro players, but also fans. Commented former Negro Leagues star Dave Malarcher: "When did integration happen? When the major leagues saw those fifty thousand Negroes in the park. Branch Rickey had something else on his mind than a little black boy. He had those crowds."

Walter O'Malley, Rickey's partner (and rival for control of the Dodgers), agreed. "Rickey's Brooklyn contract called for salary plus a percentage of the take, and during World War II the take fell off," O'Malley told Kahn. "It was then Rickey mentioned signing a Negro. He had a *fiscal* interest."

The Negro Leagues were a big, albeit disorganized, business, with total annual attendance of more than three million. Many historians have noted that integration spelled the end of the Negro Leagues, and more profits for the major leagues. In 1947, Robinson's first year in the majors, National League attendance rose 15 percent. The next year, when the Indians integrated with Paige and Larry Doby, American League attendance jumped 14 percent.

All this, however, was clear only in retrospect. In 1945, integration seemed a huge risk, financially as well as politically. Whatever his motives, Rickey could not have been certain signing Robinson would pay off. Indeed, many baseball executives feared black players would scare off white fans. As Yankee owner Larry MacPhail put it in a 1946 report: "A situation might be presented . . . in which the preponderance of Negro attendance . . . could threaten the value of the Major League franchises."

MacPhail's analysis was undoubtedly colored by racism, but there was some truth to it. Contrary to the generally accepted assumption, Rickey reaped no windfall from signing Robinson. A 1998 study by business historian Henry Fetter found that despite the image of Brooklyn fans as loyal and colorblind, most of the 1947 increase in Dodger attendance came on the road. Even that increase, Fetter argued, could be attributed to factors other than Robinson's presence. In 1947 the Dodgers played only five doubleheaders on the road, compared to fourteen in 1946; this, Fetter concluded, gave fans more chances to come to games and was the reason attendance rose.

Moreover, the attendance gains of 1947 were short-lived. By 1950, National League attendance had dropped below 1946 levels. In Brooklyn, too, the trend was down. In 1948 Dodger home attendance dropped by more than 400,000, and by 1957 the Dodgers barely cracked the 1 million mark. Many factors drove attendance down: by the fifties, Brooklyn fans were watching more games on television, and more and more of them were watching the games in their new suburban homes. Robinson did not drive all these fans away from Brooklyn, but neither could he bring them all back.

A somewhat less cynical view of Rickey's motives was that what he really cared about was not so much money, but winning. That's why he created the farm system, along with other innovations such as sliding pits and batting tees, which later became standard at training sites. And that's why he signed Robinson.

Rickey's own words provided plenty of evidence for this view. "The greatest untapped reservoir of raw material in the history of the game is the black race," he told family members. "The Negroes will make us winners for years to come."

To reporters he said: "If an elephant with pink ears were a better center fielder for the Dodgers than the best player the team had for that position, I would sign the elephant to a contract and put him in center field."

Could this be the same man who promised Charley Thomas a different world? Was Rickey interested in changing nothing more than the National League standings?

That seems to overstate the case. Rickey may have played down the political ramifications of his move to defuse conservative criticism, or to distance himself from the radical implications of integration. He may have stressed his desire to win because he knew others would spread the Charley Thomas version anyway. Besides, there's no reason why Rickey couldn't be both anti-Communist and pro-integration. He wanted to win pennants and he wanted to break down racial barriers; by signing Robinson, he accomplished both.

To Mann, the same publicist who first reported the Charley Thomas story, Rickey said: "I have never meant to be a crusader, and I hope I won't be regarded as one. My purpose is to be fair to all people, and my selfish objective is to win baseball games."

The emphasis on Rickey and Robinson has tended to obscure other factors that led to baseball integration. By the time Rickey reached Brooklyn, its soil was indeed less stony than that of St. Louis in the 1920s and 1930s.

For more than a decade, leftist writers, especially in the Communist and black press, had spearheaded a campaign against baseball segregation. Even baseball owners, never an especially progressive bunch, were increasingly embarrassed. More than anything else, though, it was World War II that transformed attitudes. Jackie Robinson was not the only soldier, black or white, to confront the illogic of a Jim Crow army fighting Hitler's racism. New attitudes were evident throughout the first half of the 1940s, well before Rickey signed Robinson. In St. Louis, the Cardinals integrated the stands at Sportsman's Park. In Philadelphia, Bill Veeck Jr. was rumored to be interested in buying the Phillies with the intention of filling the war-depleted roster with black players. In Boston, Robinson was one of three Negro Leagues players to attend a tryout at Fenway Park. None ever heard back from the Red Sox, who were more interested in defusing political pressure than in actually signing a black, but it was yet another indication of the rising pressure.

In New York, Governor Thomas E. Dewey signed into law the Quinn-Ives Act, forbidding discrimination in hiring, and Mayor Fiorello LaGuardia pushed baseball to abide by it. Rickey later insisted that neither the law nor the lobbying influenced him; in fact, he considered "the misguided labor of pressure groups" a serious threat to his carefully prepared "great experiment." At the very least, however, the pressure may have forced him to accelerate his timetable. Wrote historian Jules Tygiel: "With public pressure mounting, particularly in the New York area, it seems likely that political events would have forced the issue within the next few years. Rickey's action and his presentation of the Robinson case as an 'experiment' actually relieved the pressure on other owners and allowed them to delay while awaiting the outcome of Rickey's gamble."

Tygiel argued that Robinson's success made it difficult, then and now, to recognize that others besides Rickey could have integrated baseball. Bill Veeck, for one, finally managed to buy a team in 1946. He quickly signed a number of Negro Leaguers for the Cleveland Indians, and would surely have done so even if Rickey had not already signed Robinson. Indeed, Veeck's approach raises questions about whether it was truly necessary for Rickey to choose a single black player, or whether it might not have been easier on everyone to sign a number of blacks at once. Rickey himself apparently weighed this option, at least briefly, according to baseball historian John Thorn. In 1987 Thorn uncovered at the Hall of Fame a box of 1945 photographs featuring Robinson and other Negro Leaguers, along with a draft of an article Mann had prepared with Rickey for *Look* magazine. The draft mentioned Rickey planned to sign pitcher Don Newcombe and outfielder Sam Jethroe and bring them up to the majors at the same time as Robinson. The article and photos were never published, and Robinson became the sole standard-bearer, in the opinion of Thorn and Tygiel, because political pressure from LaGuardia and others forced Rickey to go public before he had signed Newcombe and Jethroe.

Rickey's original plan, then, was a much more radical strike at segregation than he later admitted. Even if he backed away from that plan, even if he never fully realized how radically signing Robinson would change the world, even if his motives and methods were questionable, he deserves credit for delivering on his promise to Charley Thomas. In 1942, sportswriter Tom Meany, poking fun at Rickey's often pompous piety, nicknamed him the "Mahatma." The nickname stuck, for as National Public Radio host Scott Simon put it, Rickey "could make the decision about whether to bring in a right- or left-handed pitcher to face Stan Musial in the eighth inning sound like a deliberation over supporting Chiang Kai-shek or Mao Zedong." But like the real Gandhi, Rickey sincerely believed in nonviolent revolution, and that is what he brought about.

Of course, Robinson, too, deserves credit, and not just for his playing skills. Later civil rights leaders might have preferred a more militant approach, but Robinson's way was the only one available to him at the time, and he handled the racism he encountered with remarkable restraint. In doing so, he eventually won over teammates, opponents, and fans. "I couldn't have done it," said onetime Negro Leaguer and Dodger teammate Joe Black. "I might have taken it for a few days, or maybe a week, but then I'd have grabbed one of them in the dugout runway or outside the ballpark and popped him."

So, yes, there were many historical forces at work. But there were also Robinson and Rickey, and the remarkable friendship they forged. In his 1972 autobiography, Robinson wrote: "He will always have my admiration and respect. Critics had said, 'Don't you know that your precious Mr. Rickey didn't bring you up out of the black leagues because he loved you? Are you stupid enough not to understand that the Brooklyn club profited hugely because of what your Mr. Rickey did?'

"Yes, I know that," Robinson continued. "But I also know what a big gamble he took. A bond developed between us that lasted long after I had left the game. In a way I feel I was the son he had lost and he was the father I had lost."

Clyde Sukeforth described the first meeting in Rickey's office: "The old man was so engrossed in Robinson . . . he didn't hear a damn word I said. When he met somebody he was interested in, he studied them in the most profound way. He just stared and stared. And that's what he did with Robinson—stared at him as if he were trying to get inside the man. And Jack stared right back at him."

"Oh, they were a pair, those two!" recalled Sukeforth.

To investigate further:

Dorinson, Joseph, and Joram Warmund, eds. *Jackie Robinson.* Armonk, N.Y.: M. E. Sharpe, 1998. Includes Fetter's analysis of attendance figures.

Falkner, David. *Great Time Coming.* New York: Simon & Schuster, 1995. An excellent biography, especially on Robinson's life before and after the Dodgers.

Honig, Donald. *Baseball When the Grass Was Real.* New York: Coward, McCann, & Geoghegan, 1975. One of Honig's four superb oral histories, this covers the 1920s to the 1940s and includes an interview with Sukeforth. In the interview, Sukeforth demonstrates the eye for detail that made him as good a storyteller as he was a scout.

Kahn, Roger. *The Boys of Summer.* New York: Harper & Row, 1971. Looking back at the Dodgers, above all Robinson, Kahn wrote what has become, deservedly, the most famous book in the baseball canon.

—————. *The Era.* New York: Ticknor & Fields, 1993. Kahn expands his subject to include the Giants and Yankees, but his heart clearly belonged to the Dodgers.

Mann, Arthur. *The Jackie Robinson Story.* New York: Grosset & Dunlap, 1951. Mann's job as Dodger publicist meant that the book was at least in part Rickey's version of the story.

Peterson, Robert. *Only the Ball Was White.* New York: Oxford University Press, 1992. Originally published in 1970 and still among the best works on black players and teams.

Rampersad, Arnold. *Jackie Robinson.* New York: Alfred A. Knopf, 1997. A thorough biography written with the cooperation of Rachel Robinson.

Robinson, Jackie. *I Never Had It Made.* New York: G. P. Putnam's Sons, 1972. By 1972, the year he died, Robinson had become much more pessimistic, and here he expresses doubt about some of his own positions, such as his criticism of Robeson and support of Nixon.

Robinson, Rachel. *Jackie Robinson.* New York: Harry N. Abrams, 1996. A lavishly illustrated portrait by his widow.

Simon, Scott. *Jackie Robinson and the Integration of Baseball.* New York: John Wiley & Sons, 2002. A lively account, brief but nuanced.

Tygiel, Jules. *Baseball's Great Experiment.* New York: Oxford University Press, 1983. An authoritative and lively social history of baseball integration.

—————. ed. *The Jackie Robinson Reader.* New York: E. P. Dutton, 1997. Includes Thorn's account of his detective work at the Hall of Fame, as well as the article by Arthur Mann, written for *Look* magazine but never published because political pressures forced Rickey to speed up his great experiment.

How Old Was Satchel Paige?

He won, Satchel Paige estimated, more than 2,000 games, about 100 of them no-hitters. He would sometimes call in his outfield to the pitching mound, so confident was he that he would strike out the side. In all-star games between Negro Leaguers and major leaguers, he went 13 innings to beat Dizzy Dean 1–0 and struck out 16 to beat Bob Feller.

Said Dean: "A bunch of the fellows get in a barber session the other day and they start to arguefy about the best pitcher they ever see. Some says Lefty Grove and Lefty Gomez and Walter Johnson and old Pete Alexander and Dazzy Vance . . . and some of the boys even say Old Diz is the best they ever see. But I see all them fellows but Matty and Johnson and I know who's the best pitcher I ever see and it's old Satchel Paige."

"The stories about Satchel Paige are legendary," his teammate Buck O'Neil once said, "and some of them are even true."

Even his name is shrouded in myth. He was born Leroy Paige, or possibly Page, in the black ghetto of Mobile, Alabama. As a child, he earned change carrying bags at the railroad station. As Paige later told the story, he rigged together a pole and some ropes so that he could carry three or four satchels at once. The other kids called him a "walking satchel tree," and the name stuck.

A childhood friend remembered it differently. "All those years he said he got the name 'cause he carried satchels," Willie

Hines told Paige biographer Mark Ribowsky. "Hell no—it's 'cause he stole 'em."

Paige, always eager to promote his legend, also was aware that the nickname tied him to another. "Later, some even called me Satchmo," he wrote in his 1961 autobiography, "but not because I blew a mean trumpet like Louie Armstrong. I just blow that fast ball—blow it right by the hitters."

What made it difficult to tell fact from fiction, of course, was that most of what Paige did was in the Negro Leagues, where record-keeping was, if not quite as unreliable as sometimes portrayed, by no means as meticulous as in the majors. Paige pitched professionally for more than twenty years before his first major league appearance. Finally, on July 9, 1948, he took the mound for the Cleveland Indians, the first black pitcher in the American League. He threw two shutout innings.

The *Sporting News* was indignant. "[Indian owner Bill] Veeck has gone too far in his quest for publicity," wrote J. G. Taylor Spink. "Paige said he was 39 years of age. There are reports that he is somewhat in the neighborhood of 50. . . . To bring in a pitching 'rookie' of Paige's age casts a reflection on the entire scheme of operation in the major leagues [and is] to demean the standards of baseball in the big circuits. If Satch were white, he would not have drawn a second thought from Veeck." To which Veeck responded: "If Satch were white, he would have been in the majors twenty-five years earlier and the question would not have been before the house."

Veeck also pointed to Paige's record. He was 6–1 in 1948, 4–7 the next: a perfectly respectable rookie season followed by a reasonable sophomore slump. But for a man in his forties or fifties, truly amazing.

How old was Satchel Paige? The mystery became all the more intriguing as Paige continued to retire major league batters. The Indians dropped him after 1949, but in 1951 Veeck, now owner of the St. Louis Browns, brought him back to the majors for a 3–4 year. He rebounded in 1952 to make the All-Star team with an astounding 12–10 record. "Leroy just drops his age two or three years each season," Veeck said. The Browns' record book got into the act, too, listing Paige's date of birth as 1892, 1896, 1900, and 1904, and then telling readers to "take your pick."

Paige slid to 3–9 in 1954, and it seemed the end of the line. Still, he continued to barnstorm and play in various minor leagues. Then, in 1965, Charley Finley signed Paige to the Kansas City Athletics. Finley was second only to Veeck in his disregard for baseball protocol; he would later introduce orange balls and Mustache Day. He clearly considered Paige, now in his fortieth year of professional ball, a publicity gimmick. He sent him to the bullpen with a rocking chair and a nurse. Paige surprised everyone by pitching three shutout innings against the Red Sox.

Without a doubt, that made Paige the oldest player ever to appear in a major league game. The question remained: how old?

The logical person to ask was his mother, Lula Coleman Paige, and in 1948 the *Cleveland Plain Dealer* did just that. She stated he was born in 1904, making him forty-four at the time of his major league debut. Satchel Paige quickly refuted his mother. "She must have me mistaken with my oldest brother," he said. "It's quite a job keeping up with sixteen kids."

Lula Paige herself changed her story a number of times, seemingly enjoying the attention as much as her son. In 1948, Veeck tracked her down at a general store in Mobile.

"I found out quickly enough the source of Satch's humor," he wrote. " 'I can't rightly recall whether Leroy was my firstborn,' she said, 'or my fifteenth.' Having had her joke, she told me she really couldn't remember what year he had been born, but that she could guarantee he wasn't her oldest."

A few years later she told a reporter she was sure about the 1904 date, since she had written it in her Bible. "Seems like Mom's Bible would know," Paige conceded in his autobiography, but added, "she ain't ever shown me the Bible.

"Anyway," he continued, "she was in her nineties when she told the reporter that and sometimes she tended to forget things."

Later, Paige expanded his mother's story to include a goat that ate the Bible, forever dooming any efforts to solve the mystery. (The goat, Paige was happy to offer, lived to be twenty-seven.)

Clearly Paige reveled in his reputation as ageless. If Jim Crow had robbed him of his chance to show his best stuff in the majors, he would seize immortality elsewhere. His famous one-liners repeatedly showed him to be not just wiser, but older. "Age is a question of mind over matter," he once said. "If you don't mind, it don't matter." Another: "We don't stop playing because we get old. We get old because we stop playing." And another: "If you keep moving, Old Age ain't got a chance of catching you. He moves mighty slow." And most famous of all: "Don't look back. Something might be gaining on you."

Said Veeck: "Satch's age has always been a subject of lively debate, a debate he did not go out of his way to discourage. It could even be said that he dished out his age the way he dished out his pitches, mixing his figures up nicely and always keeping his interviewers off balance."

Veeck, too, was not above using Paige's age to stoke interest in the Indians, and even more so, in the otherwise uninteresting Browns. The indignation of the *Sporting News* may have had more to do with Paige's race than his age, but there was no denying Veeck's "quest for publicity." This was the same Veeck, after all, who in 1951 sent the 3'7" Eddie Gaedel up to the plate. ("He was," Veeck asserted, "the best darn midget who ever played big-league ball.")

In fact, according to some baseball historians, Veeck knew perfectly well how old Paige was, and intentionally obfuscated the issue. He made a great show of hiring a private detective to check the records at the Mobile city hall, and announced there was no birth certificate for a Leroy Paige. There was, however, a record of the July 7, 1906, birth of Leroy *Page*.

Veeck's detective, the owner later reported, deemed this finding irrelevant. "Since the Mobile records were filled with Leroys," the detective told Veeck, "he felt confident that we could scratch that date." Veeck concluded Paige must have been born years earlier, probably in 1899 or before.

Robert Peterson, one of the premier historians of the Negro Leagues, disagreed. Noting that Paige was pitching professionally in 1926, he concluded, "it is impossible to believe that his fastball could have been kept under wraps until he was twenty-seven years old." Peterson thought the 1906 date likely.

Ribowsky accused Veeck of being disingenuous. He pointed out that until 1924, according to the Mobile city directories, Paige family members all spelled their name Page. Satchel's father was listed as John Page until 1902, the year he died, and his mother was Lula Page until 1932. Only in 1926 did Satchel's brothers John R. and Clarence change the spelling, and another brother stuck with the original version until 1942. Reports of Leroy's early pitching exploits often spelled his name without the i, though equally often skipped the surname entirely and went by Satch or Satchel or Satchell.

In his autobiography, Paige conceded, "my folks started out by spelling their name 'Page' and later stuck in the 'i' to make themselves sound more high-tone."

"I'll go by that birth certificate," he wrote.

Still, he was clearly reluctant to give 1906 a definitive endorsement, stressing, "there are all kinds of other dates floating around." Before he died, he made sure doubt would remain. His headstone read: "Dedicated in honor of Satchel Paige, '?'–1982."

Were Paige and Veeck, then, in cahoots? Perhaps. Both had much to gain from perpetuating the legend of the ageless Paige. Both enjoyed a good mystery and a good joke. But for Paige, at least, his past wasn't all funny, and there was much about the life of a poverty-stricken black child in early-twentieth-century Mobile that he was happy to forget. Perhaps, too, Ribowsky suggested, he was eager to put behind him the name of Page, since John Page periodically deserted his family.

Moreover, Paige had reason to resent the birth certificate. The Mobile records for poor black families were extremely unreliable. What records there were usually came from the families themselves, often relying on memories as protean as that of Lula Page. Like the Negro Leagues, black life in early-twentieth-century Mobile was deemed, in the white world, unworthy of record-keeping.

Ribowsky believed that it was pain more than mirth that motivated Paige to keep his origins a mystery. "It could not have been much fun at all to embrace a birthdate dug up for him," the biographer maintained, "not when it only called back to mind family divisions and the neglect of an entire city."

The birth of Leroy Page was an event neither the man nor his city cared to remember. So Satchel Paige made sure—and part of his genius lay in using his forgotten birthday to accomplish this—that the rest of his life would not be forgotten.

To investigate further:

O'Neil, Buck, with Steve Wulf and David Conrads. *I Was Right on Time*. New York: Simon & Schuster, 1996. Paige's Negro Leagues teammate and manager tells plenty of wonderful stories, including how he managed to keep Satchel's fiancée and girlfriend from meeting.

Paige, Leroy (Satchel), as told to David Lipman. *Maybe I'll Pitch Forever*. Garden City, N.Y.: Doubleday, 1962. Between the lines (and the one-liners) one can read hints of bitterness.

Peterson, Robert. *Only the Ball Was White*. New York: Oxford University Press, 1992. Groundbreaking.

Ribowsky, Mark. *Don't Look Back*. New York: Simon & Schuster, 1994. Ribowsky is superb at distinguishing the man from the myth.

Veeck, Bill, with Ed Linn. *Veeck as in Wreck*. New York: Fireside, 1989. Originally published in 1962, this was, according to Red Smith, "the best [sports] autobiography ever written." Like Veeck, the book is consistently funny and provocative.

Did Thomson Steal Branca's Sign?

Four times broadcaster Russ Hodges screamed it—"THE GIANTS WIN THE PENNANT!"—before getting around to explaining how they had done so. No one blamed him for being excited. And no one listening to the game really needed an explanation. Hodges had set up the situation for all to see.

"Bobby Thomson up there swinging," he told the WMCA radio audience. "One out, last of the ninth. . . . Branca pitches and Bobby takes a strike on the inside corner. . . . Brooklyn leads it 4–2. . . . Branca throws . . . there's a long drive . . . it's gonna be . . . I BELIEVE . . ."

Thomson's homer in the third and deciding game of the 1951 National League playoff series between the Dodgers and Giants remains the most dramatic in baseball history. Sure, you could make a case for Mazeroski in 1961 and Fisk in 1975 and Dent in 1978 and plenty of others. But Thomson's was, as the *New York Daily News* immediately and lastingly called it, the "shot heard 'round the world." Thomson's was the one the post office put on a stamp. Thomson's was in the bottom of the ninth. And Thomson's was the culmination of one of the most remarkable drives in baseball history, the "miracle of Coogan's Bluff" that saw the Giants come from 13½ back on August 11 to tie the Dodgers in the final game of the regular season.

Just an inning before his shot, Thomson appeared destined to be the game's goat. Andy Pafko's grounder bounced over Thomson's shoulder at third, scoring Duke Snider. Then Billy Cox's grounder went under Thomson's glove, bringing in Jackie Robinson.

In the bottom of the ninth, Alvin Dark and Don Mueller singled, though neither hit the ball hard. Monte Irvin popped out. The loudspeaker in the press box told writers to pick up their passes for the World Series at the Dodger clubhouse in Ebbets Field. Then Whitey Lockman doubled, scoring Dark and sending Mueller to third. Clint Harting ran for Mueller, who had broken his leg on the play. Ralph Branca relieved Don Newcombe, who had been masterful. Thomson stepped to the plate.

As Red Smith wrote, just after the game ended: "Now it is done. Now the story ends. And there is no way to tell it. The art of fiction is dead. Reality has strangled invention. Only the utterly impossible, the inexpressibly fantastic, can ever be plausible again."

Dark, who was on base when Thomson hit the homer and later became a Baptist preacher, insisted the season was part of "the Lord's plan." Giant catcher Wes Westrum surmised "it was just meant to be."

Except, from the start, there were rumors of a decidedly nondivine intervention. The Giant comeback, the story went, was the result of a sign-stealing plot involving binoculars, electric wire, and buzzers. Thomson was able to connect with Branca's high, inside fastball because he knew that's what was coming.

What Hodges should have been screaming, many believed (and they were not all Dodger fans), was: "The Giants steal the pennant!"

The rumors broke into print in a 1962 Associated Press story by Joseph Reichler. The *Washington Post* headline read: "Sign-Stealing with Binoculars Set Up Thomson's Flag-Winning Homer."

Reichler quoted an unidentified former Giant as saying that for the final three months of the 1951 season, the team had a spy in the center-field clubhouse. With the aid of binoculars, he read the catcher's signs, then passed them on via a wire to the dugout. One buzz meant a fastball, two a breaking pitch. A bench coach then gave the sign to the batters, including Thomson. "You might say," the anonymous source said, "that the shot heard 'round the world was set off by a buzzer."

Thomson's teammates quickly rallied 'round. "Anybody who knows anything about baseball knows that with a runner on second base no catcher in the business would give just one sign and stick with it," said Dark, who in 1962 was the Giant manager. "He flashes three or four phoney signs. It would take either a genius or a very lucky man to select the legitimate sign and flash it to the hitter."

Thomson himself called the accusation "the most ridiculous thing I have ever heard." If he'd been stealing signs, Thomson demanded to know, why didn't he swing at Branca's first pitch? That first pitch, Thomson said, "was a fat one right down the middle." Branca confirmed this: "The first one was right down the pipe. On the second one I tried to brush him back a bit but I didn't get the ball in tight enough. I always figured he just out-guessed me."

Many players also argued that sign-stealing was a tricky business, something the Giants and Thomson would have been foolish to depend on. Signals were complicated to start with, and managers and catchers often changed them in the middle of a game or an inning or even an at-bat. ("I ain't gonna change our signs," Casey Stengel once explained. "I'm just gonna change what they mean.") A batter tipped off incorrectly was in worse shape than one who didn't know what was coming. In 1947, Yankee coach Charlie Dressen (who managed the Dodgers in 1951) signaled Joe DiMaggio to expect a curve. After a fastball almost beaned him, DiMaggio told Dressen, "Knock it off before you get me killed." Yogi Berra once said, "I wouldn't take a sign if their own catcher sent it to me Western Union."

This was Thomson's position as well. "I never wanted to know what pitch was coming," he said in 1968. "I was so over-eager, if I'd known a fastball was coming I'd likely have swung too soon and missed it."

Implicit in these denials, of course, was an admission that *others* did steal signs. Reichler's story prompted others to recall the history of sign-stealing, which began long before Thomson did or didn't do it. In 1900, Red shortstop Tommy Corcoran, after studying the Phillies' third-base coach, darted across the foul line, fell to his knees, and started frantically digging up the dirt at Philadelphia's Baker Bowl. Before the umpires, grounds-keepers, and police could restrain him, Corcoran unearthed a wooden box with a buzzer inside and wires attached. The Phillies' third-string catcher, Morgan Murphy, had been stationed in the center-field clubhouse with a pair of binoculars. After stealing the catcher's signs, Murphy would transmit the information to the third-base coach by underground wires. Later that same month, Corcoran uncovered another spy network in Pittsburgh, where signs were relayed through the placement of an iron rod on the outfield fence.

In 1909, New York Highlander manager George Stallings rented an apartment opposite Hilltop Park. By bouncing sunlight off a mirror, Stallings' spies transmitted the signs from the apart-ment directly to the batter. The system was, admittedly, ineffec-tive on cloudy days.

Just three years before the Giant-Dodger playoffs, Cleveland pitcher Bob Feller inserted a telescope in a hole in the score-board. This was the same telescope Feller had used to pick up enemy aircraft when he was a gunnery officer on the USS *Alabama*. Feller and pitcher Bob Lemon took turns peering at opposing catchers and passing signs to a groundskeeper. The groundskeeper would signal Indian hitters through another hole in the scoreboard.

The moral of most of these stories was that if Durocher's Giants were stealing signs in 1951, it wasn't anything new. It wasn't even anything particularly immoral, at least according to some players. "The way I felt about it, it was like in the war," Feller said. "You had to decipher a code, break it down, which we did against the Germans and the Japanese."

Others distinguished between stealing signs with the naked eye and using telescopes or wires or scoreboards. The former was okay, the latter not. "There has never been a specific rule against this," wrote baseball writer Leonard Koppett, "but it is generally considered unethical, because the home team can arrange it while the visiting team cannot."

As time passed, many former Giants conceded that, yes, the team had stolen signs. In 1991, the fortieth anniversary of the home run, Thomson brought out a book that was fairly open about the scheme. He continued to insist, though, that other teams were doing it, too, and that he did not have the sign for Branca's fateful pitch.

"There has been speculation about Durocher and the spyglass for years," wrote Thomson's coauthors, Lee Heiman and Bill Gutman. "But so would [then-Dodger manager Charlie] Dressen, [then-Cub manager] Frankie Frisch, and other veteran managers of the time."

The book quoted various former teammates saying pretty much the same thing. "Sure, the Giants were stealing signs from the clubhouse," said catcher Walker Cooper. "But . . . believe me, Leo wasn't the only manager with a spotter."

How, then, to explain the Giant comeback? How did they win 37 of their last 44 games?

For starters, there was Willie Mays. Giant manager Leo Durocher brought up Mays in May, and after a horrible start, he emerged as the National League's Rookie of the Year. On August 15, the Dodgers had runners on first and third, and Carl Furillo drove a pitch to deep right center. Mays made a spectacular catch, then rocketed—"threw" would be an inaccurate word here, noted thriller writer Noel Hynd—the ball to the plate, where Westrum tagged out Billy Cox.

From that point on, Mays, it seemed, was everywhere. Indeed, he was on deck when Thomson hit his homer. Said Durocher: "If somebody came up and hit .450, stole a hundred bases, and performed a miracle on the field every day, I'd still look you in the eye and say that Willie was better."

Durocher made a number of other key moves in the course of the season. Whitey Lockman came in from the outfield to first, and Monte Irvin went to left. Both began to hit and field better. Thomson, who played center until Mays arrived, moved to third where, despite occasional errors, he performed well.

Coming from way back, the Giants also may have avoided some of the pressure on the Dodgers. Other teams were always especially eager to beat the front-runner, and some players especially disliked the Dodgers. Racism was sometimes a factor; though Mays and Irvin sometimes encountered it, Jackie Robinson and the Dodgers felt it more strongly.

New statistical analyses also backed the claims that sign-stealing wasn't the key to the Giant comeback. Statistician David Smith, in a presentation to the Society for American Baseball Research, found that though the Giants' record dramatically improved after they started stealing signs, their hitting—in particular at the Polo Grounds, where the sign-stealing system was in place—actually declined. On July 20, the Giants were batting .263 at home and .252 on the road. For the rest of the season the team hit .256 at home and .269 on the road. Smith concluded that Giant pitching accounted for the turnaround.

As the shot's fiftieth anniversary approached, most baseball historians believed that though the Giants and Thomson had stolen signs during the season, that had not been the key to the pennant drive—and certainly not the key to Thomson's homer. That consensus came under new pressure in 2001, when the *Wall Street Journal* quoted Giant backup catcher Sal Yvars as saying that from his post in the bullpen, he had stolen the sign meant for Branca and passed it on to Thomson.

This was enough for the pitcher to reverse his public position. "I've known it since 1954, but I never said anything," Branca told the *New York Times*. "I became friendly with Bobby, and I didn't want to demean his home run. I didn't want to cheapen a legendary moment in baseball."

But again, Thomson's teammates rallied 'round. Lockman, who was on second base when Thomson hit the home run, said he couldn't decode the catcher's signs, so he didn't see how Yvars could.

As for Thomson, he continued to deny, though perhaps a little less adamantly, that he knew Branca's pitch in advance.

Pressed by *Journal* reporter Joshua Harris Prager about whether he got the sign, Thomson answered, "I'd have to say more no than yes. I don't like to think of something taking away from it."

Thomson added: "I was always proud of that swing."

To investigate further:

Dickson, Paul. *The Hidden Language of Baseball.* New York: Walker, 2003. How signs and sign-stealing have changed the course of baseball history.

Durocher, Leo, with Ed Linn. *Nice Guys Finish Last.* New York: Simon & Schuster, 1975. Durocher's quote, which can be found in *Bartlett's* as well as in the title of this autobiography, referred to the Giants. He said it while he was managing the Dodgers.

Hynd, Noel. *The Giants of the Polo Grounds.* New York: Doubleday, 1988. A comprehensive history of the team through 1957.

Kiernan, Thomas. *The Miracle at Coogan's Bluff.* New York: Crowell, 1975. In search of an explanation for the miracle and in the tradition of *The Boys of Summer,* Kiernan revisits the heroes of his youth.

Koppett, Leonard. *The New Thinking Fan's Guide to Baseball.* New York: Simon & Schuster, 1991. One of the best guides to how the game is played, on and off the field.

Mays, Willie, with Lou Sahadi. *Say Hey.* New York: Simon & Schuster, 1988. Later, Mays loved to bat in clutch situations. But in 1951, waiting on deck with Thomson at the plate, this is what he was praying: "Please don't let it be me. Don't make me come to bat now, God."

Prager, Joshua Harris. "Giants' 1951 Comeback, the Sport's Greatest, Wasn't All It Seemed." *Wall Street Journal,* January 31, 2001.

Thomson, Bobby, with Lee Heiman and Bill Gutman. *"The Giants Win the Pennant! The Giants Win the Pennant!* New York: Zebra Books, 1991. A solid account of the season, though more of it seems to come from his coauthors' research than from Thomson's recollections.

Why Did the
Dodgers Move?

Newspapermen Jack Newfield and Pete Hamill once decided to collaborate on an article about the worst human beings who ever lived. Over dinner, the two decided to write their top three on their napkins.

"Each of us wrote down the same three names and in the same order," Newfield told oral historian Peter Golenbock. "Hitler, Stalin, and Walter O'Malley."

Much of Brooklyn would have heartily agreed. It was O'Malley who, in October 1957, announced he would move his Dodgers from Brooklyn to Los Angeles.

His Dodgers they were—not the city of New York's or the borough of Brooklyn's, not the fans' who had watched "da bums" for decades, watched them finally become a good team in the forties just to lose to the Yankees in Series after Series, watched them finally win it all in 1955. After years of saying "wait till next year," these fans now heard O'Malley tell them there would be no next year.

"It had always been recognized that baseball was a business, but if you enjoyed the game you could always tell yourself that it was also a sport," wrote columnist Red Smith. "O'Malley was the first to say out loud that it was all business—a business that he owned and could operate as he chose."

It was not as if the Dodgers were going broke. Unlike the Braves, who abandoned Boston for Milwaukee in 1953, or the

St. Louis Browns, who became the Baltimore Orioles in 1954, or the Philadelphia A's, who moved to Kansas City in 1955, the Dodgers made money each year from 1952 to 1957, by some accounts more than the Yankees. Nor were the Dodgers like the Giants, who joined them in their cross-country trek; the Giants drew less than half what the Dodgers did, and they would have been in even sorrier shape if not for the intracity rivalry. Dodger attendance topped 1 million every year.

That wasn't enough for O'Malley. He saw 2 million pack into Milwaukee's new County Stadium, decided he wanted that for himself, and played New York against Los Angeles until he got what he wanted.

"Other teams were forced to move by apathy, or incompetence," wrote the *New York Times*'s Arthur Daley in 1957, "The only word that fits the Dodgers is greed." "Venal and mendacious" was how Roger Kahn, author of *The Boys of Summer*, the classic book on the team, described O'Malley.

There was plenty of evidence to back that up, even before O'Malley bolted for the West Coast. Back in 1942, he ingratiated himself with George McLaughlin, president of the Brooklyn Trust Company, which held the mortgage on Ebbets Field. When the team was slow to pay, O'Malley had the bank appoint him to the Dodgers' board of directors, then lend him the money to buy 25 percent of the team's stock. In 1950, O'Malley forced out Branch Rickey, his rival for control of the team. After that, anyone who even mentioned Rickey's name in O'Malley's presence had to fork over a dollar.

Rickey loyalists didn't last long, anyway. After the 1953 season, O'Malley replaced the team's beloved announcer, Red Barber, with the much cheaper Vin Scully. "He is the most devious man I've ever met," said Barber. Also gone was manager Charlie Dressen, who dared to ask for a two-year contract. After the 1956 season, O'Malley sold Jackie Robinson to the Giants for cash and an obscure pitcher. (Robinson retired rather than report to the Giants.)

"Sentiment meant nothing," said Irving Rudd, who worked as a publicist for O'Malley. "Everything was business."

Rudd recalled O'Malley talking about McLaughlin, the man who helped him take over the team. "Irving, you'll find that it's great to have loyal friendships from the past," O'Malley said (according to Rudd), "but sometimes you have to cut the cord to seek new horizons, and you can't be tied down by the past." He might just as well, Rudd thought, have been talking about Brooklyn.

"I have never heard O'Malley discuss a second baseman's hands, the speed of someone's swing or the rotation of the curve," wrote Kahn. "O'Malley considers people, whom he manipulates, and money, which he appears to coin in incalculable quantities, while saying from time to time, 'I'm just a fan.'"

This was how O'Malley was remembered, long after he died in 1979. He was the man who, for the sake of money he didn't need, tore the heart out of the borough of Brooklyn. But there's more to the story than that. And there's another version of the story in which Walter O'Malley is more victim than villain.

Did the Dodgers need a new stadium? A strong case can be made that they did.

Ebbets Field had grandeur and intimacy. There was a rotunda made from Italian marble, yet fans were so close to the field they could talk to the players. It was the kind of stadium designers now try to imitate. But it also was aging—it was built in 1913—and uncomfortable.

"The aisles are too narrow," O'Malley explained to Kahn in 1953. "The stairs are too steep. Poles obstruct the views. . . . We need twice as many seats. The bathrooms smell. The girders holding up the whole thing are rusting away." Outside Ebbets, there was parking for only seven hundred cars, an increasingly serious problem as more and more Dodger fans left Brooklyn for suburban Long Island and New Jersey.

A close look at attendance figures—and O'Malley surely took a close look—also painted a picture less rosy than nostalgia would have it. True, the Dodgers consistently drew more than 1 million, but the trend was definitely downward. In 1947, the year

Robinson joined the team, attendance peaked at 1,807,526. By
1955 it had dropped to 1,033,589 and in 1957, the team's final
year in Brooklyn, it was 1,026,158. Some of the decline was due
to the advent of television as fans, especially in the suburbs,
decided to watch the game at home. For O'Malley, this was not
a financial hardship; what he lost in ticket sales he gained in television revenue. Still, the downward trend was a definite and
legitimate worry.

O'Malley must have envied the Braves, who were not only
setting attendance records in their new stadium but also were
threatening to supplant the Dodgers as the dominant team in
the National League. By the second half of the 1950s, the Braves
had put together a team of young sluggers such as Hank Aaron
and Eddie Mathews and crafty pitchers such as Warren Spahn
and Lew Burdette. In contrast, the Dodgers were aging, not as
fast as their stadium, but enough to add to their owner's worries.
Robinson and Pee Wee Reese and Roy Campanella were nearing
the end of their careers, with no replacements in sight. Their
departures would likely further sink attendance.

"The history of the Brooklyn club," O'Malley told Kahn, "is
that fiscally you're either first or bankrupt. There is no second
place."

O'Malley also was worried about the changing demographics
of those who came to Ebbets Field and who lived nearby. As
whites moved to the suburbs, blacks and Puerto Ricans took
their place. This made O'Malley uncomfortable. "It is excessive to
accuse him of bigotry," Kahn wrote, perhaps with more generosity
than the owner deserved, "but he did harbor stereotypes. Brooklyn blacks were moving southward out of Bedford-Stuyvesant
toward Eastern Parkway and Crown Heights. Ebbets Field stood
in the path of the black advance. This became another reason he
wanted to move."

Whatever his reasons, whatever their legitimacy, O'Malley
clearly wanted a new stadium. In October 1953, he sold Ebbets
Field and took a five-year lease on the stadium, a clear statement
that he wasn't planning to stay longer than that. The question,
then, is whether he genuinely wanted a new stadium in New

York, or whether he was using the city to get what he wanted from Los Angeles. Certainly O'Malley made a great show of wanting to stay. As early as 1946, he met with Brooklyn Borough president John Cashmore to discuss the matter. In the years that followed, he chose a site—near the intersection of Atlantic and Flatbush Avenues and conveniently near two subway lines and the Long Island Railroad terminal. He put aside $6 million for construction and said he'd raise the rest through bonds. He even commissioned a model—a futuristic domed stadium that many labeled "O'Malley's Pleasure Dome."

And then O'Malley asked for the help of Robert Moses, the man many reporters and historians now consider the true villain of the story.

Moses, though never elected to any post, was the most powerful official in New York. He headed the Triborough Bridge and Tunnel Authority, the New York Parks Commission, the Construction Commission, and the Slum Clearance Committee. In these various capacities he oversaw billions of dollars that went toward building everything from bridges and expressways to housing projects and playgrounds. As Slum Clearance commissioner, Moses, under Title I of the 1949 Federal Housing Act, could condemn the land on which slums were built in order to replace them with new housing, parks, hospitals, schools, libraries, or other works that served a "public purpose." In September 1953 O'Malley invited Moses to the Brooklyn Club, and asked him to condemn the land at Atlantic and Flatbush.

In one sense, O'Malley was asking less of New York than others had given their teams. In Milwaukee, for example, the city government built the Braves their new stadium. O'Malley didn't want New York to pay for the stadium. He merely wanted the city to condemn the land so he wouldn't have to buy it in an open market (where the price was likely to escalate once the various landowners realized O'Malley wanted it). O'Malley's motive was hardly altruistic; he wanted to own his stadium, not pay rent to New York City. Still, as he explained to Moses, it would cost the city a lot less to condemn the land and sell it to the Dodgers than it would to build a stadium. And the result would surely serve a public purpose: not only would the team stay in Brooklyn, but also the stadium would stabilize the entire neighborhood.

Moses didn't see it that way. A private stadium was not a public amenity. Despite years of pleading by O'Malley and his friends, Moses stuck to that position. "A new ball field for the Dodgers cannot be dressed up as a Title I project," Moses wrote O'Malley in August 1955. O'Malley responded the next day by announcing that the following season—1956—the Dodgers would play seven "home games" at Roosevelt Stadium in Jersey City, New Jersey. This was clearly intended as a warning. O'Malley wanted to make it clear that if New York wouldn't cooperate, he had other options.

Moses was unmoved. In a *Sports Illustrated* article, he was blunt. "Walter honestly believes that he in himself constitutes a public purpose," said Moses. "Let me in my own words give you briefly what I believe will be the conclusion as to the Atlantic terminal site. It won't happen."

Moses' indignation was disingenuous. He had certainly stretched the definition of "public purpose" for some of his projects. He condemned the land for what became Lincoln Center, for example, even though that performing arts center was built by private, albeit nonprofit, agencies. Charles Abrams, who helped create the New York City Housing Authority, quipped that "under present redevelopment laws, Macy's could condemn Gimbel's—if Robert Moses gave the word."

Why wouldn't Moses help O'Malley? There are many theories. He wasn't much of a baseball fan. He liked building highways, and didn't like a stadium whose proximity to the Long Island Railroad terminal would have instead depended on mass transit. Or maybe he sincerely believed a private stadium was an improper use of public funds. In any case, he wouldn't budge.

O'Malley looked elsewhere for help. In May 1956, New York mayor Robert Wagner raised the hopes of Brooklyn fans when he asked the state legislature to form the Brooklyn Sports Center

Authority. The Authority would have the power to condemn land for a public stadium. This wasn't O'Malley's first choice—he still wanted a private stadium—but he professed a willingness to work with the Authority. Unfortunately for Brooklyn fans, so did Moses. Acting as an adviser to the Authority, Moses urged its members to move cautiously. They followed his advice, commissioning various studies and acting on none of them.

Finally, in April 1957, Moses announced his solution. He would build a new stadium at Queens' Flushing Meadows. This was the site of the 1939–1940 World's Fair and the future site of Shea Stadium, convenient to many highways and to Long Island. Unlike O'Malley's, this would be a public stadium, owned and operated by Moses' Parks Department and thus a legitimate use of public funds. Some reporters and historians suspected this was why Moses had been so set against O'Malley's plans for a new stadium in Brooklyn. Maybe all along Moses had in mind his own stadium in Queens. In any case, he offered to lease the stadium to the Dodgers.

O'Malley was not pleased. He didn't like the idea of paying rent, and he wasn't sure what to make of Moses' site. "If my team is forced to play in the borough of Queens," he told Kahn, "they will no longer be the Brooklyn Dodgers."

By then, O'Malley was already negotiating with Los Angeles. He began doing so during the 1956 World Series, while the Dodgers were hosting the Yankees. Among the spectators was Kenneth Hann, a Los Angeles County supervisor who had come east to try to interest a major league team in moving west. Hann assumed his best prospect was the Washington Senators, a team that was, as usual, doing poorly both on and off the field.

"When I was attending the game at Ebbets Field, Walter O'Malley sent me a note and said he is interested in coming to Los Angeles," Hann recalled years later. "I never dreamt we could get a world champion." Soon after, O'Malley visited Hann in Los Angeles to confirm his interest. He also warned him—this still according to Hann—that he would deny their discussions, since

Brooklyn fans "would murder me" if they found out he was planning to move the team.

The next step was to secure the territorial rights to Los Angeles, then held by the Chicago Cubs. In February 1957, O'Malley struck a deal with Cub owner Philip Wrigley. The Dodgers took over the Los Angeles Angels, until then a minor league affiliate of the Cubs. With that, they also got the rights to put a major league team in the area.

Next O'Malley persuaded Giant owner Horace Stoneham to move to California. This didn't take much. The Giants, with attendance half the Dodgers' and a stadium in worse shape, were planning to move somewhere in any case. O'Malley pointed out the benefits of the two teams sticking together. They could continue their rivalry and save on jet fare. In July 1957, Stoneham announced he was moving to San Francisco, where the city would build his team a new stadium.

Back in Los Angeles, officials were looking at land they could offer the Dodgers. They settled on three hundred acres of Chavez Ravine, centrally located and already owned by the city. The city had bought the land for housing, but here there was no Robert Moses to determine what other uses might be in the public interest. Indeed, there was little support for public housing among California officials. Some, among them Congressman Richard Nixon, thought public housing was suspiciously socialistic. So Los Angeles officials were eager to get rid of the land. On October 7, 1957, the City Council approved a deal to sell it to the Dodgers. The next day, O'Malley announced the team was moving to Los Angeles.

To O'Malley's many detractors, the owner's simultaneous talks with officials on both coasts proved his treachery. They saw the New York talks as a sham, meant only to wring the best possible deal out of Los Angeles. O'Malley's public stance throughout 1957—that he was talking to Los Angeles but was not committed—was a lie. His warning to Hann that he would deny their plans was further proof that O'Malley was a liar.

"Never was the owner of the Dodgers more devious or cold-blooded than in the summer of 1957," wrote pseudonymous baseball writer Damon Rice. "He had already made up his mind to move to Los Angeles but continued to deceive the City of New York and the people of Brooklyn. He told us there was still a chance the Dodgers would stay long after the chance was gone. All he cared about now was squeezing the last nickel out of the Faithful."

And yet, O'Malley may very well have wanted to stay in Brooklyn. He may even have been willing to consider Queens, given the right rent. Despite Moses' resistance, despite the unwillingness or inability of New York officials to offer him any-thing (except the still dubious Flushing Meadows), despite the open arms of Los Angeles officials, O'Malley kept trying to per-suade New Yorkers to help him stay. He just couldn't get anyone in New York to make him a concrete offer. Even as the Los Angeles City Council prepared to offer O'Malley Chavez Ravine, many of its members were not sure he would take the offer. Years later, Councilwoman Rosalind Wyman recalled, "No one knew if he really wanted it."

"O'Malley was, in fact, a man not nearly as powerful as he would have liked to be, a man without the muscle and influence to get what he wanted," wrote journalist Michael Shapiro. "So he had to scheme, playing people and cities off each other because otherwise he would have ended up the loser, the owner of a team that fewer and fewer people were willing to go out of their way to see."

In retrospect, the move to California worked out for O'Mal-ley. In 1958, despite the team's worst finish since 1944, atten-dance was 1,845,268, and from there it only went up. But in 1957, O'Malley didn't know that. Other teams, including the Braves, Browns, and Athletics, had thought about moving to the West Coast but had decided Milwaukee and Baltimore and Kansas City were better options. Los Angeles was a distant and untested market. O'Malley didn't even know for sure, at least until October 7, that he would get the land to build a stadium there. So he kept open the New York option, dwindling though it was, for as long as he could.

"O'Malley was more a reactor to events around him than an instigator," wrote Neil Sullivan, who wrote the most comprehensive account of the team's move. "The passionate anger Walter O'Malley continues to inspire in old Brooklyn Dodger fans stems from the fact that the team's departure to Los Angeles demonstrated more conclusively than any other event that Brooklyn had been irrevocably transformed."

None of this makes O'Malley a hero, a loyal Brooklynite, or even a true baseball fan. He was none of these things. But he wasn't the devil, either.

To Investigate further:

Caro, Robert. *The Power Broker.* New York. Alfred A. Knopf, 1974. This classic biography of Moses tells the story of the making and breaking of New York City.

Cohen, Stanley. *Dodgers!* New York: Birch Lane Press, 1990. The first hundred years.

Dorinson, Joseph, and Joram Warmund, eds. *Jackie Robinson.* Armonk, N.Y.: M. E. Sharpe, 1998. Includes business historian Henry Fetter's study of attendance figures, which challenges the traditional image of the loyal, color-blind Dodger fan.

Golenbock, Peter. *Bums.* New York: G. P. Putnam's Sons, 1984. This wide-ranging oral history quotes players, fans, reporters, and team executives—few of whom had anything good to say about O'Malley.

Helyar, John. *Lords of the Realm.* New York: Villard Books, 1994. An entertaining history of the business of baseball. O'Malley may have lacked influence in New York, but not among his fellow lords. At one ownership meeting, the Cubs' Phil Wrigley turned to O'Malley and asked, "Walter, what do I think?"

Kahn, Roger. *The Boys of Summer.* New York: Harper & Row, 1971. A classic.

———. *The Era.* New York: Ticknor & Fields, 1993. The era "when the Yankees, the Giants, and the Dodgers ruled the world."

Shapiro, Michael. *The Last Good Season*. New York: Doubleday, 2003. Shapiro's thoughtful and moving chronicle of the 1956 season pays equal attention to the Dodgers' successful battle against the Braves and to O'Malley's unsuccessful battle against Moses.

Sullivan, Neil. *The Dodgers Move West*. New York: Oxford University Press, 1987. A thorough history of the maneuverings on both coasts and a convincing revisionist defense of O'Malley.

Why Didn't Castro Sign with the Senators?

What if Fidel had ended up on the Giants' pitching staff, as he so nearly did?" wondered Charles McCabe of the *San Francisco Chronicle* in 1982. "John F. Kennedy would have been spared the Bay of Pigs and the missile crisis of 1962. The whole Marxist alignment of Castro's Cuba with Soviet Russia would probably never have happened."

This type of counterfactual—or "what if?" history—is tantalizing. What if Pocahontas had not saved John Smith? What if the Nazis had won the Battle of Britain? What if Lincoln (or Kennedy) had not been shot? Part of the fascination comes from the realization that history is not inevitable, that had some small detail been different, so might everything else be.

Castro's aborted baseball career is one of those small details on which history supposedly turned. Had he signed with the Giants, McCabe wrote, "instead of hating Yankees, he'd be hating the Dodgers."

By some accounts, it was not the Giants but Washington Senator scout Joe Cambria who almost signed Castro. "Cambria . . . turned Fidel Castro down twice," the Phillies' supervisor of Latin scouting, Ruben Amaro, told baseball writer Kevin Kerrane. "He could have changed history if he remembered that some pitchers just mature late." Or, as Tina Rosenberg wrote in the *New York Times* in 1999, "Had Cambria been more patient with a developing prospect, baseball might have prevented [Castro's regime]."

Such speculation, of course, belongs more to the realm of fantasy than history. We can't know for sure that the Dodgers would have won the World Series in 1941 if Mickey Owen had stopped one ball, or the Red Sox in 1986 if Bill Buckner had stopped another. And we surely can't know what it would have meant for the Senators or the Giants—or the world—if Fidel Castro had made it to the majors.

But there are questions history *can* answer. For example: Did the Senators or the Giants or any major league team scout him? Did they come close to signing him? And how good a pitcher was Fidel Castro?

There's little doubt that Castro was a fine pitcher in high school. The yearbook for Belen, a Jesuit prep school in Havana, describes him as "a true athlete, defending with valor and pride the banner of the school." Sigfrido Medina, who played against him back then, told political scientist Milton Jamail that Castro "was kind of like 'El Duque' [Yankee and Expo pitcher Orlando Hernandez]. He had a great curveball on the outside corner. And a low breaking ball that came in on the knees."

So it wouldn't be surprising if Cambria saw him play. Cambria was one of the few scouts based in Cuba during the 1940s and 1950s. He signed more than four hundred Cubans for the Senators, including Pedro Ramos, Camilo Pascual, and Zoilo Versalles. Edel Casas, an expert on Cuban baseball, told Jamail that Cambria offered Castro a contract in 1942 or 1943. "Fidel turned him down," Casas added.

Sports historian J. David Truby quoted Cambria: "Fidel Castro is a big, powerful young man. His fastball is not great, but passable. He uses good curve variety. He uses his head and can win that way for us, too."

The Giant version of the near-signing depends on the recollections of owner Horace Stoneham and scout Alex Pompez. Stoneham remembered Castro as "a real prospect." Pompez, again according to Truby, said the Giants offered Castro a $5,000 bonus but that Castro decided to go to law school instead.

The best-known account of Castro pitching is by Pittsburgh Pirate third baseman Don Hoak. In the June 1964 issue of *Sport* magazine, Hoak reminisced about his minor league days in Cuba.

"Cuba was an American baseball player's paradise when I played there in the winter of 1950–51," Hoak wrote. "But even in those days, the students at the University of Havana were politically restless. At the Havana ballpark they'd frequently interrupt our games by staging demonstrations on the field."

It was during one anti-Batista demonstration, Hoak continued, that he came face to face with Castro.

"It was approximately the fifth inning, as I recall, when . . . down from the stands came the students—perhaps 300 of them. As fate would have it, I had just stepped into the batter's box when all hell broke loose."

Next thing Hoak knew, the students' leader was on the mound.

"Castro toed the rubber, and as he did so his appearance on the mound was so ridiculous that I cannot forget a single detail of it. He wore no glasses then, but he did have a beard—a funny little beard at the point of his chin that he obviously had taken great care to groom. He was tall and rather skinny.

"Castro wound up with a great windmill flourish, whirling his pitching arm overhead about six times. Obviously he considered himself an ace hurler, as the sportswriters say. Left-handers as a breed are eccentric, but Castro, a right-hander, looked kookier than any southpaw I have known."

Castro's first pitch to Hoak was a curve. "Actually, it was a pretty fair curve," he recalled. It had a sharp inside break to it— and it came within an inch of breaking my head."

Hoak then fouled off two pitches. "Castro had two strikes on me and he was stomping pompously around the mound as though he had just conquered Washington, D.C."

At this point, the umpire decided he'd had enough of Castro. "He marched over to the *policía*, who were lazily enjoying the fun from the grandstands, and ordered them in no uncertain terms to clear the field. . . . A knot of cops moved briskly on pitcher Castro. Briefly, he made a show of standing his ground, but the cops shoved him off the mound." Thus ended Hoak's at-bat.

"Looking back," Hoak concluded, "I think that with a little work on his control, Fidel Castro would have made a better pitcher than a prime minister."

Hoak's often-anthologized piece solidified Castro's reputation as a talented, albeit wild, pitcher. Until his death in 1969, Hoak maintained the story was true. Yet others' investigations proved otherwise. The most thorough debunking was that of Everardo Santamarina, a Cuban and American baseball archivist. Santamarina itemized numerous errors and inconsistencies in Hoak's account.

For starters, an anti-Batista demonstration could not have taken place at a ballpark or anywhere else in 1950 or 1951, since Batista did not seize power until 1952. Such a demonstration could have taken place in 1953, but Hoak wasn't on the roster of any Cuban team that year. Hoak *did* play in Cuba in 1953–1954, but Castro couldn't have participated in a demonstration then, since he was in prison from July 1953 until May 1955.

Jamail, following Casas again, thought it possible that Hoak mistook some other student revolutionary for Castro. More likely, especially given how funny the piece is, Hoak made up the whole thing.

Other reports of Castro's baseball prowess are equally suspect. In telling Jamail that Castro turned down Cambria, Casas gave no indication that he was doing more than passing on an oft-told story. And except for Truby, no one has been able to find any scouting report with Castro's name on it. Baseball historian Mark Rucker concluded that Truby's story was as much a hoax as Hoak's. That seems likely, though it's impossible to know for sure, since both scouts he quoted—Cambria and Pompez—are dead.

Moreover, not everyone was so impressed by Castro's pitching. Some high school teammates recalled him as consistently wild.

"I was scouted by Joe Cambria with a lot of other players, and if he had been we would have known," insisted Preston Gomez, later an executive with the Angels. "We never heard his name. We never saw him."

"In his senior year [at Belen] he had some extravagant notion of playing for the major leagues," wrote Castro biographer Robert Quirk. "If Castro did indeed dream such dreams, they soon evaporated. He was never as talented as he thought he was. And he could not be a team player."

Historian Roberto González Echevarría searched in vain for press about the alleged phenom. "In a country where sports coverage is broad and thorough, in a city such as Havana with a half-dozen major newspapers (plus dozens of minor ones) and with organized leagues at all levels, there is no record that Fidel Castro ever played, much less starred on any team," he wrote. Echevarría did find one box score from a 1946 intramural game played between the law and business schools at the University of Havana. "F. Castro" was listed as the pitcher. But since Castro is a common surname in Cuba, Echevarría wasn't even sure this was the future dictator.

Despite all the evidence to the contrary, the image of Castro-as-pitcher persisted.

One reason is that, whatever his abilities as a youth, Castro continued to follow and play the game as an adult. As president, he was a huge fan of the International League's Havana Sugar Kings, at least until the team moved to Jersey City and Castro embraced amateur baseball. Castro also took the mound himself in various exhibition games. One instance—in contrast to his earlier appearances, this one was amply documented—was in a July 1959 game between the local military police and Castro's Cuban army team. Wearing a uniform with the team name, Barbudos (Bearded Ones), Castro went two innings and struck out two. He bounced to short in his only at-bat.

Photos of Castro pitching for the Barbudos appeared widely in Cuba and America, solidifying his reputation as a pitcher. And like many an aging man, Castro may have encouraged the stories of his youthful prowess.

Then, too, there was the propaganda value. Castro surely found it satisfying to have excelled at the sport that Americans considered their national game. Here was a way to remind the world that baseball also was Cuba's national game. (Indeed, some Cubans believe it evolved from *batos*, a bat-and-ball game played by the island's original inhabitants. This is as much a myth as Abner Doubleday's invention of the game, since *batos* was more like tennis than baseball.) Long after he stopped playing, Castro took great interest and pride in Cuban baseball, and Cuban national teams dominated international play for several decades, at least partly because of government support.

Perhaps, too, the image of Castro-as-pitcher persists because it suggests how closely linked Cuba and America remain, despite decades of embargoes and defections and assassination attempts. Castro was never a potential major leaguer, but had history happened just a bit differently, relations between the two countries surely might have been different. It's entirely appropriate, therefore, that Castro is so frequently seen wearing military green . . . and a baseball cap.

To investigate further:

Fainaru, Steve, and Ray Sánchez. *The Duke of Havana*. New York: Villard, 2001. El Duque's flight to freedom and wealth.

González Echevarría, Roberto. *The Pride of Havana*. New York: Oxford University Press, 1999. González Echevarría argues, without condescension, that Cuban baseball and culture, even after the Revolution, were defined by American baseball and culture.

Hoak, Don with Myron Cope. "The Day I Batted against Castro." *Sport*, June 1964. "Incredible but true," was how editor John Thorn introduced the piece in his superb anthology *The Armchair Book of Baseball*. That it's incredible is certainly true.

Jamail, Milton. *Full Count*. Carbondale: Southern Illinois University Press, 2000. Baseball after the Revolution.

Kerrane, Kevin. *Dollar Sign on the Muscle*. New York: Fireside, 1989. The world of baseball scouting; originally published in 1984.

Merriman, John, ed. *For Want of a Horse*. Lexington, Mass.: Stephen Greene Press, 1985. A collection of counterfactual histories, including McCabe's on Castro.

Price, S. L. *Pitching around Fidel*. New York: Ecco Press, 2000. An appealingly intimate view of Cuban sports culture.

Quirk, Robert. *Fidel Castro*. New York: W. W. Norton, 1993. A balanced biography.

Rucker, Mark, and Peter Bjarkman. *Smoke*. Kingston, N.Y.: Total Sports Illustrated, 1999. An illustrated look at Cuban baseball's lore and history.

Santamarina, Everardo. "The Hoak Hoax." *The National Pastime* 14, Summer 1994. Hoak never faced Fidel Castro. Though Santamarina didn't investigate the possibility, Hoak also never faced Bill Castro, who pitched for the Brewers, Yankees, and Royals in the 1970s and 1980s.

Szulc, Tad. *Fidel*. New York: William Morrow, 1986. Challenging the liberal consensus, Szulc argues that Castro was already a Communist when he took power. U.S. hostility did not push Castro into the Soviet orbit (nor did a major league rejection).

Truby, David. "Castro's Curveball." *Harper's*, May 1989. The Giants' scouting report noted, according to Truby, that Castro was "a polite, well-spoken young man."

18

Why Was Steinbrenner Banned?

As the news spread throughout Yankee Stadium that George Steinbrenner had been banned from baseball, the crowd began chanting "No More George!, No More George!" Wrote *Time* magazine: "July 30 may become a patriotic holiday in New York City." "Not since the resignation of President Nixon had there been such unabashed glee at the fall of a public figure," agreed baseball historian Dan Gutman.

There were good reasons to cheer the demise of the Boss, or as Red Smith called the Yankee owner, King George III. His initial promise to leave the running of the team to baseball people was, in retrospect, merely the opening line in a long-running farce. As his partner John McMullen noted, "There is nothing so limited as being a limited partner of George Steinbrenner." For nearly two decades, Steinbrenner was responsible for a parade of firings and rehirings, locker room tirades, and public bashings of his own players. "As a player you can always tell when George is in town," said outfielder Dave Winfield, a frequent victim of Steinbrenner's outbursts. "It's like knowing when it's raining."

By July 1990, the team's performance had sunk as low as its morale. The month's highlight was a no-hitter by Yankee pitcher Andy Hawkins—in a game the team lost 4–0 after three eighth-inning errors. The Yankees went on to lose ten of their next twelve games, en route to a last-place finish. "The Yankees are only interested in one thing," outfielder Luis Polonia said. "And I don't know what it is."

No wonder, then, that the Stadium crowd, on learning of the ban, gave a standing ovation. Steinbrenner had been suspended before—for illegal contributions to Richard Nixon's 1972 campaign. But this time was different. This time he was gone for good. As Commissioner Fay Vincent explained at a press conference the next morning, Steinbrenner "is to be treated as if he had been placed on the permanent ineligible list." He would be allowed to retain partial ownership of the Yankees, but only as a limited partner. He could not even attend a major league game without Vincent's approval.

Vincent was clear about why Steinbrenner was banished: "a working relationship with a known gambler in furtherance of a private investigation aimed at a ballplayer." The gambler was Howard Spira; the player, Dave Winfield. There was no doubt of Steinbrenner's guilt; he admitted paying Spira $40,000 for information about Winfield. What was surprising was the severity of the punishment. As Vincent later recalled, he had considered suspending Steinbrenner from one to five years. But when the commissioner and owner met on the thirtieth, Steinbrenner proposed that he instead be put on the permanently ineligible list. "My preference was for the two-year suspension," Vincent said, "but I let George have the more severe penalty because that's what he wanted."

Vincent's press conference left many questions unanswered. Why was Steinbrenner so desperate to get dirt on Winfield? Why did he choose the more severe penalty? What dirt did Spira have on Winfield . . . and was it true?

The first question was the easiest to answer. Steinbrenner's feud with Winfield dated back to 1981, when the Yankees signed the former San Diego Padre outfielder to a ten-year contract. The contract included a cost-of-living clause that increased its value from about $21 million to $23 million. Steinbrenner, who hadn't understood how the clause worked before signing the contract, felt Winfield had tricked him. Winfield agreed to defer some of the cost-of-living payments, but Steinbrenner was still paying more than he'd expected.

The deal also called for Steinbrenner to donate about $300,000 a year to the David M. Winfield Foundation, a charitable organization that sponsored health fairs, nutritional counseling, scholarships, field trips, and other programs for underprivileged children. Steinbrenner, claiming the foundation was misusing funds, was consistently slow to pay. Winfield took him to court and won, further embarrassing the owner.

Steinbrenner also was dissatisfied with Winfield's performance on the field. He now longed for Reggie Jackson, with whom he'd also feuded but whose postseason performances had led the Yankees to two World Series championships and led the press to call him "Mr. October." After Winfield went 1 for 22 in the 1981 World Series, Steinbrenner dubbed his new star "Mr. May."

Winfield suspected that Steinbrenner's fury stemmed from a player showing him up, not only in negotiating a contract but also in setting himself up as a philanthropist. "George wants to 'own' his players, wants them up on their flippers barking for fish like trained seals," Winfield said. "And from the beginning I refused to bark."

Vincent described Steinbrenner as "crazed" on the subject of Winfield. "For an owner to start an investigation of one of his own players defies logic and decency," he wrote. "Winfield had outmaneuvered him on the contract—a ballplayer had outmaneuvered an owner—and now Steinbrenner was trying to destroy him."

"It is simply a strange quirk of the Boss that when he loves, he loves all out and when he hates, watch out," explained sportswriter Maury Allen. "So Steinbrenner could never accept Winfield as a productive Yankee."

Whatever drove him, Steinbrenner was ready to listen when he was approached by Spira, a clubhouse hanger-on who had worked for the Winfield Foundation and had plenty of stories to tell about his ex-boss. Spira claimed that Winfield had indeed misused foundation funds and that the outfielder and his agent, Al Frohman, had fabricated phony death threats to give Winfield an excuse for his poor World Series performance. Spira also told Steinbrenner that Winfield had loaned him $15,000 to cover his gambling debts and that Winfield threatened to kill him if he didn't pay it back. Steinbrenner met with Spira in 1986 and 1987, and in 1990 paid him $40,000.

Spira took the money, then demanded another $110,000. He threatened to go to the press if Steinbrenner didn't pay. Steinbrenner balked, and Spira carried out his threat. So—just six months after banning Pete Rose—baseball had another gambling scandal on its hands. Steinbrenner was not in trouble for paying for sleaze on one of his players; there was no rule against that. But as Rose had learned, the game's cardinal rule was to stay away from gamblers. Steinbrenner had paid a gambler $40,000.

Vincent had no doubts about the facts of the case. Steinbrenner admitted meeting and paying Spira. Steinbrenner claimed he was "scared stiff" of Spira, but Vincent listened to a tape of a conversation between the two and noted that the owner "never mentioned that he made the payment out of fear, nor did he claim he was extorted." The only question before Vincent was what the sentence should be.

"None of Steinbrenner's actions went to the heart of baseball . . . as Rose's misdeeds did," Vincent noted, presumably referring to the fact that Steinbrenner was associating with a gambler but not involved in gambling. On the other hand, "he was already a convicted felon because of the illegal campaign contributions. . . . You could make a case that he was a recidivist." That balanced out to a moderate sentence.

So did the opinions of other owners, though Vincent would undoubtedly deny that they played a role and later proved himself capable of acting independently of his bosses. Recalled Vincent: "Some owners and others were saying, 'Throw him out for life. You'll be doing baseball a service.'" Some owners undoubtedly found Steinbrenner obnoxiously egocentric; more were probably irked by his free-agent signings, which were pushing player salaries ever upward. Yet most owners, however much they disliked Steinbrenner, were probably uncomfortable with throwing him out for life or making him sell the team. If Vincent could do that to one owner, he could do it to another, and that was more power than most owners were willing to cede to a commissioner. So owner sentiment, too, pointed toward a moderate sentence. Vincent settled on two years.

Then Steinbrenner surprised everyone by asking for more. The reason, he explained to the commissioner, was that a suspension could cost him his membership on the U.S. Olympic Committee.

"That's the most important thing to me in my life right now," Steinbrenner told Vincent (according to Vincent). I'd rather leave the game than have a two-year suspension. In fact, that's what I want to do. I want out of baseball. I'm sick and tired of it."

Like Rose, Steinbrenner was willing to take a harsher punishment if he could control the wording of the deal. He didn't want the words "suspension" or "ban" used, since he feared they would disqualify him from the USOC. His only other condition was that one of his sons be allowed to run the team. Vincent agreed, and Steinbrenner signed the deal that put him on baseball's permanently ineligible list.

Almost immediately, Steinbrenner regretted his decision. He may have been momentarily sick and tired of it, but he did not want out of baseball forever. He may not even have fully understood what he was signing, just as he didn't understand the cost-of-living clause in Winfield's contract. The Boss, while priding himself on his business acumen, apparently had a tendency to put too much trust in his lawyers.

"George made a series of bad decisions," Vincent wrote, "but . . . his ultimate failing was in choosing his legal counsel. . . . I saw no indication that they understood how baseball operates, that they had studied the Rose case, or that they understood what it means to be on the permanently ineligible list. They simply seemed unprepared. And more than anything, they didn't appear to have their eye on their client's ultimate goal. George's objective was to keep his position on the USOC and to stay in baseball. They should have worked out something with the USOC before they saw me."

A year after Vincent sentenced Steinbrenner to the permanently ineligible list, a federal judge sentenced Spira to two and a half years in prison for extortion. Steinbrenner might have hoped the verdict against Spira would buttress his case for reinstatement. After all, if he paid Spira under duress, then it wasn't his fault. During Spira's trial, Steinbrenner testified he'd paid Spira out of a mix of fear and charity.

"He was harassing my children, my family, my friends with phone calls," Steinbrenner told the court. "Second, I was told his mother was sick with cancer. His father had borrowed money from people in the building and couldn't face them. I felt sorry for his parents."

Steinbrenner also claimed he was worried that Spira would go public with allegations of gambling by other Yankees, specifically manager Lou Piniella. "I didn't want that," he said. "And I wanted him to start a new life and get out of my life. Get away from the Yankees, get away from New York, get away from me and leave me alone."

None of these explanations did Steinbrenner any good, nor did they ring true. Spira was prosecuted for demanding an additional $110,000—and Steinbrenner may very well have feared him at that point. But the original $40,000 wasn't part of the case against Spira, presumably because prosecutors didn't believe that payment was the result of extortion. Like Vincent, prosecutors believed Steinbrenner willingly paid the $40,000 in return for information with which he could smear Winfield.

Steinbrenner continued his efforts to get reinstated. One of his partners sued baseball and Vincent, arguing it was illegal to remove a team's general partner. Steinbrenner repeatedly called Vincent, telling the commissioner his life was empty without baseball. Eventually Vincent relented.

"People still say to me, 'You kicked George out of baseball and then you let him back in,'" Vincent wrote. "That really is not correct. I never suspended him; he made an agreement to leave. Moreover, he served his time."

After two and a half years, Steinbrenner was back. Since then, he has been, if not a new man, surely a more restrained one. The Yankees, too, were back. Much of the credit belonged to the calming influence of manager Joe Torre, but in fairness to the Boss, Steinbrenner was less disruptive and maybe even more productive. Even Spira deserved a tiny share of the credit. As he explained after getting out of jail: "People have told me that it was because I got rid of George for three years that the Yankees were able to develop, instead of him being Godzilla and trading everyone."

Not everyone was satisfied with this happy ending.

Marvin Miller, the former head of the players' union, questioned why the commissioner's office did nothing about the Steinbrenner-Spira assocation until 1990, even though Steinbrenner had mentioned Spira's allegations to Commissioner Peter Ueberroth as early as 1987. Ueberroth said he ignored the allegations because he considered Spira unreliable (and though he didn't say it explicitly, he probably felt the same held for Steinbrenner). Miller didn't buy this. "Just how exactly was it in 'the best interests of baseball,' " he demanded to know, "for *three* commissioners to know about an owner's 'involvement' with a known gambler and not pick up the phone and warn him of the consequences?"

Miller suspected that the baseball establishment was giving Steinbrenner the rope to hang himself, hoping he'd give them reason to get rid of him (and his free-agent spending). "In the end, Steinbrenner was gone because the other owners wanted him gone," Miller wrote. "Steinbrenner had been a loose cannon on the owners' ship for a long time. . . . It would take quite a leap to believe that Fay Vincent (with some important help from Steinbrenner) forced George out of baseball on his own."

The most extensive investigation into the scandal, other than Vincent's, was by *Sports Illustrated*. The magazine concluded that though Steinbrenner certainly got what he deserved, the commissioner's office failed to thoroughly investigate Spira's accusations. After all, it wasn't just Steinbrenner who had dealings with Spira. So did Winfield.

Like Steinbrenner, Winfield gave money to Spira. Back in 1981, when Spira was working for Winfield's former agent, Al Frohman, the outfielder loaned him $15,000. Winfield said he didn't know Spira was a gambler, and that he loaned him the money at Frohman's request. But Frohman's widow later told a *Sports Illustrated* reporter that Winfield knew Spira owed the money to bookies. The magazine also quoted four sources, two unnamed, saying that they had either heard Winfield talk about betting or seen him place bets (though not on baseball).

Sports Illustrated also concluded that Frohman had indeed fabricated the death threat against Winfield, just as Spira had claimed. A former secretary at the Winfield Foundation told a reporter that she had helped prepare the threat, and that Winfield, though angry when he found out about that, had gone along with it.

"Baseball did not do itself proud in the Steinbrenner case," wrote the magazine's Jill Lieber and Craig Neff. *Sports Illustrated* stopped short of accusing the commissioner of a cover-up, arguing instead that baseball chose to investigate and punish the unpopular Steinbrenner while largely ignoring the accusations against the well-liked Winfield. "It is a tale of contradictions and double standards," wrote Lieber and Neff.

Newsday weighed in with a report criticizing the Winfield Foundation for excessive administrative costs.

Winfield responded by saying that the foundation's problems had been corrected and by denying any sports betting. Vincent defended his office. "We did, despite what *Sports Illustrated* said, investigate," he said. "As far as we're concerned at this point it's not a serious issue."

In retrospect, it's possible to fault Vincent for putting a lot more effort into investigating Steinbrenner than Winfield. But it's hard to dispute his conclusion. The case against Steinbrenner, even granting baseball's dubious motives in pursuing it, was open and shut. In contrast, the case against Winfield would have depended heavily on the credibility of Howard Spira, a man who was willing to sell out Winfield for $40,000 and to try to extort $110,000 from Steinbrenner. Like Ueberroth, Vincent put a lot of stock in the credibility of his witnesses, and—despite the secondary sources uncovered by *Sports Illustrated*—Spira did not merit much trust.

Winfield was delighted to get away from both Spira and Steinbrenner. Traded to the Angels in 1990, he had two good seasons in California. Then he signed as a free agent in Toronto, where he finally got his World Series ring. In 2001 he was inducted into the Hall of Fame, where he had to decide what cap he should put on his bust there. Not surprisingly, he chose one from the Padres, not the Yankees.

To investigate further:

Allen, Maury. *All Roads Lead to October.* New York: St. Martin's Press, 2000. A beat reporter's anecdotal history of Steinbrenner's reign; Allen is much more forgiving of the Boss than most Yankee fans and employees.

Gutman, Dan. *Baseball Babylon.* New York: Penguin, 1992. Baseball and sex, murder, drugs, booze, gambling, crime, fights, and other scandals. On Winfield, Gutman covers not just Steinbrenner's smear campaign but also Winfield's 1983 arrest in Toronto. While warming up with Yankee teammate Don Baylor, Winfield spotted a seagull sitting in right field. He threw a ball at it, hoping to scare it away. The ball killed the bird, and Winfield was charged with cruelty to animals. Steinbrenner, for once, came to his outfielder's defense. But the best line came from manager Billy Martin: "First time he hit the cutoff man all year."

Lieber, Jill, and Craig Neff, "Bad Job, Baseball." *Sports Illustrated*, October 8, 1990. Lieber and Neff first published the results of their investigation in the August 13 issue, but this was their most thorough presentation of the case against Winfield.

Miller, Marvin. *A Whole Different Ball Game.* New York: Carol, 1991. Miller received writing help from Allen Barra, who was one of the sources *Sports Illustrated* quoted as having heard Winfield talk about gambling.

Vincent, Fay. *The Last Commissioner.* New York: Simon & Schuster, 2002. Vincent was the last commissioner with any pretense of independence from the owners. His reminiscences about Joe DiMaggio, Ted Williams, Bart Giamatti, and others are revealing and poignant, and his accounts of the Rose and Steinbrenner investigations are clear and convincing.

Winfield, Dave, with Tom Parker. *Winfield.* New York: W. W. Norton, 1988. A better-than-average baseball autobiography that includes a perceptive portrait of Steinbrenner.

19

What Took the Red Sox So Long?

The day after the Red Sox won the World Series, the sun did not rise in the west and hell did not freeze over. Because, as Red Sox fans always knew during their more rational moments, there never was a curse. How, then, to explain eighty-five years of frustration? Well, even if Harry Frazee didn't bring on a curse, he deserved his share of the blame.

When the Red Sox won the World Series in 1918, it was business as usual: the team had also won in 1903, 1912, 1915, and 1916. It was a team and a town that expected to win. Enter Frazee, the debt-ridden owner of the Red Sox, a Broadway producer who cared only about his shows and not a bit about his team. In January 1920, for $100,000 cash and a $300,000 loan for a mortgage on Fenway Park, Frazee handed Babe Ruth to the Yankees.

"I believe the sale of Ruth will ultimately strengthen the team," Frazee assured reporters.

Instead, it formed the basis for the Yankee dynasty and the "curse of the Bambino." Having angered the baseball gods by scorning the greatest of them all, Frazee doomed his team to wander in the desert. Forty years would not nearly suffice.

"The memory of Babe Ruth does not fool around," wrote *New York Times* columnist George Vecsey. "His departure cast a spell that festered in the crevices and eaves of Fenway Park."

It would not be enough for the Red Sox to simply be bad; for that, you could watch the Cubs. No, the Sox would have to come painfully close, making it to the World Series four times before 2004, each time losing in the seventh game. Their playoff losses would have to be at least as excruciating.

The Sox would have to lose key games in unimaginably bizarre ways. Better yet, they should at the last moment self-destruct, some fatal flaw finally exposed. In the seventh game of the 1946 World Series, slick-fielding shortstop Johnny Pesky would hold the relay a moment too long as the Cardinals' Enos Slaughter scored from first on a single; in the 1948 playoff against the Indians, manager Joe McCarthy would pass over ace Mel Parnell and instead hand the ball to journeyman Denny Galehouse (the *immortal* Denny Galehouse was how the *Boston Globe's* Martin Nolan sarcastically referred to him), the next year, the Sox would head into the final two games against the Yankees needing only a split, and lose twice; in the 1978 playoff, a gust of wind would carry Bucky Dent's fly (he was hitless in his last thirteen at-bats, a .243 hitter on the year, as he stepped to the plate, this Bucky *Bleeping* Dent) into the left-field net behind the Green Monster; in 1986, the Sox would be *one strike away* from winning the Series, and Mookie Wilson's ground ball would somehow skip through Bill Buckner's legs (and why did manager John McNamara, who routinely replaced Buckner on defense with a late-inning lead, this time have to leave him in?); in the seventh game of the 2003 league championship series, manager Grady Little would stick with a clearly worn-out Pedro Martinez and watch the Yankees *(who else?)* come back to win it.

For New Englanders, for whom some are chosen and some are not, this sometimes seemed a suitably Calvinistic punishment for their—or at least for Frazee's—sin. The team's frustrations also appealed to the area's many writers, from John Updike to Stephen King, who recognized that losing was a more interesting subject than winning. Said then-National League president Bart Giamatti during the pennant race of 1986 (and remember, this was pre-Buckner): "Somehow the Sox fulfill the notion that we live in a fallen world. It's as though we assume they're here to provide us with more pain." All New England understood what was meant by "the curse of the Bambino," especially after *Globe* writer Dan Shaughnessy's popular book with that title.

To Sox fans, it must have seemed as if Frazee had sold his soul—or theirs—to the devil. It was not just that he sold Ruth to the Yankees. He followed that with the 1920 trades of pitcher Waite Hoyt and catcher Wally Schang, the 1921 trades of pitchers Sam Jones and Joe Bush and shortstop Everett Scott, the 1922 trades of third baseman Joe Dugan and outfielder Elmer Smith, and the 1923 trade of pitcher Herb Pennock. When the Yankees won the World Series in 1923, eleven of the twenty-four players on their roster were former Red Sox.

"They talk about the Yankee dynasty," said pitcher Ernie Shore, who also went from Boston to New York, "but I still think of it as a Red Sox dynasty in Yankee uniforms."

Still, even before 2004, it was clear that something more than a curse was operating here. Even if Frazee was to blame for the trades that dismantled the Boston dynasty of the teens and created the Yankee one of the twenties, they can hardly explain the next seven-plus decades.

For that, we must look beyond Harry Frazee or Babe Ruth.

Tom Yawkey, who bought the Red Sox in 1933, was as eager to buy players as Frazee had been to sell them. Heir to a lumber and mining fortune, Yawkey happily opened his checkbook to acquire future Hall of Famers such as Joe Cronin, Bobby Doerr, Jimmie Foxx, and Lefty Grove. World War II sent the heart of the team into the armed services, but in 1946 the Sox were back. Led by Doerr, Pesky, Dom DiMaggio, and Ted Williams, they won 104 games and the pennant. In the seventh game of the Series, DiMaggio doubled, scoring two runners, tying the game, and apparently giving the Sox the momentum.

Now came the first of the Sox's famous bad breaks. Running to second, DiMaggio pulled a muscle. Leon Culberson went in to run for him. That meant that it was Culberson, not DiMaggio (whom many considered as great a fielder as his brother Joe) who was in center the next inning, when Harry Walker singled to left center and Enos Slaughter took off from first and scored. Had DiMaggio been in center, Red Sox fans believed, he would have gotten the ball to Pesky quicker, and Pesky would have thrown out Slaughter at home, or maybe Slaughter wouldn't even have tried to score. As it was, Pesky got the ball and, after a moment's hesitation, became the first in a long line of Sox goats.

Was this fair to Pesky? Probably not. Films of the play don't show him pausing, though he seems to look toward third before realizing that Slaughter is already heading home. Certainly he did not make an error; what he did was make an average play when an extraordinary one was needed.

In any case, disappointed though Pesky and the Sox were, this was well before the team became known for their bad luck, let alone a curse. The Sox were confident they'd have a chance to redeem themselves in another Series soon.

To make sure, Yawkey bought pitchers Jack Kramer and Ellis Kinder and slugging shortstop Vern Stephens. In 1948, the Sox finished tied with the Indians, forcing a playoff. McCarthy could have gone with Kramer, who was 18–5, or Kinder, who was 10–7, or Joe Dobson at 16–10, but the obvious choice was Parnell, who was 15–8 and had pitched well against Cleveland. Why McCarthy went with Galehouse, a spot starter who was 8–7 on the year, is one of the abiding mysteries of Red Sox history. Indian manager Lou Boudreau couldn't believe his good fortune; when McCarthy announced his starter just prior to the game, Boudreau checked under the stands to see if Parnell was secretly warming up.

After the game, McCarthy said he chose Galehouse because he was a veteran. Later, he reminded baseball historian Donald Honig that Galehouse had pitched well in his last outing against the Indians. Galehouse also was a righty, which might have helped him against Cleveland's righty power hitters. Another story was that McCarthy sent catcher Birdie Tebbetts to talk to each of the pitchers, and except for Galehouse, they all backed off. Galehouse later confirmed that Tebbetts asked him how he felt about pitching and that he answered that if McCarthy wanted him to pitch, he'd do so. Parnell vehemently denied Tebbetts approached him. "McCarthy would never ask anybody if they wanted to pitch a ball game," he insisted. "He told you. He was the manager."

Tebbetts wouldn't say. "There are only two people who know what happened," he said. "One of them is Joe McCarthy and he's dead, and I'm not going to say anything."

In any case, Galehouse didn't get through the fourth, and the Indians sailed to an 8–3 win.

The next year, another controversial pitching choice backfired for McCarthy, this time against the Yankees. The two teams were tied going into the final game of the season. In the top of the eighth, with the Yankees up, 1–0, McCarthy pinch-hit for Kinder. Parnell, who had been battered the day before, and then Tex Hughson relieved, and the Yankees blew the game open with four runs. The Red Sox scored three in the ninth, losing, 5–3. This time McCarthy's decision was more easily defended—trailing in the eighth, there's a strong case for pinch-hitting for the pitcher, even one pitching as well as Kinder. But the result was the same: in their season's final game, the Red Sox had lost the pennant.

Those fingers that weren't pointed at McCarthy were pointed at Ted Williams. "It has been popular in making the Red Sox favorites year after year to say they have 'everything,'" wrote Joe Williams in *Sport* magazine. "This isn't true. If they had 'everything,' there would be no . . . Red Sox mystery."

Why didn't the Sox win? "I think the answer is Williams," Joe Williams answered. Many other Boston writers agreed, accusing their star of failing in the clutch.

"There was his flop in the 1946 World Series when he hit only .200 and arrogantly jested at the shift the Cardinals used against him," Joe Williams continued. "There was his one, lonely shabby hit in the historic play-off game in '48. There was his bloomer-girl mark of .215 down the stretch in the steaming '49 race, capped by his utter helplessness in the two wind-up games with the Yankees with the pennant virtually hanging on every swing of his bat."

This was unfair to Williams. In 1948, when the Sox won three straight to force a playoff, Williams went 6 for 8. In 1949, when the Sox won nine in a row to temporarily overtake the Yankees, Williams won four games with home runs. His performance in his one World Series was undeniably a disappointment, but he was playing with a seriously sore left elbow.

McCarthy and Williams made easy scapegoats, but the underlying problem was neither a manager nor a player. It was the man who paid their salaries.

No one could accuse Yawkey of being cheap; for his era, he spent as lavishly as George Steinbrenner later did. But the Red Sox were a toy for Yawkey, not a business. Sometimes he even put on a uniform and took batting practice at Fenway, which was not in itself a problem. But he also surrounded himself with the people he wanted to hang out with, which was. There was Joe Cronin, for example, his player-manager and shortstop, who insisted on getting rid of future Hall of Famer Pee Wee Reese because Reese also played shortstop. Or there was Pinky Higgins, who managed the team for eight seasons and was also, crucially, Yawkey's drinking buddy.

Tempted by the proximity of Fenway's left-field wall, Yawkey and his advisers consistently opened their coffers for right-handed sluggers. These sluggers were in turn tempted by the wall, often striking out as they tried to pull everything.

"Instead of first basemen, the Sox favored power forwards," Nolan wrote. "For decades Red Sox policy built a row of condominiums down the right-field line—Foxx, Walt Dropo, Vic Wertz, Dick Gernert, Mickey Vernon, Norm Zauchin, Dick Stuart, Lee Thomas, George Scott, Tony Perez."

"The team's strategy has been a prisoner of Fenway, or at least of the Wall," Nolan continued. "Big-boom right-handed hitters were always courted (many of whom dented the Wall for singles)." At the same time, the team often found itself short a good pitcher or two.

Even when the slugging paid off with homers, it backfired on the road, where the Sox regularly had a losing record. What Yawkey and his advisers failed to note was that Fenway's large right field offered plenty of space for balls to drop in. It was no coincidence, though the Sox management never seemed to notice, that the team's most successful hitters, such as Williams and Carl Yastrzemski and Wade Boggs, were lefties.

Red Sox management suffered from a much greater blind spot when it came to black players. "There will never," manager Pinky Higgins told reporter Al Hirshberg, "be any niggers on this team as long as I have anything to say about it."

Jackie Robinson tried out for the Sox in 1945 before Branch Rickey signed him for the Dodgers. No one in Boston bothered to call him after the tryout. A Red Sox scout received a tip about Willie Mays in 1949 but declined to check it out. The Sox waited until 1959, after every other major league team, to sign their first black player.

True, the Yankees were also slow to sign blacks. But they were otherwise so efficient that they were able to compensate, at least until the mid-1960s, when they, too, felt the effects of their racism.

By the time the Sox were willing to sign blacks, many didn't want to play there. "I never felt welcome in Boston," recalled outfielder Reggie Smith, who played on the Sox's 1967 pennant winner. "I remember after the Celtics won the world championship, someone asked me to respond to Bill Russell's feeling that Boston was a racist city. I made comments to the effect that it was, and I was immediately considered a troublemaker."

The Sox's racism may even have pushed blacks on opposing teams to give a little extra. "We knew Boston's reputation," said Yankee second baseman Willie Randolph. "You want to win every game, of course, but believe me, every black player in that Yankee clubhouse wanted to beat Boston even more."

After Yawkey died in 1976, Red Sox management tried to change the team's reputation among black players. But many black free agents chose not to listen to offers from Boston. Outfielders Marquis Grissom and David Justice insisted on language in their contracts precluding a trade to Boston. As late as 1990 and 1991, Ellis Burks was the only black on the roster.

"The price the Red Sox would pay . . . was winning," wrote journalist Howard Bryant in his 2002 history of race and baseball in Boston. "Surely a club with Mays, Robinson, Doerr, and the Splinter would have beaten those Yankees at least once."

Nineteen sixty-seven was the year it all came together for the Red Sox. After a decade in the second division, the Sox, 100–1 shots as the season opened, won a three-way race on the final day of the season. Yaz led the league in batting average and runs batted in and tied for the home run lead. Manager Dick Williams, equally antagonistic toward his white and black players, somehow united the team behind him. Even losing the seventh game of the World Series, with a tired Jim Lonborg overmatched by Cardinal ace Bob Gibson, barely dampened the spirit of Sox fans. The Cardinals were clearly the better team, and the Sox made it as far as they did because, for a change, they got the breaks.

The era of good feelings returned in 1975, at least through the sixth game of the World Series, when the born-and-bred New Englander Carlton Fisk willed his game-winning, Series-tying home run into the left-field net. True, the Sox yet again lost a seventh game, this time after manager Darrell Johnson, following in his predecessors' footsteps, made the questionable decision to replace his most effective reliever, Jim Willoughby, with rookie Jim Burton, in the ninth inning. Joe Morgan quickly drove in the winning run for the Reds. True, too, there were bitter feelings left over from game three, which umpire Larry Barnett cost the Sox by muffing an interference call. But the sixth game was what stuck in the memories of Sox fans.

"The seventh game, which settled the championship in the very last inning, probably would have been a famous thriller in some other Series, but in 1975 it was outclassed," wrote Roger Angell in the *New Yorker.* "It was a good play that opened on the night after the opening night of *King Lear.*"

There was no such consolation in 1978, the year the Sox, crippled by injuries to Fisk, Yaz, outfielders Dwight Evans and Fred Lynn, third baseman Butch Hobson, second baseman Jerry Remy, and shortstop Rick Burleson, let the Yankees come from fourteen back to force a playoff. In the seventh inning, just after the wind had started blowing out to left, came Dent's home run. And in the bottom of the ninth, with the Sox trailing 5–4 and Burleson on first, Yankee right fielder Lou Piniella lost Remy's drive in the sun, just to have it hit in front of him and hop into his glove. That kept Burleson on second instead of third, preventing him from scoring on Jim Rice's long flyout. Luck, it seemed, had again deserted the Red Sox.

The worst was yet to come. In 1986, the Sox had a 3–2 lead in games and a 5–3 lead heading into the bottom of the tenth. Calvin Schiraldi was on the mound for the Sox (and Calvinist New England couldn't help but note his first name). Schiraldi retired the first two hitters. Then came three hits and a run. Bob Stanley relieved Schiraldi and threw a wild pitch. Tie score. Then came Wilson's grounder to—and through—Buckner. Another game seven defeat inevitably followed.

Some criticized McNamara for leaving Buckner at first. It seemed the manager had put sentiment over sense. "There is only one logical explanation to account for Buckner's presence on the field at that moment," wrote Shaughnessy. "McNamara wanted his veteran war horse in the victory celebration photographs. The manager and Buckner have always bristled when this subject is raised, but leaving Buckner in the game simply didn't make sense and was a departure from the way McNamara had managed in every other postseason victory. Boston won seven playoff and Series games in 1986, and in the final inning of each victory, Dave Stapleton was playing first base."

Finally, there was the 2003 championship series against the Yankees, game seven, when Little stuck with his ace and Martinez blew a 3-run lead in the eighth. By then, you could forgive even the most rational of Sox fans for bemoaning, if not the curse, at least the remarkable string of bad decisions and bad luck stretching back almost a century. This was a team whose story was a classic tragedy, and we all know how those end. "The hero must go under at last," explained Harvard classicist Emily Vermeule after the 1978 playoff, "after prodigious deeds, to be remembered and immortal and to have poets sing his tale." To which Angell replied: "I understand that, and I will sing the tale of Yaz always, but I still don't quite see why it couldn't have been arranged for him to single to right center, or to double off the wall. I'd have sung that, too."

Why couldn't Yaz and the Sox have their happy ending? "I think God was shelling a peanut," Angell concluded.

And yet: for all that went wrong, there were plenty of explanations that required neither a classical nor a religious education. Not just big explanations, like too many right-handed sluggers and too few blacks, but specific ones to answer what might otherwise seem like fate. Take Dent's homer, for example. The same wind that blew his into the net had carried many a Sox homer there. And the Sox perhaps took Dent too lightly; he went on to become the 1978 World Series MVP with a .417 batting average and 7 runs batted in. Or as Angell put it: "Those who live by the wall must die by the wall."

Besides, the Yankees scored two more runs after Dent's homer, including a home run by Reggie Jackson that was not windborne. And Piniella, though undeniably lucky, was also remarkably poised and quick to grab Remy's hit after he finally spotted it.

As for leaving Buckner in, remember this: the game was already tied when Wilson grounded the ball to first. Also, as McNamara pointed out in his defense, it was Buckner's legs that were shot, not his hands. Nor was it clear that even if Buckner had stopped the ball, Wilson wouldn't have beaten the throw to first. Buckner always maintained Wilson would have beaten Stanley to the base (though Stanley disagreed). Remember, too, this was the sixth game; the Sox still had a seventh game to lose, and they did so without any otherworldly intervention.

What the Sox suffered from was a history of bad judgment by its ownership and management, compounded by a series of bad breaks. What the Sox had in 2004 was an owner, in John Henry, who wasn't afraid to shell out Yankee-like dollars; a general manager, in Theo Epstein, who wasn't afraid to trade Nomar Garciaparra, the team's popular but sulking shortstop; a pitcher, in Curt Schilling, who shut down the Yankees and the Cardinals in his blood-soaked sock; and righty *and* lefty sluggers, both black, in Manny Ramirez and David Ortiz. The Sox also had, for a change, a bit of luck: a call against the Yankees' Alex Rodriguez that, though correct, could have gone the other way; clutch homers from second baseman Mark Bellhorn whose previous power numbers, if not quite Bucky Dent-like, were hardly those of Ramirez or Ortiz; and a team that got hot just when it mattered most.

To investigate further:

Angell, Roger. *Once More around the Park*. New York: Ballantine, 1991. A selection of baseball essays by the master of the form, this includes his 1975 and 1986 masterpieces.

Boswell, Thomas. *How Life Imitates the World Series*. Garden City, N.Y.: Doubleday, 1982. Includes Boswell's essay "The Greatest Game Ever Played" (the 1978 playoff).

Bryant, Howard. *Shut Out*. New York: Routledge, 2002. A perceptive history of Red Sox racism.

Gammons, Peter. *Beyond the Sixth Game*. Boston: Houghton Mifflin, 1985. How free agency, established just weeks after the 1975 World Series, tore apart the Sox dynasty-in-the-making.

Golenbock, Peter. *Fenway*. New York: G. P. Putnam's Sons, 1992. An oral history of the Sox.

Gould, Stephen Jay. *Triumph and Tragedy in Mudville*. New York: W. W. Norton, 2003. One essay by the eminent evolutionist traces how the facts of Buckner's error became part of Red Sox mythology.

Halberstam, David. *Summer of '49*. New York: William Morrow, 1989. How the Sox battled the Yankees to the final game.

Honig, Donald. *The Boston Red Sox*. New York: Prentice Hall Press, 1990. An illustrated history.

Linn, Ed. *The Great Rivalry*. New York: Tickner & Fields, 1991. The Yankees vs. the Red Sox, 1901–1990.

Riley, Dan. *The Red Sox Reader*. Boston: Houghton Mifflin, 1991. A collection of classic essays.

Shaughnessy, Dan. *The Curse of the Bambino.* New York: Penguin, 2000. Originally published in 1990, this helped create the image of the cursed Sox. Highly entertaining.

Stout, Glenn, ed. *Impossible Dreams.* Boston: Houghton Mifflin, 2003. A collection of pieces on the Sox, mostly by sports reporters, not the literati.

Stout, Glenn, and Richard Johnson. *Red Sox Century.* Boston: Houghton Mifflin, 2000. Not only the most comprehensive history of the team, but also one that takes a fresh look at many of the myths surrounding the Sox. Stout and Johnson document, for example, that the standard view of Frazee is unfair. He was not in financial trouble when he sold Ruth, and he genuinely believed he could build a better team without him. The sale of Ruth came about not because of Frazee's lack of concern for his team but as part of an ongoing power struggle that pitted Frazee, White Sox owner Charles Comiskey, and Yankee owner Jacob Ruppert against American League president Ban Johnson and the five other American League teams. That did not, of course, make it a good deal for the Sox.

Why Can't the Cubs Win?

In 1945, William Sianis, the founder of Billy Goat's Tavern and a diehard Cub fan, tried to bring his pet goat to a World Series game at Wrigley Field. He was turned away. Sianis put a curse on the team, declaring they would never win another World Series. And though Sianis tried to remove the curse during the 1969 pennant race, it has remained in effect, most notably in 2003.

How else to explain the Cubs' collapse in the 2003 National League championship series? Up 3 games to 2 against the wild-card Marlins, with a 3–0 lead, the Cubs were 5 outs from the pennant. Cub left fielder Moises Alou appeared to have the next of those outs within his grasp as he reached for Luis Castillo's foul ball. So did a fan, knocking the ball away from Alou. Given another life, Castillo walked. The Marlins rallied for 8 runs and went on to win the National League championship and the World Series.

Poor Steve Bartman. The lifelong Cub fan reacted as would anyone seeing a foul ball coming his way. He was pelted by peanuts and doused with beer, and had to leave Wrigley Field amid a police escort and talk of joining the witness protection program. But Bartman was only a scapegoat, the latest manifestation of the goat's revenge. The Cubs, who had not won a Series since 1908 or a pennant since 1945, were, many an otherwise rational fan concluded, cursed.

"Fate wasn't on our side," said Cub center fielder Kenny Lofton, who had joined the team fewer than three months before but now seemed fully immersed in its history. "The plan was set beforehand."

"The Bleat Goes On," wrote the *Chicago Tribune.*

It was not always so. William Wrigley, who was part of a syndicate that bought the Cubs in 1916 and who gained full control of the team in 1921, was determined to win the Series and, having made a fortune on chewing gum, he had the resources to make that happen. In Bill Veeck Sr., Wrigley found a savvy president and general manager. By 1927, Wrigley and Veeck had put together a powerful lineup that included outfielders Hack Wilson, Riggs Stephenson, and Earl Webb, and catcher Gabby Hartnett. The next year they added future Hall of Famer Kiki Cuyler. When that wasn't enough, Veeck engineered a blockbuster trade and Wrigley chipped in $200,000 for Rogers Hornsby.

In 1929, Hornsby hit .380 and Wilson .345, each with 39 homers. Pat Malone won 22, Charlie Root 19, Guy Bush 18, and the Cubs coasted to the pennant. In the World Series, it was defense that did the team in. Against Connie Mack's Philadelphia Athletics, the Cubs led 8–0 and seemed on their way to tying the Series at two games apiece. Then Wilson, who hit .471 in the Series, lost two balls in the sun. The Athletics won the game 10–8 and the Series 4–1.

Still, the Cubs were clearly a force to be reckoned with. They won the pennant again in 1932, this despite a year that began with Wrigley's death and then saw Hornsby fired as manager (for gambling) and shortstop Billy Jurges shot in his hotel room by a jilted showgirl. Mark Koenig, a former Yankee who replaced Jurges at short, hit .353 down the stretch but generated some controversy of his own after his teammates, noting that he hadn't played the full season, voted not to give him a full share of their pennant winnings. In the Series, Koenig's ex-teammates came to his defense, hurling insults at the Cubs (it was amid this bench jockeying that Babe Ruth allegedly pointed to the stands—though the Cubs maintained he was pointing to their dugout—

and hit his called shot). The Yankees took four straight from the Cubs.

In 1935, the Cubs won 21 in a row in September, again advancing to the World Series. This time they lost to the Detroit Tigers, partly because in the ninth inning of the sixth game, with the score tied, Cub manager Charlie Grimm had no one to pinch-hit for his pitcher. Earlier in the game, umpire George Moriarty, angered by the insults coming from the Cub bench, had ejected all of Grimm's potential pinch hitters.

Continuing their every three years pattern, the Cubs won the pennant again in 1938, this time aided by Hartnett's "homer in the gloamin'," a shot hit in the near darkness of an early evening at unlit Wrigley Field. Again the Cubs faced the Yankees in the Series, again the Yankees swept them.

And that was all. There would be one more pennant, in 1945, but only because the aging and injured Cubs had more players ineligible for the military than other teams. (World War II, political columnist and Cub fan George Will explained, was fought to make the National League safe for the Cubs.) Fans would have to wait until 1984 to see the team in the playoffs, and they're still waiting to see them back in the World Series. The Cubs are not, of course, the only team with a history of losing. The Red Sox have won only one World Series since they defeated the Cubs in 1918. But even before 2004 the Sox had won four pennants since 1918 and were a perennial contender, with decades of near-misses and missed chances. Not so the Cubs. It's not just that they haven't won the Series since 1908, or that they haven't been in one since 1945; it's that they rarely came close. Year after year, while Fenway's fans braced for heartbreak, Wrigley's—despite living in what could only be called a major sports market—could relax in the sun and take in the scenery, knowing full well that their team was out of the race.

For Philip K. Wrigley, who inherited the team after his father's death, the sun and the ivy and some hot dogs and beer made for a perfectly reasonable marketing strategy. "A team that isn't winning a pennant has to sell something," explained Bill Veeck Jr.

(who worked for Philip Wrigley, just as his father had for William Wrigley). "We sold 'Beautiful Wrigley Field.'"

Veeck also noted that a beautiful stadium did not necessarily make for a winning team. Indeed, Wrigley was a lot more eager to spend money on the stadium than on the team.

"It is hard to understand how a father and son can be as completely different as William and Phil Wrigley," wrote Veeck. "His father left the club to him . . . so Phil Wrigley assumed the burden out of his sense of loyalty and duty. If he has any particular feeling for baseball, he has disguised it magnificently."

One by one, Phil Wrigley traded away his stars, usually for players past their prime, such as a sore-armed Dizzy Dean, who won only 16 games in three seasons with the Cubs. Wrigley refused to invest in a farm system, continuing to buy individual players from independent minor league teams. When he finally did acquire some minor league teams, he insisted that they be financially independent. That meant he was perfectly willing to sell some of his best prospects to the highest bidder, rather than promote them to the Cubs.

Similarly, the gum company was run separately from the team, and none of the former's profits could be directed to the latter. "There are a great many stockholders in the Wrigley Gum Company who would be the first to complain if any of their money was used in baseball," he explained.

Many historians of the Cubs, among them Peter Golenbock and George Castle, date the team's decline to William Wrigley's death in 1932. The 1935, 1938, and 1945 pennants were flukes, they believed, the last gasps of a once-powerful team. Wrote Golenbock: "Had it not been for three miracles—a twenty-one-game winning streak, a seemingly impossible home run hit in darkness, and a season in which all the teams except the Cubs lost their best players to a world war—Philip Wrigley would have presided over a 35-year stretch in which the Cubs were submerged in the bottom half of the National League standings."

Philip Wrigley's philosophies imbued the entire organization. "It seemed like when Wrigley owned the Cubs, the feeling was it would be super if you won the pennant, but if not, no big deal," said Glen Hobbie, who pitched for the team in the late fifties and early sixties. In 1980, the team's highlight film opened with the song "Tomorrow."

Well before then, the Chicago press was on Wrigley's case, and he insisted he did care about the team. "It's pretty hard to do anything right in baseball," he complained in a 1959 interview. "If you don't butt in, you're not interested; if you do, it's front office interference. . . . I'm generally working with the future rather than with the present. I'm out ahead somewhere like an advance man for a circus. I suppose that's why people don't think I'm interested in things—-because I don't hang around."

But that missed the point. The problem wasn't Wrigley's absence but his presence. He didn't want to spend his money on major league players or minor league teams, but he had plenty of other ideas about how to build a winner. These were either innovative or downright weird, depending on whether you wanted to work for Phil Wrigley or not. There was, for example, his decision to hire a man who would put a hex on opposing teams. Veeck, always on the lookout for a good promotion (it was he who later sent a midget to bat for the St. Louis Browns), was enthusiastic until he realized his boss was completely serious.

"We carried our Evil Eye around the league with us," Veeck recalled. "At home, he sat directly behind the plate, gesturing furiously at opposing pitchers, none of whom seemed disposed to enter into the spirit of the thing at all."

Wrigley's weirdest innovation was a "college of coaches." In 1960, tired of hiring and firing managers, he decided to eliminate the position. Instead, he created a pool of eight coaches who would rotate to various major and minor league jobs. Every few weeks one of these would get his turn as "head coach." In theory, this made sense; players would receive consistent coaching at all levels. As the team's 1961 media guide explained: "The core of the new Cubs program is a standard system of play, administered by a stable, good-sized group of coaches." In that way, when a minor leaguer is promoted, "he will know personally—and be known by—the coaches who have worked with him on his way up."

In practice, however, the college of coaches had just the opposite effect. As each coach took his turn in charge, he would change tactics and lineups in an effort to prove he was better than his predecessors. The players ended up confused and disgruntled.

"Not one of them helped one of the others," recalled pitcher Don Elston. "My impression was that whoever was the manager—or the head coach—was pretty much on his own. All they did was wait until it was their turn."

"For a four-game series in Pittsburgh . . . I went 11 for 16 and caught 18 innings in a doubleheader on Sunday," said catcher Dick Bertell. [Elvin] Tappe was the head coach. Then we go back to Chicago, and Lou Klein takes over. I sat for a week. What did I do, hit my way out of the lineup?"

Perhaps the biggest victim of the college was Lou Brock, who was buffeted by constant changes as to whether he should swing for power or get on base and run. After two frustrating seasons in Chicago, the Cubs traded Brock to St. Louis, where he led the team to the World Series. In return, the Cubs received Ernie Broglio, who in three seasons in Chicago won 7 and lost 19.

The Cubs finished 64–90 in 1961 and 59–103 in 1962, behind the expansion Houston Colt .45s. This despite a pretty good team that included Ernie Banks, Ron Santo, George Altman, Billy Williams, and Brock. Quietly, Wrigley abandoned the college.

In 1966, Wrigley finally hired a manager who was both knowledgeable about baseball and willing to stand up to the owner. Leo Durocher put together the Cubs' first pennant contender since 1945. With Williams still in left and Banks and Santo still at the corners, Durocher added All-Stars Glenn Beckert and Don Kessinger up the middle. By 1969, the pitching was equally impressive with Ferguson Jenkins (21–15, 3.21), Bill Hands (20–14, 2.49), and Ken Holtzman (17–13, 3.59). On August 15, the Cubs led the Mets by 9½ games. When the season ended, the Mets were up by 8.

What happened?

Cub fans pointed to a questionable call that allowed Met center fielder Tommie Agee to score from second during a September showdown against the Cubs. But that can hardly explain the Mets' amazing 23–8 run . . . or the Cubs' 8–17 record for the month. Many blamed Durocher for not giving his regulars enough rest during the season. Santo, Kessinger, catcher Randy Hundley, and Banks, now 38 years old and playing on bad knees, were clearly tired by September.

"Leo had stuck with his horses, and maybe that hurt us the last month of that season," recalled Beckert. "That's second-guessing now. But there was no platooning with Leo."

The 1969 season also focused attention on a twenty-year pattern of late-season collapses. Before then, this didn't bother anyone, since the Cubs were out of contention well before the September swoon. If the pattern was mentioned at all, it was to show that the Cubs were not only a bad team, but also a team that choked. But 1969 prompted more serious study of the pattern. Bill James tracked it over three decades. In the 1950s, the Cubs had a winning percentage of .465 in May, .439 in September. In the 1960s, it was .474 in May, .424 in September. In the 1970s, it was .532 in May, .436 in September.

The culprit, according to the general wisdom, was Beautiful Wrigley Field. Its ivied walls, however beautiful, were nightmarishly close for pitchers. More importantly, it was the only major league stadium without lights— "a passing fad" was how Phil Wrigley described night games—so the Cubs played all their home games during the day. Over the course of the summer, the players wilted in the heat and humidity. The fact that the trend dated back to the late forties—just about the time other stadiums added night games—seemed to confirm the thesis.

"An understanding of fatigue is one of the largest gaps in our comprehension of what takes place during a pennant race," wrote James. "Is it not possible that . . . extensive platooning succeeds, in part, because it reduces fatigue?"

In addition to the heat, Cub players had to adjust to the back and forth between night and day games.

"The constant changing of the schedule hurts," said Holtzman. "It's the change of the body clock. Pro athletes are highly disciplined athletes. . . . I'm a fan of Wrigley Field as much as anyone. But . . . it's radically different."

"Your sleeping habits change," agreed Williams. "When we went on the road to play a night game, it affected us because at the time you'd normally be out at the ballpark . . . you'd be taking a nap here in Chicago because you'd finished the game."

In 1987 statistician Don Zminda analyzed the batting performances of Banks, Williams, and Santo from 1960 to 1971 during the first game of a road trip, when they had to adjust to playing at night. Williams hit .277 (compared to .297 overall), Santo .248 (compared to .281), Banks .220 (compared to .264).

Said Gary Nicholson, who was the team trainer from 1972 to 1976: "They drank a lot of caffeine and Cokes . . . to keep 'em going."

In the eighties, there was less focus on the heat and the lights. One reason was that the Tribune Corporation, which bought the team from the Wrigley family in 1981, added lights and eighteen night games in 1988. This diminished (though it didn't eliminate) the team's problems adjusting when they hit the road or returned home. The main reason for the new attitude, though, was that the Cubs were, for the first time since the 1930s, a good team.

Unlike the Wrigleys, the Tribune was willing to invest some of its money in players. New general manager Dallas Green, who was as strong-willed as Durocher, brought to Chicago Ryne Sandberg, Larry Bowa, Ron Cey, Dennis Eckersley, and Steve Trout. In June 1984 Green traded Joe Carter and Mel Hall to Cleveland for Rick Sutcliffe. Sutcliffe, who was 4–5 with the Indians, went 16–1 for the rest of the year.

With the right pitchers, Wrigley didn't seem like such a bandbox. With the right team, the heat and lights didn't seem such obstacles. In 1984 the Cubs were 52–31 after July 1. In 1989 they were 52–32. Neither team appeared to tire down the stretch, and each won the division title. Cub manager Jim Frey summed up the new attitude after the team clinched in 1984. "It wasn't too hot this year," he said.

Still, there was no pennant, no World Series. The 1984 defeat in the deciding game of the championship series was enough to revive talk of the goat. With the Cubs up 3–2 in the sixth and Sutcliffe on the mound, San Diego's Tim Flannery grounded to first. In a play that foreshadowed the turning point of the 1986 Series, when Red Sox first baseman (and ex-Cub) Bill Buckner watched Mookie Wilson's grounder go through his legs, this one got by Leon Durham. Then came a check-swing single, a bad bounce past Sandberg, and a grounder up the middle. The Padres won the game 6–3, and the Cubs went home.

Some critics also questioned whether the Tribune was truly committed to going all the way, especially after Green left in 1987. Blue Jay general manager Pat Gillick, who interviewed with Tribune executives in 1991, made them sound a lot like Phil Wrigley. "Some of the mystique of the Cubs is ineptitude," Gillick said. "If they win, there might be an expectation level to win again. It's not a big deal to the company. The Cubs are a pimple on the Tribune Company's financial statement."

The failure to hold on to Greg Maddux, who led the team to the division championship in 1989 and won 87 games for the Cubs between 1988 and 1992, fueled the doubts. Maddux signed with the Atlanta Braves despite his stated desire to stay in Chicago.

Some Cub fans were reassured when the team appointed Andy MacPhail president in 1994. MacPhail was a respected third-generation baseball executive. Powered by Sammy Sosa's 66 homers, the team won the East in 1998, though some fans clung to the old image of the lovable losers. At Wrigley you could still find plenty of T-shirts saying "Any team can have a bad century."

Other Cub fans were less patient. After the heartbreak conclusion to the until-then heartening 2003 season, some decided to take matters into their own hands. Two months after the Marlins beat the Cubs, a Chicago restaurant group named for Cub sportscaster Harry Caray paid $113,824 for the ball Bartman deflected away from Alou. (Bartman received none of this money.) In February 2004, the Caray group, with the help of a Hollywood special-effects expert and in front of a crowd of Chicagoans, blew up the ball.

Hopes that they might thus have exorcised the curse of the goat soared in 2004. With the return of Maddux and the mid-season addition of shortstop Nomar Garciaparra, the Cubs had a one-and-a-half-game lead in the wild card race with nine left to play. Still, Cubs fans could not help but fear the chunks of concrete that fell from Wrigley's crumbling upper deck on three occasions during the season. This had to be an omen. The Cubs, too, crumbled, losing seven of their last nine games and finishing three out.

To investigate further:

Castle, George. *The Million-to-One Team*. South Bend, Ind.: Diamond Communications, 2000. Repetitious but damning: Castle dismisses arguments that the field or sun or wind or luck have anything to do with the Cubs' failures, and lays the blame on the shortsighted policies of Philip Wrigley and (to a lesser extent) the Tribune Corporation.

Fulk, David, and Dan Riley. *The Cubs Reader*. Boston: Houghton Mifflin, 1991. Essays by Roger Angell, Jon Margolis, Harry Stein, Lonnie Wheeler, George Will, and others.

Golenbock, Peter. *Wrigleyville*. New York: St. Martin's Press, 1996. A satisfying oral history.

Honig, Donald. *The Chicago Cubs*. New York: Prentice Hall Press, 1991. An illustrated history.

James, Bill. *Baseball Abstract*. New York: Ballantine, 1982. James changed the way we think about the effects of parks on performance, as he did the way we think about so much else about the game. See also his comments on Wrigley in his 1986, 1990, and 1992 annuals, as well as his *Historical Baseball Abstract*.

Veeck, Bill, with Ed Linn. *Veeck as in Wreck*. New York: Fireside, 1989. Originally published in 1962, still hilarious and incisive.

Will, George. *Bunts*. New York: Fireside, 1999. Essays on baseball, many on the Cubs, by the conservative political columnist. Will is open-minded enough to consider the benefits of affirmative action, at least when it comes to his team. He approvingly quotes Cub fan John Nies asking "whether it is really fair to retire a Cub hitter after three called strikes, which is the same standard used to judge the skills of a Ted Williams or a Reggie Jackson."

21

Who Threw the Spitter?

In the thirteenth inning of the second game of a doubleheader, with the Giants and Mets tied at 6, Giant manager Alvin Dark had only two pitchers left. One, Bob Hendley, was scheduled to start the next day. So Dark turned to Gaylord Perry, whose 4.77 ERA couldn't have instilled confidence.

"Frankly, there was nobody else left," Perry recalled. "I was the eleventh man on an eleven-man pitching staff."

Remarkably, on that very long day in 1964, Perry threw 10 shutout innings. In the 23rd, the Giants finally scored 2 to win.

That Perry had added a new pitch—a spitball—to his repertoire was clear from the start.

"Like any kid with a new toy, I was overdoing it," he wrote in his 1974 book *Me and the Spitter.* [Met manager Casey] Stengel kept yelling to [plate umpire Ed] Sudol, "Call out the ground crew, Ed. Spread the rain tarp under him." Even Giant catcher Tom Haller warned Perry, "Sudol's getting suspicious of that splashing sound in my mitt."

Yet Perry persisted, winning 314 games and the Cy Young Award in both leagues. In 1968, when baseball changed its rules so a pitcher could no longer touch his fingers to his mouth anywhere near the mound, Perry turned to other substances, ranging from Vaseline to K-Y jelly. Opposing managers and umpires tried in vain to prove he was greasing the ball.

"I've had to take off my pants, my shirt, one shoe and even my cap," Perry wrote. "I've had to towel-dry my face, neck and arms before as many as 50,000 fans. . . . And I've been the selected short subject of stop-action movies in two cities and the target of still photographers hired by ball clubs in other cities."

They found nothing. In 1971, reporters went so far as to question Allison Perry, the pitcher's then-five-year-old daughter. "Does your daddy throw a greaseball, honey?" one asked. "It's a hard slider," Allison answered.

Even his book-length confession did opponents and umpires no good, since Perry maintained that he didn't throw the spitter anymore. To which manager Gene Mauch replied, "But he doesn't throw it any less, either."

In *Me and the Spitter*, Perry explained why it was so tough to find any proof. "Often the ball would dry on the way to the plate," he wrote. "If it didn't, it would get wiped off in the pocket of the catcher's mitt. If the umpire wanted to check the ball, the catcher gave it a quick smear with his thumb to clean off the spot while handing it to the ump. And the umpire himself unconsciously would provide the final wipe, just handling the ball to look for a foreign substance. I needed so little grease toward the end of my greaseball career that it was undetectable.

"They have never found a thing on the ball. And they never will," he gloated. "They've never thrown me out of a game while pitching."

Perry spoke too soon. In 1982, while Perry was pitching in Seattle against the Red Sox, umpire Dave Phillips watched the bottom drop out of a series of fastballs. Fed up, Phillips ejected Perry. Still, the $250 fine and ten-day suspension was hardly a sentence likely to strike fear in the hearts of spitballers, grease-ballers, mudballers, or anyone else. It seemed more like a concession that baseball either would not or could not put an end to illegal pitches, that they were as much a part of the game as stealing a sign or even stealing a base. And that raised the question of just how big a part of the game these pitches—and pitchers— have been.

* * *

The spitball appears to have been invented around the turn of the twentieth century. By some accounts, Frank Corridon of the Eastern League's Providence club was the first to throw it. New York Highlander Jack Chesbro was definitely throwing it by 1904, the year his record improved from 21–15 to 41–12. In the following years the pitch was fairly common—and perfectly legal. Its history becomes trickier after the 1919 season, when the pitch was outlawed.

Some continued to throw the spitter legally, since the 1919 decision allowed each team to grandfather two pitchers. Of these, Burleigh Grimes, Stan Coveleski, and Red Faber made the Hall of Fame. Grimes lasted the longest, throwing the last legal spitball in 1934. After that, spitball historians had to depend more on rumor and the occasional, usually postretirement, confession.

One of the first to confess was Dodger pitcher Preacher Roe, in a 1955 *Sports Illustrated* article. Like Perry, Roe seemed destined to mediocrity. He was 34–47 when he decided to throw the spitter, 95–38 after.

Yankee pitcher Whitey Ford confessed in his 1987 autobiography *Slick*. Ford said he experimented with a spitter early in his career but never mastered it. Then Milwaukee Braves pitcher Lew Burdette taught him the mudball. First he rubbed saliva on the ball, then dirt, which stuck to the wet ball.

"I couldn't believe the movement I was able to get," Ford wrote. "This was the new pitch I was looking for."

Opposing pitchers occasionally took advantage of Ford's handiwork. "When I was with the Angels and pitching against the Yankees in the Stadium, I loved to watch Whitey strike out our last hitter in an inning with his mudball," said Bo Belinsky. "[Yankee catcher] Elston Howard would roll the ball back to the mound. I would go out there, pick up the ball and see this big wad of mud glued to the ball. My first pitch to the first Yankee hitter was usually a beauty."

The pitch baffled hitters because, unlike a spitball or a knuckleball, it rotated. The mudball came in looking like any other pitch. And even if batters suspected something, there was no way they could prove it.

"Usually, by the time the ball hit the catcher's mitt, or the batter made contact, the blow would knock the mud off and it wouldn't be detected," Ford wrote. "If somebody asked the umpire to check the ball after I had 'loaded' it up with mud and before I pitched, just as I was reaching up to throw it to the umpire, I would hit the ball on the side of my pants leg and the mud would come off. By the time the umpire got the ball and looked at it, all he saw was a little dirt on the baseball."

Ford also tried scuffing the ball with a half-inch-long file embedded in a ring covered with flesh-colored Band-Aids. This was even more effective than the mudball. "One little nick was all it took to get the baseball to sail and dip like crazy," he wrote.

Many pitchers didn't mind being suspected of throwing an illegal pitch, especially if it kept batters off balance. "The reason I didn't have to use the super-sinker too often was that I worked so hard on developing my decoy—a series of motions designed to make the batter think you're throwing a spitter even when you're not," explained Perry. "The effectiveness of the super drop depends on the decoy as much as on the pitch itself."

Dodger pitcher Don Sutton also reveled in his reputation for scuffing balls. An umpire searching Sutton's glove once discovered a note inside that read, "You're getting warm, but it's not here!"

Still, when umpire Doug Harvey found a quarter-size rip in a ball and ejected Sutton, the pitcher denied he did it and threatened to sue if he was suspended. He wasn't.

One of the few pitchers who was suspended was Twin Joe Niekro. In 1987, during a game against the Angels, umpire Tim Tschida told him to empty his pockets. Out flew an emery board and a piece of sandpaper. "The guy was so blatant," said umpire Dave Palermo, "it was like a guy walking down the street carrying a bottle of booze during Prohibition."

Niekro parlayed the incident into an appearance on the David Letterman show, where he showed up wearing a utility belt with a sander, shoe polish, and jar of Vaseline, as well as emery boards. Still, Niekro adamantly denied doing anything illegal. He claimed he needed the emery board and sandpaper to keep his fingernails trim, which enabled him to get a better grip on his knuckleball.

"Maybe it looked worse on television, like I was a high school kid trying to ditch a cigarette," Niekro wrote in a letter to his fellow knuckleballer and brother Phil. "But let's be serious: where am I going to flip it, out of the stadium? I knew the emery board was coming out. I was making no attempt to fake anybody out or try to get away with anything. If I knew I had something to hide, I wouldn't have pulled the emery board out."

Niekro was suspended for ten games.

Mostly, though, umpires weren't as lucky. During the 1986 season, Harvey searched Astro Mike Scott sixty-five times but found nothing. Opponents collected dozens of scuffed balls Scott threw, but there was no way to prove he was the one who scuffed them.

"Does Scott doctor the ball?" asked catcher and broadcaster Tim McCarver. "The answer is yes, of course. But so do a lot of good pitchers. You'd be surprised at the names."

The problem was there was no way to prove it. So in a game that prides itself on its statistics, the incidence of spitballs—or if we take Perry's word about the effect of the 1968 rules change, other illegal pitches—remains a question answered mostly by impressions and anecdotes. Even those who have ventured a numerical guess have no way to prove it. Rogers Hornsby, one of the game's greatest hitters, estimated that 95 percent of pitchers threw something illegal. But Hornsby was himself a notorious cheater and may have assumed others had an equal knack for it.

"Not nearly as much . . . trickery goes on today," wrote Nolan Ryan after twenty-four years in the majors. "Players today don't have the same appreciation of the cunning that another generation put into winning." Ryan denied ever altering a ball himself but admitted he took advantage of "whatever edge that fate may have provided" in the form of scuffed-up balls.

Met manager George Bamberger disagreed with Ryan. "Right now, we're in the heyday of illegal pitches," he told sportswriter Tom Boswell in the early 1980s. "Any pitcher who doesn't seriously consider an 'extra' pitch, you got to wonder if he really wants to win."

Bamberger guessed about half of pitchers cheated. Oriole pitching coach Ray Miller, himself an admitted former spitballer, guessed that about a dozen American Leaguers threw something illegal regularly, and another fifty occasionally.

One reason why there aren't more illegal pitches is that they aren't easily mastered. Said Nolan Ryan: "Other than Burdette and Gaylord Perry, I doubt many pitchers made a living throwing the spitter or a variation of it. The reason is basic. Most pitchers find it hard enough to control the legal ones."

Perry agreed. "Improperly loaded or thrown, the spitter will arrive at the plate and pause with 'hit-me-here' written all over it." Belinsky said much the same thing. "Every pitcher has fooled with it at certain times," he said. "Only a few have ever thrown it in a game because it's a dangerous pitch if it isn't controlled. If it doesn't drop, it just hangs up there like a balloon."

Dodger pitcher Hugh Casey may have thrown the most infamous spitball-gone-awry. In the 1941 World Series, Casey threw a third strike by Tommy Henrich, whose swing didn't even come close. The pitch apparently gave the Dodgers the game and tied the Series. But the ball got by Dodger catcher Mickey Owen, Henrich ran to first, and the Yankees came back to win the game and the Series. To Dodger fans, Owen is forever a goat, perhaps unfairly. For though Owen and Henrich both claimed the pitch was a curve, Casey later admitted it was a spitter.

Many pitchers don't even want a scuffed ball. "What you will see most of the time is the pitcher himself lobbing the ball back to the umpire and asking for a new one," Ryan observed, "because he really doesn't have the confidence of knowing how the ball will move when he throws it."

Baseball is a game of skills more than one of raw athletic talent," wrote Boswell, "and the spitball is clearly one of the game's most difficult and chancy skills. For every career it salvages, there is probably another that it helps to ruin." That fear has undoubtedly dissuaded many from throwing the pitch.

What about the ethics of the pitch? Has that given pause to any would-be spitballers? Perhaps. But those who have thrown the pitch have certainly come up with plenty of justifications.

"I thought of my wife, Blanche, our very young children, and Mamma and Daddy back home on the farm," said Perry, recalling that fateful day in 1964. "All counting on me."

Ford, too, felt he had no choice. "I didn't begin cheating until late in my career, when I needed something to help me survive," he said.

Then there was reliever George Frazier's appeal to patriotism. "I don't put any foreign substances on the baseball," he said. "Everything I use is from the good old U.S.A."

Mostly, though, spitballers have argued that what they're doing, though technically against the rules, was very much in the spirit of the game. "The main ethic of baseball is simple: win," said Perry. "I can't see what's wrong with throwing a pitch few other people can master that helped me win."

As Preacher Roe put it, "I didn't sin against God."

Baseball, after all, is a game that depends on deception. The pitcher who looks toward the plate and then makes his pickoff move, the catcher who quickly moves his glove to make an outside pitch look like a strike, the second baseman who executes the double play by touching second without the ball: all these are honored parts of the game, and only the last is technically against the rules. Why, many a pitcher has asked, should a properly concealed spitter be treated any differently?

In fact, it hasn't been. The few punishments handed out for illegal pitches have hardly signaled that major league baseball considers this a serious crime. An occasional ejection, a short suspension, a token fine: they're all part of the game.

"The game has strict and clearly written rules, but they are not enforced and in some cases are almost completely ignored," wrote Dan Gutman in *It Ain't Cheatin' if You Don't Get Caught.* "Except for blatant offenses that cannot be overlooked, cheating is tolerated, and is actually considered to be just another skill, like hitting to the opposite field."

What would be unacceptable would be for pitchers to cheat in a way that throws off the game's balance, that gives them such an edge that batters have no recourse. And, as many a pitcher has pointed out, batters have plenty of tricks of their own.

For more than half of the twentieth century, batters looked for ways to make their bats heavier, figuring this would give them more power. In the 1920s Brown first baseman George Sisler hammered phonograph needles into his bat. In the 1950s, Red first baseman Ted Kluszewski tried nails. Such techniques were not only illegal but also perhaps counterproductive, since heavier bats meant slower swings.

By the 1960s, the pendulum had swung the other way. By drilling a hole and filling it with cork, or some substance lighter than wood, batters could make the bat lighter, thus giving them more control of and speed on their swing. Like pitchers, batters tended to wait until after they retired before confessing. Detroit first baseman Norm Cash was one of the first to do so, admitting he used a corked bat in 1961 when he hit .361 to win the American League batting title.

That Cash hit .243 the next year, presumably while still corking, makes one wonder whether his method was any more effective than Sisler's or Kluszewski's. "Almost all interesting scientific problems involve conflicting factors," wrote scientists Robert Watts and Terry Bahill. "In the case of hitting a baseball with a bat, we found that, strictly from the point of view of momentum considerations, the speed of a baseball leaving the bat with a given bat speed is maximized by making the bat mass (or weight) as large as possible. From the standpoint of bat control and accuracy, the bat should be extraordinarily light."

In other words, no one knows for sure what works.

But some batters thought they did. Gutman thought that 5 to 30 percent of batters stuffed their bats, though these were really just guesses. The modern preference is clearly for lighter-than-wood substances, including sawdust and Styrofoam as well as cork. Graig Nettles, according to some reports, went so far as to insert Super Balls in his bat, perhaps in the mistaken belief that they'd add spring to the bat. In a 1974 game, Nettles singled to left, his bat broke open, and out bounced six balls. Wrote *Time* magazine: "Nettles was the first man to bounce out to the third baseman, the shortstop, and the second baseman at once."

At first, Nettles claimed a fan gave him the bat, and he had no idea it had been doctored. Later, he admitted he knew it was corked, but maintained the Super Balls were a myth. "That never happened," he wrote in his autobiography *Balls*. "Nothing came out. He [the fan] had sawed an inch off the end of the bat and then plugged it down the middle with cork, and then glued the top back on."

In 1987, Astro left fielder Billy Hatcher was ejected when his bat split, revealing cork. Hatcher claimed he had borrowed the bat from reliever Dave Smith. After the incident, Hatcher's average dropped 40 points. Also in 1987 many suspected that Met third baseman Howard Johnson was corking, since his home run total jumped to 36, from 12, 11, and 10 the three previous years. Johnson's power was especially evident in the first half of the season, perhaps because by August opposing managers were routinely checking his bats. They found nothing, and in Johnson's defense, 1987 was the year offense so soared that many suspected a livelier ball was in play.

Most shocking of all corkings, of course, was Sammy Sosa's. In 1998, it seemed as though the entire country was rooting for the joyful Cub outfielder as he, along with Cardinal first baseman Mark McGwire, successfully pursued Roger Maris's home run record. Five years later, Sosa's bat cracked open during a game against Tampa Bay, revealing a piece of cork. ESPN titled its special on the controversy, "Say It Ain't Sosa."

Sosa said he had accidentally picked up a bat meant only for batting practice, when he liked to put on a show for the fans. X-rays of his other seventy-six bats seemed to confirm Sosa's story.

"We're very confident that all those bats were clean and had no foreign substances in them," announced baseball executive vice president Sandy Alderson. "This is consistent with Sammy's explanation."

Others were skeptical. Sosa had been slumping before the incident, leading some to conclude he was desperate enough to cheat. It also didn't help that the corked bat hadn't been specially marked to make sure it didn't end up in a game.

Sosa was suspended for seven games. When he returned, he won over most fans with a barrage of home runs, leading the Cubs to the playoffs. "He admitted he committed a crime, unknowingly, but it's still a crime," Cub manager Dusty Baker said. "And he went ahead with his business."

To investigate further:

Allen, Maury, with Bo Belinsky. *Bo*. New York: Dial Press, 1973. Belinsky was better known as a playboy than a pitcher, and what seemed refreshingly open in the 1960s now just seems sexist.

Boswell, Thomas. *How Life Imitates the World Series*. Garden City, N.Y.: Doubleday, 1982. Boswell's essays are on a par with those of Roger Angell. This collection, Boswell's first, includes "Salvation through Salivation."

Bouton, Jim. *Ball Four Plus Ball Five*. New York: Stein & Day, 1981. Originally published in 1970, *Ball Four* changed the way we look at the game and, perhaps, the nation. Bouton's struggle to prolong his career with a knuckler (he apparently never tried a spitter) is at once hilarious and moving. "You see," he wrote, "you spend a good piece of your life gripping a baseball and in the end it turns out that it was the other way around all the time."

Brosnan, Jim. *The Long Season*. New York: Harper & Row, 1960. A decade before *Ball Four*, Brosnan earned acclaim, deservedly, for his frank portrayal of a season in the bullpen. But you have to wonder why he never mentions a spitter, though he was frequently accused of throwing one.

Ford, Whitey, with Phil Pepe. *Slick*. New York: William Morrow, 1987. Whitey's nickname and book title wasn't meant to describe his spitballs, or the fact that he was pretty slick on the mound. According to Mickey Mantle, "Casey Stengel . . . used to have a favorite expression that he used when he thought some of his players were getting a little too big for their britches and needed some toning down. He called us 'whiskey slick.' . . . After a while, Billy [Martin] and I picked up on it and we began to call Whitey 'Slick,' and the name just stuck."

Gutman, Dan. *It Ain't Cheatin' if You Don't Get Caught*. New York: Penguin, 2000. Scuffing, corking, spitting, gunking, and other baseball fundamentals.

Nettles, Graig, and Peter Golenbock. *Balls*. New York: G. P. Putnam's Sons, 1984. "Some kids dream of joining the circus, others of becoming a major league baseball player," Nettles wrote. "I have been doubly blessed. As a member of the New York Yankees, I have gotten to do both."

Niekro, Phil and Joe, with Ken Picking. *The Niekro Files*. Chicago: Contemporary Books, 1988. The letters of baseball's knuckleballing brothers.

Perry, Gaylord, with Bob Sudyk. *Me and the Spitter*. New York: E. P. Dutton, 1974. "Do I still wet them?" teased Perry. "I sure know how. But that doesn't mean I do it—or even that I ever did it. Maybe I'm just kidding. Maybe I got the Mets out in 1964 on sheer talent."

Ryan, Nolan, with Mickey Herskowitz. *Kings of the Hill*. New York: HarperCollins, 1992. Ryan's top ten pitchers with the "right scuff": Gaylord Perry, Lew Burdette, Kevin Gross, Don Sutton, Bill Singer, Joe Niekro, Mike Scott, Don Drysdale, Rick Honeycutt, and Dave Smith.

Thorn, John, and John Holway. *The Pitcher*. New York: Prentice Hall Press, 1987. Statistics, analysis, anecdotes, and everything else you wanted to know about pitchers.

Watts, Robert, and Terry Bahill. *Keep Your Eye on the Ball*. New York: W. H. Freeman, 2000. The science of baseball.

22

Does a Curveball Curve?

Most authorities, including the Hall of Fame, credit Candy Cummings with the invention of the curve. Like many who followed, the 5-foot-9, 120-pound Cummings turned to the pitch because he had neither the size nor the strength for a good fastball. Cummings claimed he started experimenting at boarding school in 1864.

"My friends began to laugh at me, and to throw jokes at my theory of making a ball go sideways," Cummings recalled. "I fear that some of them thought it was so preposterous that it was no joke and that I should be carefully watched over."

In 1867, pitching against Harvard for an amateur Brooklyn team, Cummings seemed to have mastered the pitch. "A surge of joy flooded over me that I shall never forget," he said. "I felt like shouting out that I had made a ball curve. . . . But I said not a word, and saw many a batter at that game throw down his stick in disgust. Every time I was successful I could scarcely keep from dancing from pure joy."

Cummings later played for the Hartford Dark Blues, whose manager, Bob Ferguson, said, "God never gave him any size, but he's the candy."

From then on, the curve was an irrefutable presence for many a hitter. "Get out my work clothes, Mom," the apocryphal postcard home from spring training read. "They've started to throw curveballs."

Still, there were always those who sided with Cummings' friends and considered the curve a joke. In a 1941 issue of the *New Yorker*, R. W. Madden recounted a conversation he had with an old man who denied there was such a thing as a curveball:

> "I've *seen* curves," I told him. "Every game I've ever been to, the pitcher has had *some* kind of curve."
>
> "Well, son," the old man said, not unkindly, "you *think* you seen curves. And why? Because you expect to see them. When a pitcher spends ten seconds winding up; and the ball goes fast, with a bat zipping across the plate, and the catcher makes a show of moving his mitt to pick up the curve, no wonder you think you see it. Ever see a magician? . . . Baseball's better for fooling people than magic because by now most of the players believe in it themselves."

It wasn't just a few old-timers who were skeptical. There were plenty who believed, as *Life* magazine argued in 1941, that a curveball was a theoretical possibility but that pitchers had neither the finger nor the wrist strength to put enough spin on a ball to make it curve. A Ping-Pong ball or a tennis ball could curve, sure. A golf ball could obviously hook, after it was struck by a golf club. A baseball, too, could curve—if the batter connected right. But a baseball was simply too heavy for a pitcher to do it on his own.

The curve, this line of thinking concluded, was an optical illusion.

It seemed an easy enough proposition to test. So in 1870, at Brooklyn's Capitoline Grounds, baseball writer Henry Chadwick set two stakes between the pitcher's box and the plate. Then he challenged Fred Goldsmith, a Chicago pitcher who claimed he started throwing curves before Cummings, to throw a pitch to the right of the first stake and the left of the second. Goldsmith did just that.

Chadwick's demonstration satisfied the crowd, but there were still skeptics. In 1941 *Life* stepped up to the plate. The magazine enlisted two top curveballers, Cy Blanton of the Phillies and Carl Hubbell of the Giants. Then it set up three cameras to photograph a pitch at one-thirtieth of a second intervals. The resulting prints showed a sagitta—the largest deviation from the straight line drawn from the beginning to the end of the ball's flight— that was smaller than the diameter of the baseball. From that, *Life* concluded there was no horizontal curve. (The ball did curve downward as gravity took its toll.)

"Possibly there is an infinitely small side movement of the ball," the magazine said, "but these pictures fail to show it."

Martin Quigley, author of the 1984 book *The Crooked Pitch*, summed up the dismay and derision that followed with an exchange that was probably repeated after many a homer:

"What did you hit?"
"A hanging optical illusion."
"Well, that's Life for you."

In 1949, *Life*'s rival *Look* conducted its own experiment, this time with Red curveballer Ken Raffensberger. *Look* also painted half the ball black, to be able to see and count its spins. The pictures showed the ball turned at 1,400 revolutions per minute. And this did make the ball curve, though in such a gentle arc that many wondered how it could fool a major league hitter. Almost thirty years later, *Science 82* tried again, using Oriole pitching coach Ray Miller and pitcher Scott McGregor. *Science 82*'s conclusions matched *Look*'s: the ball curved, though less than a foot and in a gentle arc.

By then, no one was questioning that pitchers could put enough spin on the ball to make it curve. Clearly, pitchers not only could throw curves, but also did. By putting a spin on the ball, they caused more air pressure on one side of the ball than on the other, forcing the ball to one side. How much a ball curves depends on how fast it's spinning (the faster the spin, the more the curve) and how fast it's thrown (the faster the pitch, the less the curve, since there's less time for the lateral force to act on the ball).

But a question remained. If the curve broke as gradually as these experiments suggested, why didn't batters see it coming and react accordingly? The curves of Raffensberger and McGregor, as *Look* and *Science 82* described them, seemed so gentle, Quigley wrote, that a "Little Leaguer could clobber" them. Robert Watts, one of the scientists who conducted the latter experiment, later conceded it might have been flawed, since the night before, McGregor had pitched for the Orioles and might not have been in top form. But that didn't really solve the problem. Even if McGregor's pitch curved more, it was still a gradual curve.

To batters, the explanation was clear: the curveball did not curve gradually, but broke suddenly. "A curveball comes straight in," said Oriole first baseman Terry Crowley, "then about four or five feet from home plate it breaks straight down."

Oriole outfielder John Lowenstein agreed that curves broke. "All a physicist has to do is stand up there with a bat to convince himself," he said.

Yet the break, scientists adamantly maintained, was against the laws of physics.

As scientists explained it, the force on the ball was constant, so the ball had to curve constantly. Watts noted that if not for gravity forcing the ball to the ground, the curve would eventually travel a full circle—in McGregor's case, he calculated the circle would have a diameter of more than 2,000 feet—and end up back in the pitcher's glove. Said Watts: "There's no way the force is going to suddenly take effect 10 feet from the plate."

What, then, accounted for the batter's perception?

Watts suggested the apparent break was the result of a batter misjudging how fast a pitch is, and therefore where it will cross the plate.

Science writers Eric Schrier and William Allman used a railroad analogy to show why, though the ball is always curving at the same rate, its circular path becomes clearer to the batter as it approaches him. "Think of a train traveling at a constant speed on a circular track," they wrote. "If a viewer stands at the center of the circle, the train appears to be moving at a constant rate. If the viewer stands near the perimeter of the circle, however, the train at first appears to be traveling a straight line as it comes toward him and then seems to move sideways as it passes him and heads upward."

Yale physics professor Robert Adair explained that though the radius of curvature is nearly constant throughout the ball's flight, the deflection from the original direction increases approximately quadratically with distance. In other words, there's four times the deflection at twice the distance. Moreover, the batter has little time to react to this, and he has to do so while coping with the pitcher's changing speeds and the ball's downward drop. Coming at you at 70 or 75 miles per hour, the deflection appears anything but "gentle."

Wrote Adair: "Does a curveball then travel in a smooth arc like the arc of a circle? Yes. Does the ball 'break' as it nears the plate? Yes. Neither the smooth arc nor the break is an illusion; they are different descriptions of the same reality."

Adair also explained where *Life* had gone wrong. The magazine had confused the sagitta with the full deflection of the ball. Of Blanton and Hubbell, Adair wrote: "These fine pitchers threw their major league curveballs . . . with about 8-inch left-right breaks that could be seen clearly by laying a ruler along the ball trajectories shown in the two-page foldout. But the editors of *Life*, looking at the two-inch sagitta, smaller than the diameter of the baseball, concluded that the balls did not curve."

Since Adair was an old friend of Commissioner Bart Giamatti, who in 1987 named him "physicist to the National League," this is as close as we're likely to get to the official position of baseball—and of science.

The focus on whether a ball curves to the right or to the left is sort of ironic, considering that a *vertical* curve is the more common and more effective pitch. The reason is clear: a horizontal curve moves the ball toward or away from the batter, meaning he'll connect with a different part of the bat. A ball that drops or rises, in contrast, would cause the batter to swing over or under it for a grounder or a pop-up, if not a strike.

No one questions that a ball can drop; even if there's no spin at work, gravity will push it down. The rising fastball is another matter. More blatantly than any other curve, it seems to defy the law of physics, specifically the law of gravity. Sure, backspin could push a ball upward, but not nearly enough to counteract the downward force of gravity. Consider this: assuming the pitch is thrown overhand, the ball falls about three feet from where it leaves the pitcher's hand to where it crosses the plate. That means a rising fastball would have to hop up more than three feet. No one claims that a horizontal curve moves three feet laterally, so there's no reason to assume a vertical one could do so. Watts figured that a ball would have to spin at about 3,400 revolutions per minute to rise, about 1,100 rpm more than the highest rate measured. Adair guessed that backspin could cause a ball to rise up to seven inches, not nearly enough to offset a three-foot drop.

This upward break, then, is a matter of perception. Seven inches may not be enough for the ball to rise, but it still puts it higher than it otherwise would be, thus throwing off a batter. Moreover, a very fast pitch has less time to drop en route to the plate, and a batter who underestimated its speed also might miscalculate its height.

Explained engineer Terry Bahill: "The hitter develops a mental model of how fast the ball is traveling, its course and where it will be when it crosses home plate. With a fastball that appears to rise, the mental model is simply wrong."

If the ball is thrown at 95 or 100 miles per hour, especially sandwiched between a couple of slower pitches, one can certainly forgive a batter for saying it rose.

To investigate further:

Adair, Robert. *The Physics of Baseball*. New York: Perennial, 2002. In addition to explaining the curve and rising fastball, Adair delves into such questions as the ideal trajectory of the bat (35 degrees) and how many feet more a 400-foot homer will travel for every inch a barometer drops (about 6 feet). Originally published in 1990.

Life. "Baseball's Curve Balls." September 15, 1941.

————. "Camera and Science Settle the Old Rhubarb about Baseball's Curve Ball." July 27, 1953.

Look. "Visual Proof That a Baseball Curves." June 19, 1949.

Madden, R. W. "Our Skeptical Correspondents." *New Yorker,* May 24, 1941. It all started, Madden's acquaintance explained to him, when over a few beers some pitcher told a few friends he could throw a curve. Pretty soon, everyone was claiming they could throw one or hit one or see one. "Oh, maybe here and there there's somebody that, if he's honest with himself, he'll admit to himself he ain't never really seen a curve. But by then he's afraid to talk about it for fear of making a fool of himself."

Quigley, Martin. *The Crooked Pitch.* Chapel Hill, N.C.: Algonquin Books, 1984. "The story of the curveball is the story of the game itself," Quigley wrote in this history of the pitch and its pitchers. "Some would say of life itself." At the very least, the book makes clear how much intrigue the pitch, this "creator of abiding uncertainty," has added to the game.

Schrier, Eric, and William Allman. *Newton at the Bat.* New York: Scribner, 1984. Science in football, basketball, wrestling, tennis, golf, and Frisbee, as well as baseball.

Watts, Robert, and Terry Bahill. *Keep Your Eye on the Ball.* New York: W. H. Freeman, 2000. The title may offer good advice, but as Watts and Bahill demonstrate in their study of the science of baseball, it's impossible advice to follow. Watts was one of the scientists who conducted the 1982 study of McGregor and Miller's pitches.

23

Where Did "Fungo" Come From?

You don't have to know anything about baseball to talk about playing hardball or pinch hitting or striking out. Baseball words are everywhere in America, which is perhaps part of what Reggie Jackson meant when he said that "the country is as American as baseball." Baseball's rich verbal tradition has also been more carefully studied than that of any other sport, most notably by Paul Dickson, whose interest in both baseball and language resulted in his 7,000-word dictionary. Yet even Dickson was unable to track down the origins of every baseball word. Sometimes, even with fairly common words, you *can't* look it up.

Take, for example, "fungo." As early as 1867, the pioneering baseball writer Henry Chadwick described fungo as "a preliminary practice game in which one player takes the bat and, tossing the ball up, hits it as it falls." This was, Chadwick accurately added, "useless as practice in batting, but good for taking fly balls." By 1892 the word was being used as a verb (in the *Brooklyn Daily Eagle*), and it soon came to refer to the bat used in the game and the act of batting without a pitcher, as well as the game itself. Its etymology, however, remained a mystery.

That didn't mean you couldn't find an array of theories, some quite scholarly and others—well, let's put it this way—remarkably creative.

*   *   *

One set of theories traced fungo to its Latin roots as *fungos*, or spongy. Fungo bats were traditionally made with a lighter, softer wood than game bats, leading some to think of them as more like a fungus—also derived from *fungos*—than wood. That the knob at the end of a fungo bat resembled the head of a mushroom also seemed to fit. Moreover, the balls hit by fungo hitters tend to be hit pretty softly—one tends to think of a coach lifting a lazy fly ball, not driving one into the gap.

An alternative, albeit amorphous, Latin etymology focused on the verb *fungor*, to produce or to execute. After all, a fungo hitter is producing or executing a fly ball or a ground ball. There also could be ties to *fungible*—meaning something that can be replaced by something else—since a fungo bat can replace a regular one.

One advocate of fungo's Latin roots was Stephen Fulkerson, who presented his case in a letter to *New York Times Magazine* columnist William Safire. "Among rural folk, the term relates to 'fungus,' which lacks the character of being a real plant," wrote Fulkerson. "Instead of getting its roots in the ground as it should, it prefers to 'graft' off a log or an old stump; it has no green leaves, and as often as not it is poisonous. It has no flowers and lacks vigor or strength and so crumbles if one tries to pick it up."

Continued Fulkerson: "The notion is a pejorative one, somewhat as fungoes are a whole lot less than real baseball flies."

A second set of theories found the word's roots in Scotland. The Scots' most formidable advocate was Joan Hall, associate editor of the *Dictionary of Regional English*. Hall conceded that the Scots were better known for golf, but claimed fungo as well. The Scottish verb *fung* has two definitions. One is to pitch or toss, which is what fungo batters do themselves before hitting. The other is to whiz, which is what some fungo hitters make the ball do.

Wrote Hall (also to Safire): "I fung this your way, hoping it will put to rest those left-field speculations about tropical woods."

The German case was based on the verb *fangen*, to catch. Granted, to fungo is to hit the ball, not catch it. But someone has to catch it, too, and kids still sometimes play a game in which the object is to catch a certain number of balls, then take a turn at bat. As Chadwick noted, that game, too, was called fungo. Gerald Cohen, an etymologist who compiled a dictionary of 1913 baseball lingo, cited various nineteenth-century references to make the case that the game, not the hitting, may have been the original meaning of fungo.

As with all things baseball, there were plenty of efforts to locate the word's roots in America. Safire correspondent George Clahr suggested it was named after Dolph Fungeau, allegedly a coach for the New York Highlanders in the early years of the twentieth century. Clahr added that Dolph's wife, an Indian woman named Shahageen Singh, gave rise to the term "shag," since she so liked chasing down the balls her husband fungoed. Another Safire correspondent, Elsie Plotkin, made the only-slightly-more credible suggestion that it started with Van Lingle Mungo, a Dodger pitcher in the 1930s. According to Plotkin, Mungo so enjoyed hitting practice flies to the outfield that his teammates would ask whoever was batting to "Mungo me a few." Explained Plotkin: "One day a player (who may have been standing out in the Ebbets Field sun too long) somehow twisted his tongue and said, 'Hey, fungo me a mew.'"

Other Safire correspondents suggested acronyms, such as "For U No-Good Outfielders" or "FUN for Good Outfielders" (both from Clahr) or "For Use in Nurturing Green Outfielders" (from Miles Klein).

The most widespread theory combined the words "fun" and "go." Early versions of the game might have included a rhyme including the words "run" and "go." Or fielders might have chanted, "One goes, two goes, fun goes"—remember, they had to keep track of how many balls they caught because once they reached a certain number they got to bat. The fun-go/run-go theories made some sense, or at least were less convoluted than most. But they, too, lacked any definitive proof.

*   *   *

Fungo was by no means the only baseball term of uncertain origin. Others included "ace," generally tied to Asa Brainard, who went 56–1 for the Cincinnati Red Stockings in 1869. But lexicographer David Shulman noted that Brainard's nickname was Count, not Ace, and suggested that the term may have evolved from the ace in a deck of cards. Then there was "battery," designating the pitcher and catcher collectively. Most assumed it was borrowed from the military, though some thought it followed more directly from telegraphy, the pitcher being the transmitter, the catcher the receiver.

"Bullpen" has spawned almost as many theories as fungo. The most popular has to do with the Bull Durham tobacco signs that were prevalent on outfield fences around the turn of the century. Relief pitchers would often warm up under the signs. The problem with that theory was that the word was around before the signs. Baseball writer Lee Allen found the word used in the *Cincinnati Enquirer* as early as 1877, though to denote a place where unruly crowds, not relief pitchers, were penned in. Outside baseball, bullpen usually referred to a makeshift prison, which would support Allen's view. Another theory found the roots in bullfighting; reserve bulls, like pitchers, had to be kept somewhere until matadors or batters knock them out.

Then there's "fan." Dickson, following etymologists Barry Popik and Gerald Cohen, thought it came from fanatic. In 1896 Ted Sullivan traced the origin to 1883, when he managed the St. Louis Browns. According to Sullivan, he told Brown owner Chris von der Ahe that he didn't "propose to be advised by a lot of fanatics." Von der Ahe, a native German speaker, couldn't pronounce the word and so shortened it to fan.

There are various problems with this theory, as etymologist Peter Morris explained in a 2003 presentation to the Society for American Baseball Research. For one thing, the German for fanatic is *fanaticker*, so it's hard to see why von der Ahe would have trouble pronouncing the word. Moreover, at various times Sullivan gave two other versions of the word's origin. In his 1898 telling, it was Charles Comiskey (who managed the Browns after Sullivan) and not von der Ahe who abbreviated fanatic. And in 1891, in Sullivan's earliest version, it was Sullivan himself (in a conversation with Comiskey) who coined the term. This time it had nothing to do with fanatic. Instead, Sullivan was referring to people who talked lengthily and boringly about baseball. "The most likely scenario," Morris thought, "is that Sullivan thought to himself that the men were 'windbags,' asked himself what else just blows wind around, and settled upon a fan." Morris also noted that scorecards once had handles so that fans could use them to fan themselves.

Baseball, clearly, is an etymological jungle. The roots, even of common words, seem hopelessly twisted and tangled. Yet this is not cause for despair. Some usages have clearly grown out of more than a single root, adding not just confusion but also richness to the language of the game.

"If there is a bias lurking in this book," Dickson wrote in his *Dictionary*, "it is that words and phrases can have a motley assortment of etymologies that have acted corroboratively to give the term momentum and popularity. One of them may, in fact, be the original, but that does not mean the others did not have important influence."

In other words, bullpens may have existed before Bull Durham, but they might not have become so prevalent without the tobacco ads. And fungoes may have arisen without Van Lingle Mungo, but that doesn't mean that someone—and not just Elsie Plotkin—didn't have Mungo in mind when they saw someone playing fungo.

To investigate further:

Allen, Lee. *The Hot Stove League*. Kingston, N.Y.: Total Sports Illustrated Classics, 2000. Originally published in 1955 and still entertaining.

Coffin, Tristram. *The Old Ball Game*. New York: Herder & Herder, 1971. "Old ladies who have never been to the ballpark . . . men who think athletics begin and end with a pair of goalposts, still know and use a great deal of baseball-derived terminology," wrote folklorist Coffin.

"Perhaps other sports . . . have two strikes on them before they come to bat."

Dickson, Paul. *The New Dickson Baseball Dictionary.* San Diego: Harcourt, Brace & Company, 1999. Originally published in 1989 but with about 2,000 words added for the new edition, this is the rare reference book that is both definitive and fun. This chapter is much indebted to Dickson.

Ercolano, Patrick. *Fungoes, Floaters, and Fork Balls.* Englewood Cliffs, N.J.: Prentice-Hall, 1987. Useful but far surpassed by Dickson.

Morris, Peter. "What It Means to Be a Fan." Address to the 2003 Society for American Baseball Research convention.

Safire, William. *What's the Good Word?* New York: Times Books, 1982. A collection of Safire's "On Language" columns from the *New York Times Magazine,* along with letters from his readers.

24

Can Small-Market Teams Compete?

Imagine the Mariners with Randy Johnson on the mound, Alex Rodriguez at short, a healthy Ken Griffey Jr. in center. Imagine the A's with Jason Giambi still at first. This is Commissioner Bud Selig's utopia, an alternative universe in which, with revenues shared and luxury taxed, his own Milwaukee Brewers would have as good a chance to sign free agents and reach the World Series as the Yankees.

It's always been a bit disconcerting to watch Selig and his fellow small-market team owners, millionaires all, embrace baseball's version of socialism. Still, it's not just a few owners complaining about rich teams taking their pick of the best players. By signing Japan's Hideki Matsui and Cuba's José Contreras, Yankee principal owner George Steinbrenner signaled he considered the whole world to be part of the Yankee farm system. Well before that, plenty of fans and writers and economists worried that teams from smaller markets could no longer hold on to their best players, let alone sign others' free agents. Even Rudy Giuliani must occasionally have felt, or at least winced, for fans of the Tigers or Royals or other teams doomed to an unending stretch of "rebuilding" years.

In 1999, Selig appointed a blue-ribbon panel to study the problem. Its members—former senator George Mitchell, Yale president Richard Levin, columnist George Will, and former Federal Reserve chairman Paul Volcker—concluded that the game was indeed in dire straits. "The growing gap between the 'have' and the 'have not' clubs," the 2000 report read, "is a serious and imminent threat to the popularity, health, stability, and growth of the game."

A year later, testifying before the Senate, Selig said the situation had worsened since the panel's report. In 2001, he said, baseball teams lost $519 million. Twenty-five of thirty teams lost money.

How could these teams, whose very survival was in doubt, hope to compete with the Yankees?

Money, of course, had always mattered, even before Harry Frazee pocketed $100,000 for shipping Babe Ruth to New York. In the 1950s, the Yankees routinely and notoriously acquired the best Kansas City had to offer, including Roger Maris, Clete Boyer, Ryne Duren, and Ralph Terry. In the midst of pennant races, the Yankees grabbed Johnny Mize in 1949, Johnny Sain in 1951, Enos Slaughter in 1954. Other rich teams did the same. In 1947, for example, the Frazee-less Red Sox were accused of trying to buy the pennant when they paid the St. Louis Browns $400,000 for pitchers Jack Kramer and Ellis Kinder and shortstop Vern Stephens.

Even Branch Rickey, whose farm system was renowned for growing St. Louis Cardinals instead of buying them, needed money to buy minor league teams. And when the Cardinals, who had to share a comparatively small market with the Browns, were strapped for cash, Rickey was willing to sell off the products of his farm system.

None of this changed when Catfish Hunter became a free agent in 1974. Free agency did not mean that rich teams would suddenly be able to buy the best players on the rosters of their poorer rivals. It merely meant that to buy the players they wanted, rich teams would have to pay the players rather than their owners. Instead of paying A's owner Charley Finley, Steinbrenner paid Hunter himself.

In fact, contrary to the owners' claims at the time, free agency brought with it an *increase* in competitive balance. In the 1980s, the first full decade without the reserve clause, St. Louis won three pennants, Kansas City and Oakland two, Minnesota and Milwaukee one. All small-market teams. The Yankees, after 1981, were nowhere to be found. It would be another fifteen years before they made it back to the World Series, a longer stretch even than their post-1964 collapse. Sure, Steinbrenner continued to spend his money, but it was on the likes of Steve Kemp and Ken Griffey Sr. and Omar Moreno, players well past their prime. "The 1984 Yankees had assembled an all-star line-up," wrote historian Henry Fetter, "but it was that of 1979."

If anyone still doubted that baseball was more balanced than ever, the 1991 season drove home the point. The Minnesota Twins met the Atlanta Braves in the World Series. In 1990, both teams had finished last in their divisions. The have-nots had become the haves in a single year.

Other measures proved much the same thing. Economist Andrew Zimbalist calculated standard deviation of win percentage from 1903 into the mid-1990s. The deviation, if you insist on doing it yourself, is equal to the square root of the difference between each team's win percentage and the average win percentage squared, divided by the number of teams. Zimbalist found a steady improvement in competitive balance. Statistician and historian Bill James noted that in the 1970s, twenty divisional champions successfully defended their titles; in the 1980s, only three did so.

Wrote James: "The 1980s . . . were by far the most competitive years in baseball history up to that point, and also the decade in which the small-city markets enjoyed their most success ever."

There were varying explanations. Zimbalist argued that free agency made it too expensive to hold together a dynasty, and easier to improve a team quickly. James noted that lots of teams, not just the richest ones, turned out to be able to pay the players' new going rates. Lots of teams were making lots of money, as attendance steadily rose and television revenue jumped almost fourteenfold between 1975 and 1991.

"What we didn't realize is that major league teams in 1975 had the potential to earn so much money that the salaries they paid to players at that time were relatively trivial," James wrote in his 1992 *Baseball Abstract*. "We thought . . . that teams in small markets would lose their best players because they couldn't afford to double their salaries, when in fact they could. They could afford to double them, and triple them, and quadruple them and keep going."

In the mid-1990s, all that changed. The Yankees were back, making the playoffs every year from 1995 to 2003, and winning four World Series and six American League championships. In 2003 the *Onion*, a satirical newspaper, ran this headline: "Yankees ensure pennant by signing every player in baseball."

Again, a range of statistical measures, from standard deviations to championship concentrations, confirmed the trend. Increasingly, the teams playing in the postseason were big-market teams.

What changed?

This time the rich really did get richer, and the poor poorer. Big-city teams continued to rake in television money, while revenues from baseball's national television contract—on which the smaller-market teams depended—dropped (by more than 60 percent in 1994). In 1989, the difference in revenues between the richest and the poorest teams was about $30 million; by 2001, it was more than $200 million. Meanwhile, salaries continued to soar.

"The error of the 1970s was that we thought that the anti-competitive aspects of free agency would arrive immediately," wrote James. "The error of the 1980s was that we thought that since the anti-competitive aspects of free agency had not arrived immediately, they were not going to arrive at all."

"Perhaps more troubling than the increase in the statistical measure of unequal performance," wrote Zimbalist, "is the clear evidence that the relationship between team performance and team payroll has grown stronger."

There were, of course, exceptions. The Rangers, Orioles, Dodgers, and Mets all spent fortunes to no avail. The Twins and A's, with comparatively tiny payrolls, were consistent winners. When Michael Lewis's *Moneyball* became a best-seller in 2003, A's general manager Billy Beane became the poster child for low-budget success. Lewis calculated that the A's spent about $500,000 per win, the Twins $675,000. The Orioles and the Rangers spent nearly $3 million for each game won.

"At the bottom of the Oakland experiment was a willingness to rethink baseball: how it is managed, how it is played, who is best suited to play it, and why," Lewis wrote. "In what amounted to a systematic scientific investigation of their sport, the Oakland front office had reexamined everything from the market price of foot speed to the inherent difference between the average major league player and the superior Triple-A one. That's how they found their bargains."

Beane rejected his scouts' traditional measures of player potential, along with many of the stats other general managers prized. Drawing on the work of James and others, he decided, for example, that saves were vastly overrated and walks vastly underrated. At one point, the A's front office played with a system that replaced all traditional batting statistics with a matrix of points on the diamond. Instead of a double, the system merely recorded that a ball hit with a certain force landed at a certain point. Then you checked how often such a hit went for an out or a hit, and what percentage of a run it meant for the team. It made no difference whether, in any particular case, that hit had been caught by the center fielder or fallen for a double. This was, as Lewis put it, less a hit than a Platonic idea of a hit. Yet even Beane's less radical statistics led the A's to value players very differently than other teams did.

"We don't get the guys who are perfect," Beane aide Paul DePodesta explained to Lewis. "There has to be something wrong with them for them to get to us."

Ironically, Beane himself had been exactly the kind of player he later rejected as a general manager. "Billy never looked bad, even when he struggled," said Met scout Roger Jongewaard, who signed him. In the minors, playing in an outfield with Lenny Dykstra and Darryl Strawberry, Beane was considered the one with the most promise. But he could never hit consistently, and at the end of 1989 his career batting average with the Twins and A's was .219. Beane seemed nevertheless likely to hold on to a job as the A's fifth outfielder. To the shock of A's general manager Sandy Alderson, he asked for a front office job instead.

Using Beane's unorthodox methods, the A's made the playoffs every year from 2000 to 2003, each time taking their opponents to a deciding game. Even when they lost Giambi to the Yankees ("Goliath, dissatisfied with his size advantage, has bought David's sling," wrote Lewis), the A's replaced him with Scott Hatteberg, a cast-off Red Sox catcher with a surprisingly high on-base average. And went right on winning.

Beane's methods came under fire each October, when the A's consistently fell short. "With just enough to prove something—five games—the real teams stand up and the second-raters go home," wrote the *San Francisco Chronicle* in 2003 after the A's lost their ninth straight potential series-ending game and were eliminated by the Red Sox (who, incidentally, had embraced a philosophy similar to Beane's and had hired none other than Bill James as "senior baseball operations adviser"). Others argued that Beane's success had nothing to do with his statistical analysis and instead depended on his trio of star starters, Barry Zito and Tim Hudson and Mark Mulder.

Beane angrily responded to critics of the A's postseason failures. "I'll tell you one thing, if you want to give me $50 million more, I'll promise you we won't blow the 2–0 lead," he said.

Maybe so. But Beane would have seemed less churlish if he'd also explained that five games weren't a statistically valid sample for judging his statistical system. Lewis offered a better defense of the A's collapse. "Over a long season the luck evens out, and the skill shines through," he wrote. "But in a series of three out of five, or even four out of seven, anything can happen. Baseball science may still give a team a slight edge, but that edge is overwhelmed by chance."

The A's success over the long run demonstrated—as did the Yankees' failures between 1982 and 1995—that good management (or bad) mattered at least as much as money. But it did *not* mean that money didn't matter. Beane surely could have used another $50 million; Scott Hatteberg's walks, however undervalued, were not nearly as useful as Jason Giambi's walks and home runs. And the A's were clearly the exception that proved the rule, or at least the rule from 1995 on: the teams that made it to the postseason were increasingly the teams with the highest revenues and payrolls.

To Selig, the solutions were obvious: cut payroll and other costs (by having cities, not teams, pay for new stadiums) and share revenues (through a luxury tax on big-spending teams or by directly passing money from richer to poorer teams). Given Selig's 2001 figure of $519 million in losses, it would be hard to argue with any of this. But that figure did not withstand close scrutiny.

Most teams, being privately held, did not have to make their finances public. But a few were public, or chose to release financial information to attract investors or buyers. This allowed economists such as Zimbalist to compare some teams' figures with what Selig provided Congress. There were numerous discrepancies. In 1998, for example, the Indians declared revenues of $140 million for 1997 and $145 million for 1998. That was $45 million less than Selig reported to Congress.

The White Sox, according to Selig, made $30 million from local television, radio, and cable, while the Cubs earned $24 million. Yet the Cubs had much higher ratings, and WGN carried their games nationwide. Why, then, did WGN pay so little to televise Cub games? Because WGN and the Cubs were both owned by the Tribune Corporation, which chose to inflate revenues at the former at the expense of the latter. This allowed the Cubs to claim poverty when it came time to share revenues with poorer teams or to negotiate contracts with players or government agencies. Other owners were also delighted to sacrifice baseball profits for the sake of other companies that did business with the team (and that happened to have the same owner as the team).

In 2002, Forbes estimated a $75 million profit for the sport, compared to the $232 million loss Selig claimed. Perhaps the truest indication that Selig was grossly undervaluing the value of major league teams was what it cost to buy one. In 2001, the Red Sox went for more than $700 million. This wasn't even the highest bid for a team that, according to Selig, was losing money.

"Fans say baseball will never see another .400 average," *Washington Post* columnist Tom Boswell wrote in 2002. "When it comes to telling a straight story, that's what Selig bats every year."

Clearly, Selig exaggerated the financial plight of the sport in an effort to wring concessions from players and municipalities. There is no need, as Selig once suggested, to eliminate two teams. There is plenty of money to go around. But it wouldn't hurt for more of that money to actually go around, and some degree of revenue sharing and luxury taxes would reverse the trend toward competitive imbalance. This was what the owners and players agreed to in 2002, and if the trend continues, the system may need further tweaking. An international draft also would help by ensuring that foreign players didn't all end up on the rosters of the Yankees and other rich teams.

Such moderate proposals would give poorer teams a better chance. To be sure, they would not have quite the same chance as the Yankees, but fairness has its limits, and even its drawbacks. Yankee dynasties, after all, are a great part of baseball history. To root for—or against—the Yankees is one of a fan's greatest pleasures. There's a reason why television ratings plummet when the Royals play the Twins.

"There is such a thing as too much competitive balance," James wrote. "If all the teams are about the same, if every team becomes as good as the next one, a sport becomes formless and indistinct, a shapeless lump of games."

There will always be favorites and always be underdogs, and that's part of the game's appeal. The goal ought not to be to level the field completely, merely to ensure that, as Yogi Berra put it, "it ain't over until it's over."

Or, as Earl Weaver said after the Mets upset his Orioles in 1969, "You can't sit on a lead and run a few plays into the line and just kill the clock. You've got to throw the ball over the goddamn plate and give the other man his chance. That's why baseball is the greatest game of all."

To investigate further:

Costas, Bob. *Fair Ball*. New York: Broadway Books, 2000. A sensible and informed perspective on revenue sharing, wild cards, designated hitters, and other controversies.

Fetter, Henry. *Taking on the Yankees*. New York: W. W. Norton, 2003. An insightful study of how management, more than money, has meant the difference for the Yankees and three of their rivals: the New York Giants, the St. Louis Cardinals, and the Brooklyn Dodgers.

James, Bill. *The New Bill James Historical Baseball Abstract*. New York: Free Press, 2001. Don't skip the annual *Abstracts* just because you've got the *Historical* one. Not only do the originals include entirely different material, but also they let you trace the evolution of James's thinking.

Lewis, Michael. *Moneyball*. New York: W. W. Norton, 2003. It's tremendous fun to watch Beane wheel and deal with general managers who don't really buy his methods but who also don't want to be embarrassed by trading him someone who will somehow help the A's win. The book also raises a serious question: "if gross miscalculations of a person's value could occur on a baseball field, before a live audience of thirty thousand, and a television audience of millions more, what did that say about the measurement of performance in other lines of work?"

Miller, Marvin. *A Whole Different Ball Game*. New York: Carol, 1991. How the players won their freedom, by the man who, as executive director of their union, showed them the way.

Quirk, James, and Rodney Fort. *Hard Ball*. Princeton, N.J.: Princeton Univesity Press, 1999. Two economists look at professional sports and conclude that its problems can be solved by eliminating the leagues' monopoly power. The authors' 1992 *Pay Dirt* is also useful, though more technical and dated.

Zimbalist, Andrew. *May the Best Team Win*. Washington, D.C.: Brookings Institution Press, 2003. Like Quirk and Fort, Zimbalist believes the best way to solve most of baseball's economic problems would be to lift its antitrust exemption, but he recognizes that's unlikely so he also offers many other suggestions, such as an international draft.

25

Does Clutch Hitting Exist?

Reggie Jackson became Mr. October on October 18, 1977. Even during batting practice, before game six of the World Series between the Yankees and the Dodgers, Jackson knew it was his day.

"I hit maybe forty balls during my time in the cage," he remembered. "I must have hit twenty into the seats. Upper deck. Bullpen. Into the black in center. Didn't matter. The baseball looked like a volleyball to me."

Jackson walked his first time up. Then, with the Dodgers leading 3–2 and Thurman Munson on base, he faced Burt Hooton. "Hooton got it up, but not in far enough," Reggie later wrote. "I got it."

The next Dodger pitcher was Elias Sosa. "Sosa . . . threw me a fastball right down Broadway. I call them mattress pitches because if you're feeling right you can lay all over 'em."

Finally, Charlie Hough. "Hough threw me a knuckler. Didn't knuckle. I crushed it nearly 500 feet."

The Yankees won the game 8–4, the Series 4–2. Jackson's three homers on three consecutive swings—four, if you count his homer in his final at-bat in game five—solidified his reputation as the man you wanted at the plate when the season was on the line. Like Tommy Henrich before him and Derek Jeter after, he was a player who rose to the occasion, who came through in the clutch.

Roger Angell described it this way: "Late in a close big game—and with the deep, baying cries from the stands rolling across the field: 'Reg-gie! Reg-gie!'—he strides to the plate and taps it with his bat and settles his batting helmet and gets his feet right and turns his glittery regard toward the pitcher, and we suddenly know that it is a different hitter we are watching now, and a different man. Get ready, everybody—it's show time."

Forgotten for the moment was the season-long feud with Thurman Munson, whose followers on the team considered him a far better clutch hitter than Jackson and who were especially offended by Jackson's assertion, according to *Sport* magazine (though Jackson claimed he was misquoted) that he was the Yankees' "straw that stirs the drink" and that Munson "can only stir it bad." After October 18, even Munson was forgiving: "Anybody who can produce for my team that way," he said, "can be a teammate of mine anytime."

Yet put aside the warm feelings—as those Yankee teams could be counted on to do—and it was not so clear that Jackson was better in the clutch than Munson. Or, for that matter, that Henrich and Jeter deserved their reputations, which seemed to be based on fond memories as much as statistical evidence. What was needed, clearly, was a stat that measured clutch hitting. And as statisticians attempted to create one, many decided that the mystery was not just who was best in the clutch but whether such a thing as clutch hitting existed at all.

The stat most commonly used to measure clutch hitting was the run batted in. RBIs have been counted since 1879, and their deficiencies have been apparent about as long. Players on good-hitting teams obviously had more opportunities to knock in runs, as did those who batted third or fourth or fifth in the lineup. "The RBI total is not a measure of intestinal fortitude any more than is the runs scored total," wrote John Thorn and Pete Palmer in *The Hidden Game of Baseball*. "It is a measure of fortuity, not of clutch ability."

The game-winning RBI had the same flaw: it was situation-dependent. Worse, the GWRBI counted only the run that put your team ahead for good, which might just as easily come on a groundout in the first as a home run in the ninth. Indeed, a clutch hit in the top of the ninth that put your team ahead would count for nothing if the other team came back to win the game in the bottom of the ninth. Another RBI variant—RBI ratio—would track not just runners batted in but runners left on base, thus evening the field for leadoff hitters and Kansas City Royals. Back in 1918, the American League tracked RBI opportunities, but abandoned it after three weeks as too much trouble. More recently, *Total Baseball* presented clutch hitting index, which compared actual RBIs to the number expected, based on such factors as a batter's position in the lineup and who batted before him. This was, the encyclopedia's editors admitted, at best a rough measure.

Thorn and Palmer thought the best approach was one tried by Eldon and Harlan Mills in the late 1960s. By assigning point values to different situations, these brothers tried to give more weight to more important at-bats. They considered everything from the number of outs and bases occupied to whether it was the top or the bottom of the inning, as well, of course, as what inning it was. From this, they calculated player win averages, a stat that at least evened the field. For 1969, the only year for which the Mills brothers published their results, the league leaders in PWA were Willie McCovey and Mike Epstein.

Eight years later, statistician Richard Cramer took the Mills's PWAs, which he agreed was the best measure of clutch hitting, and compared them to players' other stats, specifically their on-base average plus slugging percentage, as well as a stat called batter win average, which Cramer himself devised. Neither on-base average nor slugging average nor BWA had anything to do with clutch hitting. Yet the leaders in those stats also tended to have the top PWAs. From this Cramer concluded that the players PWA identified as clutch hitters were merely good hitters who over the course of the season excelled both in and out of the clutch. In other words, there was no such thing as a clutch hitter.

Cramer also noted that the players whose PWAs were higher than their BWAs in 1969 did not repeat the feat the next year. In fact, some of the supposedly best clutch hitters of 1969 were among the worst in 1970, and vice versa. He interpreted this as further evidence that the performances others had attributed to clutch hitting were more likely a matter of luck.

"So fades a legend," Cramer wrote, "but after all, what was really meant when someone was called a 'clutch hitter'? Was he really a batter who didn't fold under pressure—or was he a lazy batter who bothered to try his hardest only when the game was on the line?"

In the 1980s, Bill James got similar results with a stat he called victory important RBIs. Like Cramer's PWA, the VIRBI gave more weight to RBIs in close games than runaway wins, and gave no credit at all for RBIs in losses. This was, James admitted, "an imperfect measure," but it was a lot simpler than PWA and had some of the same merits as the GWRBI without being quite as stingy about credit. James tracked the Milwaukee Brewers from 1979 to 1983 and found little difference in the importance of the runs driven in by different players. The players who drove in most of the big runs were the same players who led the team in RBIs.

James concluded that though it was impossible to prove clutch hitters didn't exist, there was no proof they did. "Can you prove that dodo birds are extinct?" he asked. "We can't prove it. The subject requires an honest search, and I'll keep looking." Palmer and Thorn were less agnostic; they called the clutch hitter an "optical illusion," much like the curveball was once thought to be.

The debate over clutch hitting revealed a divide between old-time baseball analysts and the new breed of statisticians. For decades, scouts and managers had measured not just bat speed but also intangibles such as a batter's character, including his ability to perform under pressure. Not surprisingly, many of the old-timers balked at the idea that they were measuring something that didn't exist. "Stats give you an indication of what guys can and can't do," Angel general manager Bill Stoneman said after his team won the 2002 World Series. "But you've still got to play the game on the field."

Still, the divide is not nearly as great as it seemed during the 1980s and early 1990s. More and more teams, noting the success of stats-oriented general managers such as Sandy Alderson and Billy Beane of the A's, have incorporated the new stats into their thinking and the statisticians into their organizations. And statisticians were by no means always a united front. At the Elias Sports Bureau, statisticians assailed Cramer on various grounds.

For starters, Elias didn't buy the idea of degrees of pressure. A true clutch situation, Elias argued, had to take place in the seventh inning or later with the batter's team tied or trailing by three runs or less (or four if the bases were loaded). Sure, other situations mattered, too. But only when the game was clearly on the line could you clearly gauge a batter's clutch ability. Elias dismissed complex new stats and stuck to batting averages: if a player hit well in these late-inning pressure situations, he was a clutch hitter; if he didn't, he wasn't. And, Elias reported, some players definitely hit for significantly higher averages in these situations than in nonpressure situations.

For 1984, the year Elias first studied, the best clutch hitter was Bill Buckner, who hit .272 overall but .403 in pressure situations. The worst was Harold Baines, with an overall average of .304 compared to only .194 in the clutch. So, according to Elias, clutch hitters definitely existed: "The number of players with substantial differences does, in fact, exceed the expected level, enough so to warrant the conclusion that for a given season, some players respond tremendously to pressure while others repeatedly fail in clutch situations."

Elias also took issue with Cramer's contention that clutch hitters didn't sustain their performances over many seasons. The Elias method showed many (though by no means all) of the same leaders in 1983 and 1984. A 1987 update again found some continuity among the best and the worst.

But a 2004 *Sports Illustrated* study of players who had debuted in the previous thirty years found that "while significant improvement in pressure situations was common for one season, the variations became much smaller over a career." The best clutch hitter, based on a minimum of 400 late-inning pressure-situation at-bats, was Tony Gwynn, with a clutch average of .358

compared to .335 overall. He was followed by Jason Kendall at
.328, Magglio Ordoñez at .325, Edgar Martinez at .324, and
Nomar Garciaparra at .320. For none of these hitters was the
difference between the clutch and overall average greater than
.028, and Garciaparra's overall average was actually .003 higher
than his clutch one. These were not so much clutch hitters as
good hitters who also hit in the clutch.

The 1987 Elias study, though arguing for the existence of
clutch hitters, inadvertently provided a case study of one who
was overrated: Reggie Jackson. Get this: his average when it mattered most was .170, compared to .249 overall. The .170 was
bad enough. But the .079 differential between that and his .249
made him, for the three years Elias studied, the sixth-*worst*
clutch hitter in the majors.

Does that mean that, back in October 1977, Jackson was just
lucky? Well, maybe a bit. By his own descriptions, Hooton's
pitch was up, Sosa's was right down the middle, and Hough's
was a knuckler that didn't knuckle. But there was obviously
more at work here than luck. Jackson was, as he could tell in
batting practice, hot. "When you start to hit the ball well, when
you're in one of those streaks where you just want the pitcher to
hurry up and throw the damn ball, you wonder how you ever
even spelled s-l-u-m-p," he wrote. Whether or not clutch hitters
exist, streak hitters surely do—and Jackson was one of the greatest streak hitters of all time.

To investigate further:

Angell, Roger. *Game Time*. New York: Harcourt, 2003. The master's
own all-time favorites.

Jackson, Reggie, with Mike Lupica. *Reggie*. New York: Villard Books,
1984. Before he died, the former Indian, Brown, and White Sox owner
Bill Veeck was asked what he'd like as one last perfect day in baseball.
"I'd like to see Reggie Jackson have one more great game in a World
Series," Veeck answered.

James, Bill. The 1984 *Bill James Baseball Abstract*. New York: Ballantine, 1984. See also the 1982, 1983, and 1986 editions.

Munson, Thurman, with Martin Appel. *Thurman Munson*. New York: Coward, McCann, & Geoghegan, 1979. He wasn't charming, but if clutch hitters ever existed, he was one of them.

Siwoff, Seymour, Steve Hirdt, and Peter Hirdt. *The 1985 Elias Baseball Analyst*. New York: Collier Books, 1985. See also the 1987 and 1988 editions.

Thorn, John, Phil Birnbaum, and Bill Deane. *Total Baseball*. Toronto, Ont.: SportClassic, 2004. What started as a collection of alternative statistics became the official major league baseball encyclopedia.

Thorn, John, and Pete Palmer. *The Hidden Game of Baseball*. Garden City, N.Y.: Doubleday, 1984. Useful and provocative.

26

Were Yesterday's Players Better?

A story that has been told in many versions has a fan (or a reporter), not too long before Ty Cobb's death, asking an old-timer (sometimes Cobb himself, sometimes pitcher-turned-outfielder Lefty O'Doul) what Cobb would have hit if he'd played then. "About .300," Cobb replied. The fan expressed surprise that it wasn't higher, given Cobb's lifetime average of .367.

"Well," Cobb explained, "you have to remember that I'm almost seventy years old."

In a 1952 article in *Life*, Cobb sneered at DiMaggio and Williams and other stars of the day. They couldn't have "hit the top" in his time, they "limped along on one cylinder," unable to do anything but swing for the fences, they were a "fragile lot" who couldn't have lasted in the days when men battled "to their last breath." In a moment of generosity, Cobb singled out Stan Musial and Phil Rizzuto as throwbacks, but the title of his article made clear his point: "They Don't Play Baseball Anymore."

As always, Cobb was more strident than most, but certainly not alone in bemoaning the passing of the good old days. In 1983, Met manager George Bamberger argued that expansion had diluted the quality of play. "A lot of the kids today wouldn't have made my club in the Pacific Coast League," he said. "Many of them wouldn't have made Double A." Even Hank Aaron, whose chase of Ruth's home run record ought to have instilled in him an appreciation for the present as well as the past, complained that the younger generation, though capable of occasional great years, couldn't perform as consistently over time as he and Willie Mays.

Plenty of commentators have noted that feats once common now seem virtually superhuman. No one has hit .400 since 1941, though eight players topped .410 in the fifty years before then, and Rogers Hornsby *averaged* over .400 for five years. No one has won 30 games since 1968, though pitchers once did so regularly, and old Hoss Radbourn won 59 in 1884.

Some of this is sheer nostalgia and blatantly unfair to modern players. DiMaggio's hit streak and Williams's .406 season were gigantic achievements, however little Cobb thought of them; so were the home run records of Aaron and Bonds, even if Aaron thought his was more difficult than Bonds's. If Cobb's batting records lasted longer than others, that was because, starting in the 1920s, most of the game's best hitters hit for power, often at the expense of average. Besides, Cobb's records eventually did fall, as Maury Wills and Rickey Henderson and Pete Rose outran and outscored and outhit him.

Some seemingly superhuman feats resulted from different conventions or rules. That players no longer regularly climb into the stands to punch out a spectator or stop along the basepaths to spike an infielder, à la Cobb, can be seen as a gain for sportsmanship rather than a loss of manliness. That pitchers no longer throw back-to-back complete games proves nothing about their grit; when Radbourn won 59 in 1884, many pitchers still threw underhand, and the pitcher was still only 50 feet from the plate.

Moreover, it just doesn't make sense to assume that today's players, however pampered, are inferior athletes to those of the past. True, baseball today may lose some top athletes to basketball or football. True, there are more major league teams. But the talent pool has been greatly expanded by the influx of blacks and Latinos and the overall population growth since Cobb's time. Along with improved diet and training, this means that those who make it to the majors are stronger and faster than ever. As Mickey Mantle said, after hearing once too often that his achievements were the result of a lively ball, "Maybe the players are livelier now."

The improvements are easy to see in track and field—just look at the shorter times or longer distances. In baseball, it's trickier. Batters and pitchers have presumably both improved, so their advances have canceled each other out, at least statistically. The challenge, then, is to find a way to use such statistics to compare players from different eras. Or to put it another way: to figure out what Ty Cobb would have hit had he played today.

One approach was to "normalize" statistics by figuring out how much better or worse a player was than the league average. Thus Bill Terry's league-leading .401 in 1930 and Carl Yastrzemski's league-leading .301 in 1968 could be seen as about equal, since the league average in 1930 was .312, compared to .238 in 1968. Judging by their "relative" batting averages, Terry was a mere 2 percentage points better than Yaz.

Baseball researchers David Shoebotham and Merritt Clifton pioneered the relativist approach in the early 1970s, and in 1984 baseball writer John Thorn and statistician Pete Palmer compiled new leader lists based on this work. Cobb fared very well. His relative batting average in 1912 was the highest of all time, and he made the top twenty in seven other seasons. His lifetime relative batting average also was number one. Other old-timers also excelled, with Nap Lajoie, Tris Speaker, Rogers Hornsby, and Cobb holding the nine best single-season relative batting averages. You had to wait for number ten to get to Rod Carew's 1977 season.

Did this prove the hitters of Cobb's day were, as Cobb claimed, superior? Not really. For one thing, they rarely tried to hit homers. Presumably modern sluggers could raise their averages if they chose to slash and slap at balls instead of swinging for the fences. For another, the league leaders of Cobb's time had averages significantly higher than the league average. Since then, the gap between the top and average players has steadily narrowed. This would seem to indicate that even if Cobb and Lajoie and Speaker and Hornsby were indeed among the best ever, the average player of their time was not nearly as good as the average player today.

This is exactly what you'd expect, given the larger talent pool, better training, and the evolution of the game. As evolutionary theorist Stephen Jay Gould put it in 1986, "Systems equilibrate as they improve." Or as baseball fan Gould explained it: "Baseball was feeling its way during the early days of major league play. . . . In an era of such experiment and indifference, truly great players could take advantage in ways foreclosed ever since. 'Wee Willie' Keeler could 'hit 'em where they ain't' (and bat .432 in 1897) because fielders didn't yet know where they should be."

In contrast, Gould pointed to the plight of Wade Boggs and other modern stars. "Every pitch is charted, every hit mapped to the nearest square inch," he wrote. "Boggs and Keeler probably stood in the same place, just a few inches from the right wall of human limits, but average play has so crept up on Boggs that he lacks the space for taking advantage of suboptimality in others. All these improvements must rob great batters of ten or twenty hits a year—more than enough to convert our modern best into .400 hitters."

Clifton tried to incorporate the improvement of average players into relative batting averages. He normalized averages not just to the league average, but also to the league-leading figure. This brought more modern players to the top, with Ted Williams first and Rod Carew second. Baseball researcher Wade Larkin tried a more sophisticated approach, measuring the standard deviation of batting average from the norm. Williams, Babe Ruth, and Mickey Mantle led his list of lifetime leaders, with Cobb dropping to number seven.

Researcher Richard Cramer tried another approach, comparing the batting averages of the same player in different seasons. He couldn't compare players' seasons twenty years apart, since few players lasted that long. But he could compare these seasons indirectly by comparing, for example, performances in 1950 to

1955, and in 1955 to 1960. Cramer concluded that average batting skill rose by 120 points between 1876 and 1979. By this system, if Cobb had played in the National League of 1976, his lifetime average would have been an unremarkable .289. Researcher Dallas Adams found a comparable trend in pitching and fielding statistics.

But Adams also thought that this method was unfair to Cobb and other stars of his day. Just because average players had improved didn't mean the top players had deteriorated; in fact, Adams argued, it was more likely that the best players of the past would have matched up well against their successors. Track and field again provided a useful analogy: the times and distances of world record holders have certainly improved, but not nearly as much as those of the rest of the field. Besides, Adams added, if Cobb had played today, he might very well have adjusted his game accordingly. Adams guessed Cobb would have hit .320 to .325—well below his lifetime .367, but a lot better than .289.

"How can we make fair comparison since we gaze backward through the rose-colored lenses of our most powerful myth—the idea of a former golden age?" asked Gould. "How can we know whether past deeds matched or exceeded current prowess? In particular, was Moses right in his early pronouncement (Genesis 6:4): 'There were giants in the earth in those days'?"

Gould's answer mirrored that of Adams: the skills of average players have steadily increased, while those at the top have remained about the same. The giants of the past only seemed so large, since those around them were so small. This seems a glum conclusion, Gould admitted, "almost cosmically depressing in its paradox—that general improvement clips the wings of true greatness," that "no one soars above the commonplace anymore," that "heroes are extinct." In baseball, as in history, there was, alas, no golden age.

Gould believed that the best way to compare players from different eras was the standard deviation method, first used by Clifton and updated in 2000 by researchers Robert Watts and

Terry Bahill. The Gould and Watts-Bahill lists contained players from a variety of eras, thus reinforcing the case that the immortals of the past were no better (or worse) than today's mortal stars.

Watts and Bahill ranked Lajoie's 1901 season first, followed by Hornsby in 1924, Boggs in 1985, Brett in 1980, Carew in 1977, Cobb in 1910, and Williams in 1941. Cobb would surely not have been satisfied to be sixth-best. But he might have found some satisfaction in the company of the other leaders who, however mortal, were surely remarkable. Cobb also might have appreciated the Watts-Bahill finding that he was remarkably consistent in his achievements. In a twenty-three-year career, Cobb only once finished less than 2.6 standard deviations above his league average.

As for the rest of us, Gould offered this consolation: "Do not lament the loss of the literally outstanding performance (largely a figment, in any case, of failing among the ordinary, not a mark of greater prowess among the best). Celebrate instead the immense improvement of average play."

There never was a golden age. But as Thorn and Palmer put it, "The good old days are now."

To investigate further:

Allen, Lee. *The Hot Stove League*. Kingston, N.Y.: Total Sports Publishing, 2000. Originally published in 1955, this includes one of the earliest (and still sensible) answers to Cobb's 1952 article.

Gould, Stephen Jay. *Triumph and Tragedy in Mudville*. New York: W. W. Norton, 2003. Gould uses baseball, specifically the demise of the .400 hitter, to address the general question of how to compare past and present.

James, Bill. *The Baseball Book 1992*. New York: Villard, 1992. Even James couldn't always predict the future. One of his methods for comparing past and present was to match up comparable players from different eras. Comparing Barry Bonds in 1991 to Bobby Bonds at the same stage of his career, James concluded, "Barry doesn't quite match the numbers his father put up at the same age."

Thorn, John, and Pete Palmer. *The Hidden Game of Baseball*. Garden City, N.Y.: Doubleday, 1984. Not only did Thorn and Palmer provide plenty of new ideas of their own, but they also provided excellent summaries of more obscure works on baseball statistics, such as those of Clifton and Cramer and Adams.

Watts, Robert, and Terry Bahill. *Keep Your Eye on the Ball*. New York: W. H. Freeman, 2000. The science of baseball.

Wright, Craig, and Tom House. *The Diamond Appraised*. New York: Simon & Schuster, 1989. The book sets Wright's sophisticated statistical analysis against House's on-the-field experience as a pitcher and coach. It doesn't always work—sometimes they just don't connect, and House has much less to say than Wright. But their debate about Pete Rose's chase of Ty Cobb's all-time hit record is interesting. Wright argues, convincingly, that Rose caught Cobb by keeping himself in the lineup well beyond his productive years and to the detriment of his team.

Do Managers Matter?

I t ain't like football," Yankee manager Yogi Berra explained to
reporters who wanted to know what he planned to do differently after the Yankees lost the first game of the 1964 World
Series. "You can't make up no trick plays."

Indeed, a case can be made that a manager doesn't make all
that much of a difference. He doesn't generally find the talent;
that's up to the general manager or scouts or sometimes, especially in the case of expensive free agents, the owner. He doesn't
teach fundamentals; that's up to his coaches or the minor league
managers. And, as Berra pointed out, he can't call any play that
hasn't been called countless times before.

"Sometimes it is hard to figure out exactly what a baseball
manager does that's tougher than . . . handing out a room key,"
wrote *Washington Post* sportswriter Thomas Boswell. "Sometimes
it seems the manager's function is to make himself available to
be second-guessed, then, ultimately, fired."

When he's fired, he's often just a scapegoat, one man who's a
lot easier to get rid of than an entire roster. Or as Rocky Bridges,
manager of the San Jose Bees, once told *Sports Illustrated* writer
Gilbert Rogin: "I managed good, but boy did they play bad."

So how much does a manager actually contribute to the success or failure of his team? "This is one of the great questions of
our time, on a par with what is the meaning of life and why do

birds fly?" wrote Jim Bouton, whose relationship with his own manager, the Seattle Pilots' Joe Schultz, was marred by the fact that Schultz didn't think much of Bouton's knuckleball. "The only difference is that the last two are easier to answer."

When it comes to strategy, Red and Tiger manager Sparky Anderson agreed with Berra. "Everything's been tried," Anderson wrote. "Strategy is fine and we should all know how to run a game. But strategy is dictated not by the manager but by the kind of personnel he has."

Pinch-hit? Go to the bullpen? Send the runner? Any serious fan, let alone a qualified manager, can list the pros and cons in any given situation.

New York Times sportswriter Leonard Koppett argued that a manager's field decisions rarely amounted to more than a few wins or losses over the course of a season. That didn't mean that all managers made the same decisions, merely that whatever their philosophies or tendencies—to sacrifice or not, for example—the decisions tended to work out about the same percentage of the time. Any significant discrepancies were more likely the result of the quality of their players than of their thinking.

"Second-guessing is fun, and that's all it should be," wrote Koppett. "The man making the first guess has weighed, 999 times out of 1,000, all the relevant factors, on the basis of his experience. His reasoning powers, within the framework of baseball, are usually impeccable."

Koppett wrote that in 1967, before computers and statistics invaded dugouts. By the mid-1980s, the relevant factors had multiplied way beyond what Oriole manager Earl Weaver used to keep on his index cards. Managers such as Tony LaRussa, who has been successful in Chicago, Oakland, and St. Louis, studied printouts that showed not only how each hitter fared against each pitcher, but also to what point on the field they hit each type of pitch.

How much of this information was truly relevant? Sometimes it seemed a great deal of it. In 1984 and 1985, the Mets were 70–37 in one- and two-run games, and 23–2 in extra innings, while only 29 games over .500 overall. It helped that relievers Jesse Orosco and Roger McDowell had superb years, but many credited manager Davey Johnson, who brought to the dugout a degree in math.

"It's gotten past the point where you can explain our record just by pointing at our bullpen, or our good pinch-hitting or the way we all persevere," said Met pitcher Ron Darling. "I think [Johnson] has taken some strategic stuff to a higher level."

"At first it was thought to be beginner's luck," wrote Boswell in May 1985. "Then it was a streak. Now, after two hundred games under Johnson, it's possible—just possible—that what we have here is a man ahead of his time."

A year later, Boswell found that the computer wave was beginning to recede. "We found that [statistical] stuff began to override all the other managerial tools—intuition, human relationships, recent trends and hot streaks," Oakland general manager Sandy Alderson told Boswell. "You don't want your players thinking that the manager has more faith in the machine than he has in them."

"Weaver isolated the important stats fifteen years ago," agreed Met general manager Frank Cashen. "Every hitter versus every pitcher; hitters versus left- and right-handed pitching; and recent streaks to see who's hot and who's cold. . . . When you go much beyond what Earl always used you're just confusing yourself."

Statistician Bill James's 1997 study of batting order showed that this particular managerial decision made very little difference. James programmed a computer to simulate 100 seasons with the Cubs' powerful 1930 offense. This was a team that generally had a classic batting order: shortstop Woody English (214 hits, 100 walks, 152 runs) led off, and center fielder Hack Wilson (56 home runs, 190 runs batted in) batted cleanup.

James took the same players and put them in what seemed the worst possible order. The pitchers led off; Wilson was ninth; and third baseman Les Bell, the team's weakest hitter, batted eighth to minimize Wilson's chances of driving home a run. Over James's simulated 100 seasons, the classic order averaged

6.16 runs per game, the mixed-up one 5.85, a mere 5 percent difference.

What happened? Well, Wilson's RBI totals dropped by 20 percent. But the Cubs' other hitters now had more chances to drive in runs, and they did so—not as many as Wilson, of course, but enough to make up much of that difference.

Wrote James: "If the difference between a reasonable batting order and a completely unreasonable batting order is only 5 percent, what do you suppose the difference would be between two reasonable batting orders? That's right: it's nothing."

No manager, of course, would last long writing out a lineup with Hack Wilson ninth. But Billy Martin once tried to snap the Tigers out of a slump by putting the names of his starters in a hat and batting them in the order he picked them out. Slugging first baseman Norm Cash led off and Eddie Brinkman, a career .224 hitter with no power, batted cleanup. Sure enough, Cash led off the game with a walk, and Brinkman drove him home. The Tigers won, 2–1.

Okay, so a manager's strategic decisions may not matter all that much. But that's not all he does. What about his role in deciding who's going to play?

"Talent is the ability to do some things, not all things," wrote political columnist and baseball analyst George Will. "So the right player must be in the right place in the right situation. That is very much the result of good managing."

"He can evaluate correctly each player's capacities, and try to use them in ways that bring the team maximum benefit," agreed Koppett.

And a manager not only decides who's playing, but also can push them to play their best. True, as Yogi noted, it's not football. Baseball depends more on reflexes than brute strength, so there's no equivalent to an adrenaline-pumping halftime talk from Knute Rockne (or George Steinbrenner). But there are other ways to motivate players.

"The reason [John] McGraw was a great manager," said Al Bridwell, who played shortstop for the New York Giants in the early years of the last century, "was because he knew how to handle men. Some players he rode, and others he didn't. . . . One manager knows about as much about the fundamentals of baseball as another. What makes the difference is knowing each player and how to handle him."

The clearest indication that managers *do* matter is how dramatically some teams have improved after a managerial change.

"I don't see how in the world anyone can study the history of organizations over a period of time without coming to the conclusion that, in most organizations, the hirings and firings of managers are the turning points by which the course of the franchise is plotted," wrote James in 1982. "You look at almost any case in which an organization suddenly improves or declines by 15 or 20 games and what you'll see is that at the same time a managerial change was made, that the new manager brought in a new approach to some phase of the game, that he benched somebody and promoted somebody else and that these changes led directly to the improvement or decline."

James cited Billy Martin and Leo Durocher as managers who turned around team after team. Martin did so in Minnesota, Detroit, New York, and Oakland; Durocher in Brooklyn, New York, and Chicago.

Of Martin, Boswell wrote: "No skipper of his era has approached his ability to bring competitive fire to dormant teams; no known collection of deadbeats has been beyond Martin's inspiration." As for Durocher, his will to win was so great that he once admitted that if he was covering third and his mother was heading home, he wouldn't hesitate to trip her. "Oh, I'd pick her up and I'd brush her off," Durocher said, "and then I'd say, 'Sorry, Mom.' But nobody beats me."

That level of intensity is hard to sustain, and teams managed by Martin and Durocher were notably less successful after a year or two under either—that is, if Martin or Durocher hadn't yet been fired. That's one reason skeptics think new managers get too much credit for their team's improvements. After all, new managers are generally hired when the team is doing poorly; otherwise, the old manager wouldn't be fired. The initial improvement and eventual decline are both evidence, by this line

of thinking, of a regression toward the mean, rather than managerial influence. Besides, the team may have improved because
of new and improved players, not a new manager.

But there are just too many cases of new managers turning
around teams to ignore the role of the manager. In 1986, James
studied 116 American League teams that hired a new manager
between 1961 and 1985; 35 percent had highly successful seasons, 24 percent had very disappointing ones. Both of those figures were higher than the percentages for teams without new
managers. Clearly, the new managers made a difference, though
not always for the better.

Wrote James: "When a manager like Billy Martin or Leo
Durocher can turn around team after team after team, when
managers like Mauch or Weaver keep putting the same stamp on
their teams, season after season, how can anyone defend a [los-
ing] manager by saying he was a victim of circumstances?"

The best managers make the most of their circumstances, or
are hired because their talents match the team's needs. "Harry
Walker, the teacher, would be better with a young expansion
team than with an established team of old pros," wrote Bouton.
"Leo Durocher, the prodder, is better in small doses; he should
only be hired for the second half of a season and only for a con-
tending team with talent. . . . [Ralph] Houk should be hired by
teams who've just fired guys like Walker and Durocher, teams
where the players would be ready to appreciate Houk's best
quality, which is that when he's not building you up, he's leaving
you alone."

So back to Bouton's original question: how much does a manager actually contribute? Two games a season? Five? Ten? Perhaps
the best answer was one Bill White gave in 1964, when he was
first baseman for the Cardinals.

"It depends on the manager," White said.

Who's the best manager of all time? That's really not the point
here, but rankings are hard to resist, so here goes.

Judging by career wins, it's Connie Mack, with 3,731. The
obvious problem is that Mack also *lost* 3,948, for a win percent-

age of .486. If we judge by win percentage, Joe McCarthy leads at .615—that's ignoring the undefeated records of Mel Harder (3 wins), Dick Tracewski (2 wins), and Clyde Sukeforth (2 wins).

The problem with win percentage is that some managers obviously managed better teams than others. A more sophisticated ranking would be based on how much better or worse a team did than expected. James tried this in 1997, determining a team's expected performance by combining its three previous seasons and a .500 record, then comparing that to its actual record. McCarthy was again on top, with 126 more wins than expected.

That system, too, has flaws, as James readily admitted. For one thing, plenty of other factors besides the manager come into play. For another, managers such as Martin (+98 wins), who bounced from one team to the next, had an advantage over those who stayed with one team. Walter Alston's Dodgers, for example, were 427 games over .500 during his tenure, but Alston was credited with only 26 wins more than expected, mainly because the Dodgers were always expected to do well.

The Elias Sports Bureau used a similar system, with a more complex mathematical model to determine a team's expected wins. Elias's top six, last published in 1993, were McGraw (+81), McCarthy (+64), Martin (+63), Bill McKechnie (+55), Dick Williams (+53), and Anderson (+52).

James also weighed in with an alternative method, this time using runs scored and allowed by a team to predict its record. Of the 2004 managers with at least five years' experience, the leaders were Joe Torre (averaging 3.5 more wins a year than expected), Bobby Cox (+2.2), Felipe Alou (+1.8), Dusty Baker (+1.1), and Tony LaRussa (+0.6).

To investigate further:

Boswell, Thomas. *Why Time Begins on Opening Day*. Garden City, N.Y.: Doubleday, 1984. Boswell categorized successful managers into four types. There are the "Little Napoleons," who followed in the footsteps of New York Giant manager John McGraw and are characterized by their barely controlled intensity. ("Little Napoleons are easy to spot,"

Boswell wrote, "because they usually have their teeth imbedded in an umpire's ankle.") Then there are the "Peerless Leaders," descended from the Chicago Cubs' Frank Chance and exuding discipline and dignity. The "Tall Tacticians," à la Connie Mack of the Philadelphia A's, are known for their brains. Finally, there are the "Uncle Robbies," named for the charming Wilbert Robinson, who replaced McGraw as Oriole manager in 1902.

—————. *The Heart of the Order.* New York: Doubleday, 1989. Elegantly Angell-ic essays on Davey Johnson, Dick Howser, and Sparky Anderson, among others.

Bouton, Jim, with Neil Offen. *"I Managed Good, but Boy Did They Play Bad."* Chicago: Playboy Press, 1973. New stories about managers by Bouton, old ones by James Thurber, Roger Kahn, Christy Mathewson, Bob Considine, John Lardner, Bill Veeck, and others.

James, Bill. *The Bill James Guide to Baseball Managers from 1870 to Today.* New York: Scribner, 1997. Throughout this book James is referred to as a statistician. That's far too limiting, as is the term he invented, sabermetrician (from SABR, the Society for American Baseball Research). What James is, above all, is a writer, and a consistently thoughtful and entertaining one and that.

Koppett, Leonard. *The Man in the Dugout.* Philadelphia: Temple University Press, 2000. Before the term "sabermetrics" existed, Koppett was a serious scholar of the game. Here he traces the methods of most famous managers from three seminal figures: McGraw, Mack, and Branch Rickey.

Siwoff, Seymour, Steve Hirdt, Tom Hirdt, and Peter Hirdt. *The 1993 Elias Baseball Analyst.* New York: Fireside, 1993. The annual analysts published just the sort of information that managers such as LaRussa and Johnson collected. The Elias rankings of managers, gradually refined, can be found in the 1987 and 1988 editions (published by Collier) as well as in the 1992 and 1993 editions.

28

Does It Pay to Steal?

In September 1908, the Detroit Tigers played the Cleveland Indians. With the score tied, the Tigers had Davy Jones on third and Germany Schaefer on first. Schaefer took off for second, hoping to draw a throw so Jones could score. But Cleveland catcher Nig Clarke held on to the ball. On the next pitch, unwilling to concede the strategy couldn't work, Schaefer dashed back to first. He thus became the first major league player to steal first.

"Everybody just stood there . . . with their mouths open, not knowing what the devil was going on," Jones told oral historian Lawrence Ritter. "Even if the catcher *had* thrown to first, I was too stunned to move."

Schaefer's persistence paid off. "On the next pitch darned if he didn't . . . take off again for second base," Jones continued. "By this time the Cleveland catcher evidently had enough, because he finally threw to second to get Schaefer, and when he did I took off for home and both of us were safe."

In 1920, the rules were changed to prohibit running the bases "in reverse order for the purpose either of confusing the fielders or making a travesty of the game." That same year, coincidentally, saw a decline in stolen bases—run the right way. It was a sign of the times to come: during the next forty years, the stolen base seemed headed for extinction. What stopped runners in their tracks, more effectively than any rule change could, was the rise of the home run.

"There is no use of sending men down on a long chance of stealing a bag when there is a better chance of the batter hitting one for two bases, or maybe, out of the lot," said John McGraw, who had once built the New York Giant offense on the running game but by the mid-1920s had conceded that its time was past. "Nowadays, the game has become a case of burlesque slugging, with most of the players trying to knock home runs."

Ty Cobb, typically, was less tolerant. In 1925, before a game between his Tigers and the St. Louis Browns, he told reporters he would for the first time try to hit home runs. He hit three that day and two the next. Having made his point, he then went back to hitting for average. In his 1961 autobiography, published just after he died, Cobb remained unreconciled to the power game. "The fabric of baseball is crumbling," he wrote.

There were exceptions. The Cardinals of the thirties and the White Sox of the late fifties, for example, still played a game based on speed. So did the Negro Leagues. But the major league trend was undeniable. In 1919, for every 100 games, there were 186 stolen bases and 39 home runs. By 1949, there were 59 stolen bases and 138 home runs. In 1959 it was 69 and 182.

Ironically, just one year after Cobb's autobiography was published, the trend reversed dramatically. In 1962, Dodger short-stop Maury Wills stole 104 bases, breaking Cobb's single-season record of 96. That record lasted until 1974, when Cardinal out-fielder Lou Brock stole 118. In 1982, Rickey Henderson topped that with 130. Nor was it just a few exceptional players who were doing all the running. By the seventies, dozens of players were stealing 50.

A number of factors came into play: more black and Latino players were coming into the majors, bringing with them an ag-gressive style of play; bigger ballparks were cutting some teams' home run totals; artificial surfaces meant that balls could shoot through the infield and outfield gaps, and runners could round the bases more quickly. Above all, though, there was a change in attitude. With a decline in overall offense during the sixties, there was a stronger case for playing for a single run rather than waiting around for a home run. Successful managers such as Whitey Herzog and Billy Martin embraced Whiteyball or Billyball—essentially an aggressive running game. By the 1970s, the total number of steals by all 24 major league teams routinely surpassed 3,000, quadrupling the 16-team totals from 20 years before.

Of course, home runs did not disappear, and other, equally successful managers—most notably Earl Weaver—looked with disdain on the steal, as well as the sacrifice bunt and the hit-and-run. Said Weaver, "Baseball is pitching, three-run homers, and fundamentals."

Starting in the early 1960s, for the first time in baseball history, the running game and power game coexisted. The "book"—that oft-cited yet unwritten compendium of standard strategies that managers leaf through before deciding to pinch-hit a righty to face a lefty, or to play for a tie at home and a win on the road—needed a new chapter, if not an entire revision. No one was quite sure what to make of the return of the running game. Sure, Wills and Brock and Henderson were exciting to watch. But did their steals help their teams score? Or did the times they were caught stealing end up costing their teams a big inning?

Weaver hated the idea of giving up an out, either by a caught stealing or a sacrifice bunt. These strategies were designed to push home a single run. Weaver didn't want one run; he believed in the big inning, one in which his Baltimore Orioles would score three or four runs (some suspected *his* book started with "In the big inning . . ."). The potential loss of those three or four runs, he argued, was much more significant than the one run he might get with a steal. Or as he explained to *Washington Post* sportswriter Tom Boswell, "The answer is a single, a walk, and a three-run homer."

Weaver's philosophy was embraced by many statistically minded sportswriters, including Boswell. Boswell reported that in a majority of games, the winning team scores more runs in a single inning than the loser does in nine. "Baseball," he concluded, "is a game of big innings."

A 1983 study by statistician Bill James buttressed the case against the steal. James noted that teams that led the league in stolen bases, even in the post-1960 era, finished lower in the standings than teams that led the league in any other offensive category. And teams that finished last in steals won more often than teams that finished last in any other category, except triples.

Perhaps the most damning indictment of the stolen base came from statistician Pete Palmer and writer John Thorn in their 1984 book *The Hidden Game of Baseball*. After feeding more than 75 years of stolen-base data to a computer, including how each situation turned out, Palmer and Thorn determined that a stolen base was worth about .30 run, a caught stealing −.60 run. That meant a steal was only worth attempting if the runner was likely to succeed more than two-thirds of the time. Henderson's 130 steals and Brock's 118 were thus only a marginal help to their team, since the former was thrown out 42 times and the latter 33. Wills had the best success rate of the three record-breakers: he was thrown out only 13 times.

Palmer and Thorn calculated that with a runner on first and one out, a team would on average score .478 run. A successful steal of second increased that to .699. But if the runner was thrown out, leaving none on with two outs, the run potential dropped to .095.

"The stolen base is an overrated play," they concluded, "with even the best base stealers contributing few extra runs or wins to their teams."

Defenders of the stolen base argued that its value was as much psychological as statistical.

"The theory might make sense mathematically, but I don't buy any of it," wrote Rickey Henderson in his autobiography *Off Base*. "There are all kinds of benefits to stealing a base. There's more to it than just advancing ninety feet. . . . A base stealer can distract the pitcher, break his momentum. He can also force the infield to shift, which opens holes for his hitters."

The offense benefited in other ways, too. A 1993 study by the Elias Sports Bureau, official statisticians for major league baseball, found that when the 1992 Milwaukee Brewers increased their steal totals, their opponents' passed balls, wild pitches, balks, and errors also went up. Pickoff throws may wear out a pitcher and keep a first baseman tied to the bag. With a stolen-base threat at first, the batter may get more fastballs to hit. The base stealer's aggressiveness can make the defense nervous and his own teammates more aggressive.

"The computer people have no understanding of . . . the human element of the game," said Jim Frey, who managed the Royals and Cubs. "What they don't understand is that you're dealing with twenty-four individuals, most of whom like to play an aggressive game. Nobody likes to be known as a 'safety first' player."

In his 1999 book *Long Balls, No Strikes*, television commentator Joe Morgan (who's eleventh on the all-time steal list) sounded a lot like McGraw and Cobb. "Longball is now the name of the game," he complained. "As speed becomes less of a factor in baseball . . . the game becomes one-dimensional, constricted, and less exciting."

But Morgan's argument was essentially aesthetic, not strategic. Granted, a balanced offense is more exciting, but that doesn't make it more effective. As for Henderson and Frey and Elias, they were right to point out the secondary benefits of steals but wrong to assume that the statistical analyses didn't take those into account. The formulas devised by Palmer and James measure a steal's effect on a team's runs; if a jittery catcher throws the ball over the shortstop's head and the base runner advances not just to second but also to third, that should help the offense score. Most general managers prefer homers to steals, and for good reason.

That doesn't mean, however, that steals are worthless or counterproductive. The statistical analyses accurately portray the value of stealing in general, not in a specific situation. Palmer and Thorn readily concede this. A runner with an especially high success rate stealing (such as Morgan's own 81 percent), a pitcher or catcher with a particularly slow release, a batter who's unlikely to drive in the runner on his own: all these are perfectly valid reasons to send the runner. Palmer and Thorn even advocated the occasional attempt to steal home, at least with two outs, since the potential gain is sufficiently great to outweigh the risk.

Just as certain situations merit running, so do certain teams. Herzog's Royals and Cardinals were successful not because the manager believed in the running game, but because he had Amos Otis and Freddie Patek in Kansas City and Willie McGee and Ozzie Smith in St. Louis. Moreover, both Kansas City and St. Louis had deep fences and artificial turf. Conversely, it made sense for Weaver to wait for the three-run homer because he had Frank Robinson and Boog Powell to hit them.

"The shape of his ball club is the shape of his talent and the shape of his ballpark," James wrote in 1983, referring to Herzog. "He believes in building a ball club out of ballplayers."

Like the steal, the sacrifice bunt also declined as home run totals rose. For the bunt, though, there has been no post-1960 revival. The bunt reached its psychological if not statistical nadir in July 1978 when, tied with the Royals and with a runner on first, Yankee manager Billy Martin ordered slugger Reggie Jackson to sacrifice. After Jackson squared and missed, third base coach Dick Howser gave him the sign to hit away. By then it was too late: Jackson, humiliated and out to show up Martin, tried twice more to bunt, and struck out. The Yankees suspended Jackson, and not long after, fired Martin.

It's easy enough to see why no one is especially eager to bunt: while a steal can swipe at least a bit of home run's glamour, a successful sacrifice—the name says it all—sends the batter right back to the dugout. The sacrifice didn't have a Wills or a Henderson to defend it, or even a Herzog or a Martin. Martin, though he never admitted it, may very well have been more interested in humiliating Jackson than in advancing the runner, and Gene Mauch, whose teams tended to bunt about twice as many times as the league average, was best known for managing twenty-six years without ever winning a pennant.

"I've got nothing against the bunt—in its place," Weaver maintained. "But most of the time that place is in the bottom of a long-forgotten closet."

Palmer's statistical analysis further undermined the bunt. His computer simulations showed that on average, a team with a runner on first and no one out had a run potential of .783. After a successful sacrifice, with a runner on second and one out, it was .699. In other words, *even a successful sacrifice* hurt a team's chances of scoring. For Palmer and Thorn, the conclusion was clear: while the steal was "overrated," the sacrifice bunt was, plain and simple, "a bad play."

As with the steal, Elias came to the defense of the bunt and of the running game in general. In 1987, its statisticians matched forty-two pairs of teams from the previous five seasons with slugging and on-base averages within 0.5 percent of each other. In twenty-eight of the forty-two cases, the team that advanced more bases on outs was the team that scored more runs. A year later, Elias took a close look at Mauch's Angels and found that despite the manager's tendency to play for one run, his teams had more innings with three or more runs than the league average. What led to big innings, Elias concluded, was not an absence of sacrifice bunts or steals but a presence of home runs.

"Let's get off Mauch's back," Elias urged. "To demean his style of managing with terms like 'little ball' is not only to criticize him unfairly, but to betray an ignorance of the facts as well."

James, too, ended up defending Mauch—more surprisingly, since he had previously denigrated one-run strategies. In 1986, James took a look at Mauch's record in one-run games and found it was about .500. Since his overall record was considerably worse than that, this seemed to indicate that Mauch's strategies paid off when it mattered most.

In 1997, James took on Palmer's conclusions, arguing that it was unfair to lump together all bunt situations.

"The .783 'run potential' for a man on first/none out situation is not a fixed value, constant for all occasions," James wrote. "Rather, this is the center of a range of values which represents many such situations." In other words, it didn't generally make sense to have Barry Bonds (or Reggie Jackson) bunt. But there were plenty of other situations where you wouldn't want the batter to swing away.

True enough, though Palmer and Thorn had said as much in 1984. But for James, this meant that the Palmer research proved not that the bunt is a bad play, but merely that there are more situations in which teams shouldn't bunt than in which they should. James also criticized Palmer and Thorn for considering only the possibility that a sacrifice could succeed (runner advances, batter out) or fail (runner doesn't advance). A third possibility was that the batter would beat out the bunt, thus advancing one base runner while adding another. Using Palmer's own method, James calculated that if this occurred with one on and no outs, the scoring potential would jump to 1.380 runs.

"Am I saying that Palmer and Thorn were wrong when they said flatly that the bunt was a bad play?" James asked. "No, I can't say that they were wrong. What I'm saying is that I think it's an open question."

James suggested that a better way to look at the problem would be to ask not whether a bunt was a good play, but how many times during a season a team should bunt. Was it the hundred-plus times Mauch tried it? The thirty or so of Weaver? Or a number nearer to zero, as Palmer and Thorn might suggest?

"The answer, dear class, is rolling on the grass," wrote James. "I don't think the right number is zero, and I doubt that it's near zero, but I don't know what it is."

Confused? Well, so is everyone else. Watch what happens after a successful sacrifice bunt. As James pointed out, it's one of the few times you'll see *both* sides cheer.

To investigate further:

Alexander, Charles. *Ty Cobb*. New York: Oxford University Press, 1984. Given that Cobb's mother shot his father, you can begin to see why he didn't trust anyone.

Boswell, Thomas. *How Life Imitates the World Series*. Garden City, N.Y.: Doubleday, 1982. Includes Boswell's influential essay "The Big Bang Theory and Other Secrets of the Game."

Fiffer, Steve. *Speed*. Alexandria, Va.: Redefinition, 1990. An illustrated history of the running game.

Henderson, Rickey, with John Shea. *Off Base.* New York: HarperCollins, 1992. "Call me a hot dog, but don't call me a conformist."

Jackson, Reggie, with Mike Lupica. *Reggie.* New York: Villard Books, 1984. "He wanted a bunt? He was going to get his bunt."

James, Bill. *The Bill James Guide to Baseball Managers from 1870 to Today.* New York: Scribner, 1997. James's ideas on steals and bunts also can be found in the 1982, 1983, and 1986 *Abstracts.*

Koppett, Leonard. *The New Thinking Fan's Guide to Baseball.* New York: Fireside, 1991. Originally published in 1967, and still among the most sensible studies of the game.

Martin, Billy, and Peter Golenbock. *Number 1.* New York: Delacorte Press, 1980. "I was so mad [at Jackson], it was unreal," Martin wrote. "After the game I went into the clubhouse, went into my office, and I took my clock radio and threw it against the wall." If only that had been the only time he lost his temper.

Morgan, Joe, with Richard Lally. *Long Balls, No Strikes.* New York: Crown, 1999. Besides more running, Morgan believes baseball needs to lower the mound, eliminate the DH, and hire more black managers.

Ritter, Lawrence. *The Glory of Their Times.* New York: Macmillan, 1966. Often imitated, never surpassed.

Siwoff, Seymour, Steve Hirdt, Tom Hirdt, and Peter Hirdt. *The 1993 Elias Baseball Analyst.* New York: Fireside, 1993. The Elias *Analysts* were full of interesting statistics, but never as witty or as provocative as the *James Abstracts.* The 1987 and 1988 editions referred to in this chapter were published by Collier.

Stump, Al. *Cobb.* Chapel Hill, N.C.: Algonquin Books, 1994. Stump, who coauthored Cobb's autobiography, here tells a fuller story.

Thorn, John, and Pete Palmer. *The Hidden Game of Baseball.* Garden City, N.Y.: Doubleday, 1984. The real percentages behind "percentage plays."

Weaver, Earl, with Terry Pluto. *Weaver on Strategy.* New York: Collier Books, 1984. Weaver's ten "laws" made clear what he thought of steals and bunts. Number 3: "The easiest way around the bases is with one swing of the bat." Number 4: "Your most precious possessions on offense are your twenty-seven outs." Number 5: "If you play for one run, that's all you'll get." Number 6: "Don't play for one run unless you know that run will win a ballgame."

Wills, Maury, with Don Freeman. *How to Steal a Pennant.* New York: G. P. Putnam's Sons, 1976. In San Francisco, the grounds crew would turn the infield into a swamp to try to slow him down.

Index